Graham Seal is Emeritus Professc
University. He is a leading exper
history and the bestselling author o:
*Larrikins, Bush Tales and Other Great Australian Stories, Great
Australian Journeys, Great Bush Stories, Great Convict Stories*
and *Australia's Funniest Yarns.*

———

Praise for other books by Graham Seal

Great Australian Stories

'The pleasure of this book is in its ability to give a fair
dinkum insight into the richness of Australian story telling.'
—*The Weekly Times*

'A treasure trove of material from our nation's historical past.'
—*The Courier Mail*

The Savage Shore

'A fascinating, entertainingly written voyage on what have
often been rough and murky seas.' —*The Daily Telegraph*

'Colourful stories about the spirit of navigation and exploration, and of courageous and miserable adventures at sea.'
—*National Geographic*

'A gripping account of danger at sea, dramatic shipwrecks,
courageous castaways, murder, much missing gold and terrible
loss of life.' —*The Queensland Times*

Also by Graham Seal

Great Australian Stories
Great Anzac Stories
Larrikins, Bush Tales and Other Great Australian Stories
The Savage Shore
Great Australian Journeys
Great Convict Stories
Great Bush Stories
Australia's Funniest Yarns
Condemned

GREAT
AUSTRALIAN
MYSTERIES

SPINE-TINGLING TALES OF DISAPPEARANCES, SECRETS, UNSOLVED CRIMES AND LOST TREASURE

GRAHAM SEAL

ALLEN&UNWIN
SYDNEY•MELBOURNE•AUCKLAND•LONDON

First published in 2021

Allen & Unwin
83 Alexander Street
Crows Nest NSW 2065
Australia
Phone: (61 2) 8425 0100
Email: info@allenandunwin.com
Web: www.allenandunwin.com

A catalogue record for this
book is available from the
National Library of Australia

ISBN 978 1 76087 954 9

Set in 11.5/15 pt Sabon by Midland Typesetters, Australia
Printed in Australia by Pegasus Media & Logistics

10 9 8 7

For Harriett, Millicent, Miles, Owen and Hugo

CONTENTS

Introduction A Land of Mystery   1

1 MYSTERIES OF A NEW LAND   5
   Lost and Found Continents   5
   An Unknown South Land   7
   The Seventh Sister?   10
   Sacred Stones   11
   Gonneville's Land   14
   The *Flower of the Sea*   16
   The Phantom Rocks   17
   'A New Race of Beings'   20
   Spain Settles Australia   23
   The Hairy Folk   27
   Mark of the Witch   29

2 STRANGE SEAS   33
   The *Flying Dutchman* Down Under   33
   The Deadwater Wreck   36
   The Lost Whalemen   39
   The Spectre of Armit Island   43
   The Headless Angel   45
   The Mystery of the *Madagascar*   47

Australia's *Titanic*   50
Wraith of the *København*   52
The Fate of *Patanela*   55
Finding *Endeavour*   57
The Vanishing Wrecks of War   59

3   LOST TREASURES   63
Yamada Nagamasa's Hoard   63
Treasure of the *Gilt Dragon*   65
That Cursed Shore   68
The *Hope* Treasure   73
Fatal Mysteries of the *General Grant*   75
Lost and Found in the Torres Strait   80
Bushranging Booty   82
Yankee Ned's Pearls   84
Gippsland Gold   86
The Mother Shipton Nugget   89
No Trace of the Mace   92

4   RIDDLES OF WAR   95
Lost in Celtic Wood   95
The Youngest Anzac   97
The Secret Watchers   99
Finding the Lost Submarine   102
The Molonglo Mystery   104
Why Camp X?   107
Diamond Jack   109
The Brook Islands Experiments   113
'There'll always be a *Sydney*'   116
The Hanged Man   118
The Missing Nuclear Files   121

5   OUTBACK PUZZLES   125
The Lost Wells of the Simpson Desert   125
The Stone Face   127
Leichhardt's Last Quest   130

The Wailing Waterhole   133
Lasseter's Bones   135
It's Raining Fish!   138
Seeing the Lights   140
A Desert Miracle   143
The Haunted House at Humpty Doo   145
Highways of Death   147
The Hole from Space   149
Where's the Water?   151

6 MYSTERIOUS PLACES   155
The Haunted Hawkesbury   155
The Vicar's Tale   158
A Curious Castle   162
Satan on Dead Island   164
The Concrete Casket   166
Hermits of the Reef   169
The Guyra Stonethrower   171
The Hook Island Monster   175
'A riddle, wrapped in a mystery, inside an enigma'   177
Tunnel Tales   180
The Poinciana Woman   183

7 VANISHINGS   187
The Phantom Island   187
Mystery Bay   189
Legends of the Lake   192
Vanishing Stars   194
The Lady of the Swamp   196
Who Killed Harry?   200
The Prime Minister Vanishes   202
Flight of the Moth   204
Black Mountain Myths   207
Tiger Tales   208
Beneath the Three Ugly Sisters?   210
'Good night. Malaysian three seven zero'   213

8 UNSOLVED   217
     A Queensland Ripper?   217
     Ned Kelly's Skull   220
     The Dying Light   222
     The Cryptid Files   224
     The Pyjama Girl   227
     The Unknown Man   230
     The Weeping Woman   233
     Doing A Lord Lucan   236
     Mr Brown   238
     Luna Park Ghosts   241
     Where's Paddy?   243
     The Portuguese Platypus and the Sicilian Cockatoo   245

Acknowledgements   249
Image credits   251
Notes   253

INTRODUCTION
A LAND OF MYSTERY

Australia has always been a mystifying place.

The people who began arriving here perhaps sixty or more thousand years ago encountered a natural world that differed greatly from the animals and plants in the far northern regions from which they came and through which they passed. To survive, they had to adapt and unpick the secrets of the land.

As far as Europeans were concerned, Australia was for centuries the 'unknown south land'. Was there a vast continent at the end of the world? Where? And what could it be like? Who, or what, lived there? As contact was made, followed by occupation, the land began only grudgingly to give up its secrets. Even now there are many yet to be fully explained.

Different though these experiences were, they had one thing in common. Wherever there was a mystery, whether of nature, of discovery and exploration, of the frontier, of war, or of life and death, then there was a story. The unknown always demands an explanation of some kind. If we cannot know the facts, we often make them up. And if we know some facts, we weave those into richer yarns of every kind.

This book retells a few of our many mysteries. Some are ancient, some are historical and quite a few continue to perplex us today—and will probably continue to do so tomorrow.

1

We begin with some of the many unknowns of the very long times before European settlement, as well as some early and continuing puzzles of the colonial era. Europeans began connecting with the great south land from the seventeenth century. But even though the size and shape of the continent was slowly discovered, many more riddles arose, particularly concerning the first peoples and their unwritten past.

Our island continent has always been strongly associated with the sea. It is only in the last century or so that we have been able to arrive or leave Australia other than by a ship of some kind. That nautical heritage produced a rich tradition of vanishing ships, wrecks and the supernatural.

Lost treasures and those yet to be discovered have always fascinated humankind and Australia has its fair share of buried loot and fabulous riches gone missing—somewhere. Some has sunk to the ocean depths, some has been buried or otherwise secreted in trees and caves or on islands. Wherever they are said to lie, lost treasures are some of our most enduring tales, continuing to attract hunters with metal detectors, maps and a lot of hope.

Although modern Australia is a young nation by world standards, we have a lengthy history of war. These conflicts have produced enigmatic stories from the Western Front, the seas surrounding us and quite a few from different locations around the country. Several of these are recent conundrums from the murky world of espionage and political secrets.

The unique qualities and challenges of outback life, expressed in terms such as 'the dead heart' and 'the never-never', are central to the Australian legend, with riddles of lost explorers, unexplained phenomena and yarns of fish, frogs or pebbles falling from the sky. All true, of course. The sparse population and vast distances of Australia's large inland beyond the ranges has encouraged the growth of some very strange tales, and still does today.

Some places have a truly mysterious atmosphere. The ancient landscape stubbornly refuses to give up many of its secrets, old or new. Historical buildings, islands, reefs, hidden tunnels and colonial churches may be haunted or the site of other strange happenings.

More often than most of us would like to think, things simply vanish. It's mostly people who disappear seemingly without explanation. Even if there is one, we often cannot discover what happened, or how and who might have been involved. The numbers of the missing, past and present, are unsettling and often leave a trail of heartbreak for families and friends across generations.

Finally, there are the many unsolved crimes, missing artefacts and even animal species to perplex and worry us. These and other oddities pepper our history and folklore. Some are chilling, some are disturbing, some are just plain peculiar.

Tales of mystery are part of our shared tradition of stories we tell about ourselves. Many have appeared in books, on television, in film and online, often many times, because they continue to puzzle us. You will undoubtedly have heard of some. But even the very familiar enigmas of the past have a way of developing new pieces in a jigsaw that can never quite be completed.

Others can be looked at in a different light. Recent mysteries that may not yet be as well known as those of the past are often even more intriguing. While some mysteries have been resolved, most have not. Despite a lot of time, effort and sometimes money being spent, they remain unexplained.

Perhaps you can solve them?

Amata senior custodian Stanley Douglas at Cave Hill in South Australia, 2017, where ancient rock art tells the important traditional story of the Seven Sisters. In this songline, seven sisters eventually become the star cluster other cultures call the Pleiades—but why do they refer to seven stars when only six are visible?

1

MYSTERIES OF A NEW LAND

LOST AND FOUND CONTINENTS

Well over two thousand years ago, the ancient Greek thinker, Plato, mentioned a group of sunken islands somewhere in the Atlantic Ocean. Either despite or because of the vagueness of its location, the Atlantis fable grew from an island to a continent and is now so widely known in art, literature and popular culture that many believe it to have been real.

But there are other versions of this enduring story that place a sunken continent in waters much closer to Australia. A lost land known as Lemuria (and sometimes as Mu) is said to lie somewhere between Australia and Fiji and to have once formed a bridge between the continents of Africa and Asia. This land was allegedly the cradle of humanity, populated by tribes with learning and scientific knowledge that they spread throughout the world. Like Atlantis, this Edenic place was sent to the depths by giant tidal waves.

Like many myths, Lemuria had its origins in serious science. In the mid-nineteenth century scientists suggested the idea of a former continent as an explanation for similarities in the flora and fauna of the eastern and western extremes of the Indian Ocean. From these reasonable, if inaccurate,

5

ideas the concept was taken up by occultists who envisaged the Lemurians as beings with three eyes who procreated by laying eggs and who possessed vast esoteric knowledge lost to mere mortals.

In the 1870s a French writer claimed to have gathered evidence from Indian oral traditions of another vast landmass, called 'the land of the Rutas', that once existed east of India. Although he placed the mysterious continent in the Pacific Ocean, later popularisers of the story believed it was located in the Indian Ocean and generally considered it to be another variation of the Lemuria legend. There is also a Tamil mythological tradition of a lost continent south of India called 'Kumari Kandam' that may, or may not, be related to 'the land of the Rutas'.

Pacific Island peoples also share a strong creation tradition of a land below the sea known as Hawaiki. Their creator figure first raised this land above the water in the form of a coral reef and then an island. In many Polynesian and Maori traditions, Hawaiki is the original home of the people and the place where the souls of the dead dwell. Sometimes it is said to now be submerged, as are many other islands that feature in Pacific Ocean cultural belief systems.

Australian Aboriginal coastal traditions from all around the country tell of massive flooding of the Australian landmass. Researchers have collected oral traditions about the creation of islands where continuous land previously ran and of existing islands being inundated. The stories told in these traditions appear to be remarkably consistent, regardless of their different locations and the very disparate Aboriginal groups from whom they were collected. The stories are thought to relate to events that occurred around seven thousand years ago, during which time sea levels may have risen as much as 120 metres.

Whatever version of the story is given, the essentials remain much the same: the lost continent was the cradle of humanity, it was peopled by an advanced race or races (up to 60 million people by one guess) and it eventually sank beneath the waves at some point prior to recorded history. Variations on the theme continue unabated today, widely considered to be pseudoscience.

But, seemingly right on cue, it turns out that there is a lost continent in the Pacific Ocean. It is almost five million square kilometres off the east coast of Australia. New Zealand is the largest visible section of 'Zealandia', or 'Te Riu-a-Māui' in the Maori language. This gigantic lump of continental crust broke away from the prehistoric Gondwanaland supercontinent and gradually sank perhaps 23 million years ago. Scientists will be researching and debating almost everything about Zealandia, apart from its existence, for a very long time. It has a peculiar shape. Why? What sort of plants and animals lived on it, if any? While the Earth's eighth continent has been found, its mysteries will be hard to solve.

AN UNKNOWN SOUTH LAND

The existence of a southern continent was known in ancient times, more or less. Just where it was, how extensive its spread was and who, or what, might or might not live there was a mystery that spanned millennia. As always, speculation and fantasy arose to provide some sort of story to explain what was unknown.

Some thought that the south land would be upside down. The ancients, unlike some moderns, knew perfectly well that the Earth was a sphere and not flat. To them, it made sense that if there were people, animals and plants living there, they would grow and exist in an opposite manner to their northern hemisphere equivalents. Others favoured fantastic beasts of the kind that appear on early maps: monsters, dragons and strange beings with one eye in the middle of their foreheads or having only one giant leg, on which they hopped around.

And, of course, there were hopes of riches to be had. In common with other European dreams of finding new lands of vast wealth, the south land was rumoured to be full of gold.

These stories circulated for centuries before Europeans contacted the continent. As elsewhere in the world, they spurred navigators to brave strange oceans in tiny craft. El Dorado might have been located in South America—somewhere—but its equivalent was to be found in any unknown corner of the world.

Gradually, very gradually, navigators sighted then landed on what we now call Australia. Then it was settled by Europeans and explored further. But there were still many unexplained mysteries, especially concerning the origins and occupation of the continent by the ancestors of today's Aboriginal and Torres Strait Islander peoples. Once again, a story arose to explain all these things. The first people had arrived on the continent many thousands of years earlier and had evolved here without any outside contact. The earliest non–First Nations people to walk on the land were Dutch, and the rest is history.

Like most historical narratives, this one began to unwind over time. As contact and interaction between First Nations peoples and settlers developed, so some puzzling possibilities were thrown up.

Aboriginal oral traditions contained references to 'pale' people who came to visit them. Evidence of non-Aboriginal fishing activities and of temporary, seasonal settlement by people from south Asia was found. A bronze fishhook of Macassan design was dated to around 1000AD. The Macassans were fisherfolk from the islands of what we now know as Indonesia and Malaysia. They travelled annually to northern Australia in search of trepang, or *bêche-de-mer*, a prized delicacy in many Asian countries. Pottery shards found on Groote Eylandt may date from the eleventh century, while charcoal found in the firepits of Macassan trepang hunters might date from the twelfth century and no later than the sixteenth.

Other odd finds began to be made along the northern coasts. Coins from Africa's Swahili coast have been turning up since World War II, when five were found on an island in the Wessel group. Other coins predating European settlement have also turned up, as have several cannons said by some to be Portuguese or Spanish (see 'The Portuguese Platypus and the Sicilian Cockatoo').

It began to seem that 'first contact' of Europeans with First Nations peoples took place long before originally thought. There were many candidates for this status. At first, the Spanish were favoured due to their early explorations and activities in the Indian Ocean. Then it was the Portuguese, intrepid explorers who began their maritime adventures in the early fifteenth century and were active in the same areas as the Spanish. Some have argued, without much evidence, that the great Chinese fleet of Zheng He visited Australia in the fifteenth century. There have even been claims that the ancient Egyptians and Phoenicians sailed here.

None of the more extreme theories are supported by solid evidence. But it is now established that there was ongoing contact with Aboriginal peoples and interaction with them in northern Australia, at least. Macassan trepangers were coming to northern Australia and Aboriginal people were sometimes going back with them to their islands and even establishing families there. Some Malay words and elements of Muslim belief incorporated into Aboriginal languages support this two-way interaction.

Once again, the historical story has changed, and probably will continue to change as new discoveries are made. But mysteries persist and have produced legends of lost settlements and Portuguese shipwrecks, as well as trade and cultural contacts between Australia, south Asia and, possibly, Africa. If these possibilities are confirmed, it is likely that pre-European Australia was connected to the fabled Silk Road. If so, goods, stories and perhaps even people passed along that route through the Middle East and, ultimately, into Europe. Several puzzling pieces of evidence have been found that suggest unique Australian animals may have been known in Europe as early as the thirteenth century.

THE SEVENTH SISTER?

The Aboriginal peoples' stories that make up the famed 'Seven Sisters' songline spread across the continent from west to east. Also called 'dreaming tracks', songlines are physical pathways through the land along and around which important traditional knowledge is preserved. These stories also include knowledge of how to navigate the country.

According to the various traditions of the Martu, Ngaanyatjarra, Pitjantjatjara and Yankunytjatjara peoples, the songline of the Seven Sisters is about an escape. Seven young sisters are pursued across the landscape by a shape-shifting sorcerer who wants to possess their bodies as well as their spirits. To evade the sorcerer, the sisters turn themselves into rocks and other natural features. The sorcerer also disguises himself in different ways, always trying to tempt or outwit the sisters. But they are just that little bit too smart for the wicked old lecher and mostly manage to stay out of his grasp. When the sorcerer does catch one of the sisters, the others rescue her. There are epic battles between the women, the sorcerer and other men, as the sisters fight to maintain their freedom from men. Ultimately, the sisters fly into the sky, becoming the stars in the constellation known to other cultures as the Pleiades. But the sorcerer is still on their trail and in some traditions is identified as one of the stars in Orion's Belt, a constellation not too far from the Pleiades. The chase goes on forever.

As well as their primal creation and fertility significance these stories contain vital knowledge about bush tucker and finding water in the arid regions through which the songlines pass. They are important narratives, preserved and passed on in song, dance and art as well as in oral tradition.

The trouble is that there are only six stars visible to the naked eye in the Pleiades. Where did the seventh sister come from? Or go to?

Other ancient traditions support similar stories. In ancient Greece, the Pleiades were identified as the seven daughters of the

Titan Atlas, and a sea nymph called Pleione. The great hunter, Orion, fell in love with the sisters and chased them until the chief god, Zeus, intervened on their behalf and transformed the women into birds, setting them in the night sky as the stars that make up the Pleiades. When Orion died he became the constellation named after him, from which position he continues to pursue the objects of his lust across the skies forever.

Much the same tales, featuring different characters, are told in Indonesia, in Africa, in America and in many other parts of the world. These tales often speak of seven stars as well. What is going on?

The mystery has been solved. Using the powers of the Gaia space observatory to penetrate space and time, astronomers have discovered that there is a seventh star in the constellation. It's just that we cannot see it. Now. Around 100,000 years ago, that elusive star was clearly visible from Earth.

The difficult-to-resist conclusion from this new knowledge is that the many stories that feature a seventh sister, brother or other beings twinkling in the Pleiades were first formed around one hundred millennia ago. Whether the stories were created by different groups of humans in different locations, or whether they originate from one ancient source, probably in Africa, we don't know. That mystery will probably remain with us forever. Not that it matters. We have the treasure of some of the world's greatest—and oldest—stories.

SACRED STONES

Australia is a landscape of extreme diversity and many secrets. The number, location and meaning of the many stone arrangements around the country are firm evidence of this. Mostly little known except among traditional owners and interested researchers, the locations of these arrays are often suppressed to prevent looting and damage.

At an undisclosed location on a private property between Melbourne and Geelong in Victoria lies an extraordinary stone arrangement. The Wurdi Youang site has been likened to the English Stonehenge, with reference to its antiquity and possible astronomical significance.

Wurdi Youang is an egg-shaped ring of around 100 basalt stones, aligned east–west. At just over 150 metres in circumference, it comprises stones as small as 20 centimetres in diameter and up to standing stones approaching a metre in height. Outside the main array, at the higher western edge, are three large stones.

Ancient stone arrangements are found around the country, but nothing else quite like this one. It is the traditional property of the Wathaurong (Wadawurrung) people, for whom it is a place of spiritual significance. When the array was built is not known, though the Wathaurong people are thought to have occupied the country for over 25,000 years, and possibly longer. As the area was settled in the 1830s, the site of Wurdi Youang became part of a colonial property that has remained in the same family ever since. This explains why the site does not seem to have become more widely known until the 1970s, when it was first surveyed. Since then, there have been a number of studies made, though there seems to be little consensus about the meaning and purpose of the array.

It has been speculated that the ovoid shape of the layout represents the egg of an emu or of a bird known as a plains-wanderer. The stones also seem to line up with landscape features of the country that are of significance to Aboriginal people.

Is it an astronomical observatory of some kind? Probably not. The three outlier stones do align with the setting sun at the summer solstice and winter equinox and other features of the stones fit with this interpretation. It is very unlikely that this arrangement could be an accident; it had to be planned. But that does not make Wurdi Youang an astronomical machine, but rather a kind of calendar, marking the position of the sun throughout the year. This would presumably help with any local agriculture or aquaculture activities.

The present-day custodian of the site, the Wathaurong Aboriginal Co-operative, is reluctant to agree with the notion of it being an Australian Stonehenge: 'We just don't know,' said a representative in 2008.

Early in the twentieth century, self-taught anthropologist Daisy Bates was taken to the site of a stone array around 130 kilometres from Cue, Western Australia: 'I had previously learned from the natives [sic] of a "stone man lying down," a dark scoriated heap of stone boulders that, from one aspect, appeared to be a gigantic recumbent figure.' She was told that the figure represented 'Barlieri, a legendary father', reputed to arise in anger if strangers approached.

Researchers have since located 'an incredibly complex arrangement' they believe to be the site described by Daisy Bates. The Kalli Stone Arrangement is made up of small boulders laid out in lines, clusters and cairns. It appears to be in two parts and may be related to male initiation rituals.

Another arrangement, at Kunturu, Western Australia, was described by a researcher as the most dramatic of such structures he had ever seen, either in Australia or around the world. Over 400 upright and almost 100 fallen slabs of dark-coloured schist wind in a spiral across a dry salt lake in a 'perfectly preserved serpentine rock alignment more than 250 feet long'. A group of quartz boulders lies at the centre of the spiral, which is flanked by four lines of upright stones.

The spiral is in Badimaya country in the mid-west of Western Australia. In Badimaya dreaming the figure is said to be the great serpent, Bimara, which lives in a nearby freshwater spring. The location of this significant structure is protected by Aboriginal heritage legislation.

Where traditional owners of these structures and arrays remain, stone arrangements have powerful spiritual and related meanings. Much of this knowledge is secret. But where the original inhabitants of an area no longer exist, the significance of any sacred stones is lost, and they must remain a mystery forever.

GONNEVILLE'S LAND

One of the strangest tales of the south land began early in the sixteenth century. It wound on for centuries and played a large part in the strong French interest in the *Terres australes*, as the French knew the south land.

In the early 1660s, a curious book was published in France. It was titled *Memoirs concerning the establishment of a Christian mission in the Third World, otherwise called the Austral, South, Antarctic, Unknown Land. Presented to our Holy father Pope Alexander VII. By a priest originally from that land.* The author was Abbé Paulmier, a priest from Normandy who claimed, amazingly, to be descended from a native of the *Terres australes*. Even more amazingly the man, named Essoméricq, was said to have been brought from that land to France early in the previous century. How could this be?

In his book, Paulmier includes an earlier account of the voyage of a French Captain (de) Gonneville who sailed to the Spice Islands, more or less modern Indonesia, in 1503. His ship was blown off course in a storm and he eventually found safety in an unknown land. Fortunately, the local people were friendly; they and their chief, Arosca, welcomed the French as guests. They stayed for six months, cultivating strong bonds of friendship. So strong, that when the French took their leave, the chief's son, Essoméricq, was allowed to depart with them for the journey back to France. There, he would learn French ways and act as a kind of cultural ambassador, returning in less than two years to his people with newfound knowledge and understanding of the wider world. He was also to be trained in the arts of war.

Gonneville's return voyage went well until they were almost home. His ship was attacked in the channel by the English and all the records of his amazing visit to the *Terres australes* were lost. Fortunately, Gonneville and Essoméricq were not, and managed to make their way to France. But without the records of the trip. Gonneville was unable to take Essoméricq back home. He was married to one of Gonneville's relations, making him Paulmier's great-grandfather. Because of his direct descent from Essoméricq and because he was a man of faith, Paulmier proposed that he should bring Christianity to Australia. Paulmier spent the rest of his life trying to have his ideas and proposals acted upon, but no further voyages of discovery were made by the French until much later. But by then, his enthusiastic promotion of the Gonneville story had embedded the idea that France had a serious connection with the *Terres australes* and future French voyages were inspired by his claims.

Was it true? Did a French ship land in Australia in the early sixteenth century and establish relations with First Nations peoples a century before the first known landing of the Dutch Willem Janszoon?

Historians have found no evidence of a Captain Gonneville before Paulmier published his story. The names of the people Gonneville met in Australia, Arosca and Essoméricq, are very unlike any of the languages of the first Australians. They sound more South American, if anything, raising the possibility that, if Gonneville did exist, he was not in Australia but in what is now Brazil. Another possibility is the Indian Ocean island of Madagascar. We will never know, but Gonneville became part of official French history and his voyage an odd but useful justification for later French attempts to establish new commercial enterprises and colonise new lands.

In a final twist, after James Cook charted the east coast and claimed it and whatever else of the continent there might be for Britain, the French could no longer cling to the notion that the great south land was their *Terres australes*. Nevertheless, in 1783 a con man claimed to be the descendant of Gonneville. The Baron de Gonneville, as he grandly styled himself, attacked the British claim by trying to revive the Essoméricq story. It seems that, despite his forged family tree, no one took the 'Baron' seriously and it was widely accepted that 'Gonneville's Land', as the French had taken to calling it, was just another myth of the unknown south land.

THE *FLOWER OF THE SEA*

She was a veteran Portuguese vessel of the India trade. The three-masted *Flor do Mar* (also *Flor de la Mar*), with her large forecastle and aftercastle, had seen voyages, wars, storms and dangers by the time her long career ended off the island of Sumatra in December 1511. Commanding the 'carrack', as this style of ship was known, was a buccaneering noble named Afonso de Albuquerque.

Afonso was the kind of man who made empires. Among other titles, official and unofficial, he was known as the 'Lion of the Seas' and 'Afonso the Terrible'. Born in 1453, Afonso had a spectacular military career with the expanding Portuguese forces in Africa and later in Portuguese India, where he became its second governor and consolidated the Portuguese empire in that part of the world. In 1510 he invaded Goa and the following year conquered the wealthy city of Malacca (now Melaka) on the Malay Peninsula. Plundering the riches of this trading hub, Alfonso decided to show off the treasure to his king, shoring up his political power which was being undermined by his enemies in the Portuguese court. There was so much treasure that he needed a roomy ship to transport it to his base in Goa. The best available was the leaking, lumbering but large *Flor do Mar*.

As the heavily laden vessel wallowed off the island of Sumatra a storm blew up. The ship was driven onto the shore, broke in two and sank. There was huge loss of life and the only precious thing saved was the child of one of the slaves, reportedly by Afonso himself. There was an attempt to salvage the valuable cargo, but the results do not seem to have been entered into the commander's report. Afonso was lucky to survive and went on to a further four years of conquering until his death in 1515.

But the legend of the *Flor do Mar*'s sunken hoard lived on, growing stronger with the passing centuries. The vagueness in the official record about the fate of the fabled riches fuelled speculation about the treasure and intrigued treasure hunters, armchair and real. The wreck and its riches have long been considered by many treasure hunters to be the greatest prize of all.

The usual conflicting theories have been put forward. One is that Afonso did manage to retrieve his cargo, or at least most of it, but neglected to say so. There is also the possibility that local pearl divers may have plundered the wreck. It seems that the local monarch was unaccountably enriched around the same time.

But the tantalising possibility that the gold, silver and jewels of the *Flor do Mar* still lie on the sea floor awaiting a determined seeker just will not go away. One especially enthusiastic seeker is said to have been the late President Suharto of Indonesia (1921–2008) who may have spent up to twenty million US dollars on the quest. An Australian–American expedition tried unsuccessfully to locate the wreck in 1989–90.

In 1992 a prominent maritime treasure hunter, Bob Marx, raised investment monies for a search and announced that he had been successful. According to Marx, he found the wreck after a few days of searching—100 miles away from the presumed location. Marx died in 2019, but controversy over this finding continues today. Another treasure hunter searching for the same wreck found a silver coin, once widely used in south Asia, at a different site in Sumatra in 2020, but nothing further.

The governments of the various countries involved with the wreck of the *Flor do Mar* are said to have lodged claims with the International Court of Justice. The squabble over ownership of the wreck and its treasure—if either of them now exist—has limited further exploration. But the story remains to tantalise treasure hunters from all corners of the world. It is said that the hoard of the *Flor do Mar* would be worth, in today's money, well over two billion dollars. If it is still there.

THE PHANTOM ROCKS

Somewhere around what are now known as the Tryal Rocks off the Western Australian coast lie the remains of 90 or so

English sailors. How and why they drowned there almost 400 years ago is a harrowing tale of incompetence, ruthlessness and the refusal of one man to allow these wrongs to stand.

In fair weather, an hour or so before midnight on 25 May 1622, the English East India Company ship *Tryal* (*Tryall, Trial*) sailed on her maiden voyage towards Batavia in the Spice Islands. The 500 ton (450 tonne) *Tryal* had sailed from Plymouth the previous September and stopped over at the Cape of Good Hope. Her captain, John Brooke, had no experience of this run, nor did any of his officers. They hoped to pick up mariners who did have knowledge at the Cape but were unable to find any willing to sail with them and so relied on the journal of a previous English voyager to these parts. So confident was Brooke of the accuracy of the journal that he did not bother to post a watch as his ship sped through the darkness toward disaster.

Suddenly, in what appeared to be mid-ocean with 'neither beach, land, rocks, change of watter nor signe of danger', the wooden ship splintered on partly submerged rocks off the western coast of Australia. Brooke and many of his crew were 'in such a mayze' that their ship had run aground, but the heaving of a sounding lead showed they were in only three fathoms of water. Unable to get the rapidly filling vessel off the jagged rocks, two small boats were loaded with supplies and lowered into heavy seas. They carried 46 men, a few barrels of water, some kegs of alcohol and around 8 pounds of bread.

The men in the two boats rowed desperately towards a small, low island just visible through the spray, leaving 93 men still aboard the *Tryal* or floundering in the water. Brooke had command of a skiff, or small sailing craft, along with ten others including his son, while the factor or merchant aboard the ship, Thomas Bright, and 35 men were crammed into a longboat. Half an hour later the remains of their ship began to break apart and those stranded aboard were lost to the waves. The survivors made their way to Batavia. Apart from the death of one man in Brooke's skiff, they were lucky. Both groups of survivors found fresh water on the Montebello Islands and arrived at their destination within days of each other at the end of June.

As master of the vessel, Brooke was in deep trouble with his employers. He presented a detailed report that brazenly falsified his position at the time of the disaster. He claimed to be simply following the earlier route and had just been unlucky to plough into unmarked rocks. In the crude state of seventeenth century navigation, this was a fairly common occurrence. He might have got away with it but for Thomas Bright. He wrote to the company accusing Brooke not only of negligence in failing to post a watch but also claiming that he threw incriminating charts and other papers overboard as the *Tryal* fell apart. He alleged that Brooke had stolen some of the silver carried by the *Tryal*, carrying it away in his lightly crewed skiff. Worst of all, he called Brooke 'a Judasse' who abandoned his men and his command. According to Bright, although promising the sailors loading the escape boats that he would take them with him, their craven captain waited for a moment when they were distracted. Then he launched the skiff with only nine men 'and his boye', abandoning the rest and making for the Sunda Strait without waiting to see 'the lamentable end of ship the tyme shee splitt'.

Despite this, Brooke was given another command that he took to Sumatra, apparently without incident. But the next ship he was given and her valuable cargo of spice was lost almost in sight of Dover, possibly on purpose. At least, that was the accusation of his employer, the English East India Company, which instituted legal proceedings against him that eventually involved appeals from both sides of the House of Commons and the House of Lords. A negotiated settlement was finally reached in 1626 in which Brooke admitted his failures in return for the company dropping proceedings against him. He then disappeared.

So did the rocks on which his ship had foundered. For 300 years mariners puzzled over the location of the *Tryal*'s grave. Voyagers were sent to search for them. Even Matthew Flinders could not find them in his celebrated circumnavigation of Australia. Eventually the Admiralty decided that they did not exist.

But in 1818 a small group of islands was found and named Ritchie's Rocks after the captain of the discovering ship. Even so, it was not until 1840 that the true location of the missing Tryal Rocks was charted between the Montebellos and Barrow Island. And it took almost another century for final confirmation that these were indeed the rocks on which Brooke and his unfortunate crew had been wrecked.

The mystery of the missing rocks had been solved. But what about the rest of the silver the *Tryal* carried?

In 1969 skindivers located cannon, anchors and other artefacts believed to be from the long-lost wreck. One of the group, a colourful character named Alan Robinson, subsequently tried to retrieve the treasure by dynamiting the site, causing great damage. The 'gelignite buccaneer', as Robinson was dubbed, later hanged himself in prison while awaiting trial on an unrelated offence. But his actions caused such concern that existing state shipwreck protection legislation was strengthened by further Commonwealth regulation. Official museum expeditions have tended to confirm that the site is the wreck of the *Tryal*.

But what happened to the silver is still a mystery. It possibly lies with more than 27,000 artefacts held in the maritime collections of the Western Australian Museum for safekeeping: a collection of navigational instruments, arms, personal items—and bullion. Or still deep down below with the *Tryal* and her sailors' bones.

'A NEW RACE OF BEINGS'

Was it a hoax, or was there really a European colony in Central Australia centuries before 1788?

In 1834, an article in a regional English newspaper made just this extraordinary claim. Beneath the headline 'Discovery of a White Colony on the Northern Shore of New Holland', the anonymous author spun a fine yarn. It spoke of a secret expedition funded by an unnamed 'scientific Society' in Singapore and assisted by 'the Local government'. The expedition landed at Raffles Bay in April 1832 and 'made a two-month excursion into the interior'. The article consisted mainly of extracts from the journal of a Lieutenant Nixon, said to have been one of the expedition members.

Nixon spoke of travelling for many days over barren hills and rocks. On 15 May he came over the top of another hill and saw something he did not expect:

> Looking to the southwards I saw below me at the distance of about three or four miles, a low and level country, laid out as it were in plantations, with straight rows of trees, through which a broad sheet of smooth water extended in nearly a direct line from east to west, as far as the eye could reach to the westward, but apparently sweeping to the southward at its eastern extremity like a river; and near its banks, at one particular spot on the south side there appeared to be a group of habitations embossomed in a grove of tall trees like palms.

He described many small islands threaded by small boats and canoes—'It seemed as if enchantment had brought me to a civilised country, and I could scarcely resolve to leave the spot I stood upon.' But he had to leave, answering a call of nature. As he went back to the expedition camp, presumably after relieving his bowels, Nixon got an even bigger shock. As he came round a low rock 'I came suddenly upon a human being whose face was so fair and dress so white, that I was for a moment staggered with terror, and thought I was looking at an apparition'. The young man was deep in thought and did not see Nixon until almost upon him, then he 'raised his eyes, and in an instant uttered a loud exclamation and fell insensible to the ground'.

Nixon revived him and found that he spoke 'Old Dutch', which the explorer happened to understand from having been schooled in Holland. The young man's story was 'of a most extraordinary nature'. He said he lived in a walled community of around 300. These people were descended from a group of about 80 men and ten women, survivors of a shipwreck that occurred around 170 years earlier.

The expeditioners then visited the walled village, meeting the leader, a man named Van Baerle, a descendant of one of the wrecked ship's officers. They were told that the ship-wreck survivors travelled 'towards the rising sun'. Many died but eventually, on the 'wise advice' of the women, they followed a small stream to the oasis where they now lived. The colonists survived uncertainly on maize, yams and an occasional kangaroo and observed a form of Christian belief. They had no education provision and protected themselves with a militia of young men and boys, all armed with long pikes. 'They may,' Nixon concluded, 'be considered almost a new race of beings.'

This astonishing account set off a mystery that still intrigues people today. The unlikely possibility that a group of sixteenth century Dutch shipwreck survivors could cross from the west coast towards the east across a large stretch of the world's most rugged and waterless terrain is hard to credit. There certainly were Dutch sailors wrecked on the west coast in the sixteenth century and we know that some survived and probably formed some sort of settlement. But that was not far from where their ship foundered and nowhere near the centre of Australia.

Nixon gave coordinates for the location of the colony and there is no likelihood of anyone surviving anywhere near that location. Even if the coordinates are wrong, the only place that remotely accords with Nixon's description is Palm Valley in the Northern Territory's Finke Gorge National Park. But there is no evidence there of any European occupation. Researchers have pointed out many other inconsistencies, contradictions and unlikelihoods in this account. A variety of conspiracy theories suggests that evidence was removed by Governor James Stirling of the Swan River colony and that he even had the colony exterminated due to a concern about ownership of the land. This extremely unlikely possibility is only one of the more rational speculations.

But what about Lieutenant Nixon? There was one, but he doesn't fit the facts or dates given in the letter to the newspaper. Who wrote the letter? Probably Thomas Maslen, an armchair explorer who never visited Australia but had a fascination for the place, including the then popular notion that the continent was host to a giant inland sea.

But a good story never dies, it just gets bigger, and there have been serious attempts to find the lost white colony of central Australia. We'll keep looking.

SPAIN SETTLES AUSTRALIA

The story goes that the party sent to survey the proposed township of Port Curtis in 1853 made some unexpected discoveries. A brass ship's gun inscribed 'Santa Barbara, 1596' was found at South Trees Point and, later, a Spanish wreck on Facing Island. Rock carvings, wells lined with non-Australian timber, buildings of teak and evidence of Christian burial practices were also found.

These, and other, indications of alleged European presence in Australia several centuries before James Cook's celebrated voyage have always intrigued Australians.

Spanish—or Portuguese—wrecks are plentiful along the east coast, in legend at least. They are often associated with sunken treasures and, improbably though not impossibly, with pirates. They speak to our ongoing fascination with the romantic notion that the unknown south land must hold many secrets and undiscovered tales.

Since the 1860s they have been telling stories about the wreck in Stradbroke Island's Eighteen Mile Swamp. The first settler known to have seen the remains of what would become remembered as a 'Spanish galleon' was married to a First Nations woman who told him that the wreck had been there for many years. Local oral tradition also confirms Aboriginal knowledge of the wreck.

It was rediscovered towards the end of the nineteenth century by another generation of locals who described it as having a 'high poop and forecastle', the classic image most of us have of a Spanish galleon. A large number of copper fittings were reportedly retrieved from the wreck around this time. Others also found it over the years and in the 1930s several serious attempts were made to find and document the elusive ship, which was gradually disappearing into the peat through bushfire and damage from the elements. It then seems that no further sightings were reported until the 1970s and none since.

Over this lengthy period, the story has grown and grown as all good legends should. Professional historians and archaeologists are sceptical of claims for pre-Cook European contact and the story has been frequently debunked. But the mystery lives on, with stories of local Aboriginal people having Spanish gold coins and other artefacts in their possession as well as secret knowledge of the ship's supposed treasure. Hopeful seekers continue to search for it.

The Long Island (Whitsundays) 'Spanish galleon' wreck has much the same story as that of the Stradbroke Island galleon, including First Nations traditions and yarns about Spanish coins found washed up on the beach. Victoria also has its own famous mystery wreck at Warrnambool.

Some shipwrecked sealers were the first to mention the Mahogany Ship, as it has become known. Making their way to Port Fairy after losing their craft in 1836, the sealers saw what they reportedly described as 'an ancient wreck' stranded in the dunes. This story was later related by an early pioneer of the district and printed in a local newspaper in the 1840s. Since that time, speculation has never ceased.

The favoured theory is that the wreck was that of a Portuguese caravel. Close second is a Spanish galleon. Although there are a number of seemingly credible eyewitness accounts of seeing the ship, historians who have looked closely at the legend have serious doubts. Despite the tourist appeal of the Mahogany Ship mystery for the Warrnambool area, there is no credible evidence of a Portuguese caravel or a Spanish galleon. It is even possible that there never was a wreck, mahogany or otherwise; however, if there was a wreck it is most likely to have been the *Unity*, a schooner stolen by convicts in Van Diemen's Land early in the nineteenth century but never heard of again.

Nevertheless, theories and suppositions by serious historians and armchair mysterians continue: people are still searching and the legend is alive and kicking.

In 2020, veteran skindiver Ben Cropp revealed his plans to locate a temporary Spanish settlement on Cape York Peninsula that existed long before James Cook sailed the *Endeavour* along those coasts. Ben's quest involves some early French, German and Spanish maps, some engraved stones that he thinks indicate a temporary encampment, as well as other artefacts and coins found at various remote sites along Cape York. Taken together, these indicate that the Spanish mined alluvial gold dust some-where near the present-day settlement of Bamaga. The Spanish found the gold on a visit to the area and returned to Spain with the news, stimulating the king to send an expedition of miners to exploit the discovery. They loaded their ship with the treasure but were wrecked on one of the many surrounding reefs and so lost to history.

Ben thinks Spain then sent another ship to learn what happened to the gold ship, making that a total of three seventeenth century Spanish visits to Australia. While there is no verifiable historical evidence of the Spanish ever making it as far south as Australia, Ben Cropp is well qualified to find out if they did. He has been involved in discovering more than a hundred wrecks in his long career and is a very determined treasure hunter. But, if he is successful, there will probably be none of the gold dust left on the wreckage. The treasure will instead be the first confirmation of a Spanish presence on the great south land.

Pre-1770 mysteries are frequently fuelled by discoveries of old cannons, a supposedly sixteenth century lead weight found on Fraser Island and the various old coins that turn up from time to time around our coasts. A number were found in the Northern Territory in the 1940s. In 2018 a coin thought to be used by the pre-sixteenth century African kingdom of Kilwa (Tanzania) was found in the Wessel Islands north-east of Arnhem Land. Confirmation of its origin and how it came to be where it was found is difficult, but keeps the fascination with these mysteries alive and well. Similar finds among our neighbouring Indonesian islands are also reported from time to time.

Picking through the mud for oysters in November 2013, a woman from the village of Gampong Pande in Banda Aceh found a coral-encrusted chest. She opened it up and was amazed to find it filled with 200 or so gold coins inscribed with Arabic characters. In her surprise, she tipped many of them onto the mud, from where many were scooped up by local people. Following the law, the woman handed the chest and what remained of its treasure to the authorities. But news spread quickly, and a small gold rush descended on the area. The authorities tried to control the area but to little effect and the site was covered with excited treasure hunters hoping to make a fortune, or even just a few rupiah. Anyone lucky enough to find coins could sell them to gold traders for up to 800,000 rupiah each, around 80 US dollars, a considerable amount to the impoverished people of the island.

Historians confirmed that the area was in the heart of the Islamic kingdom of Aceh. From the thirteenth century, the village had become an industrial centre, manufacturing gold coins for the extensive trade carried on in the region and beyond. The find may have been a hoard of coins from a workshop or had perhaps been buried in a grave from a local cemetery ripped apart by the 2004 tsunami. Like this accidental event, some of the many remaining mysteries of the unknown south land may be solved in the future.

THE HAIRY FOLK

One, or perhaps several, of the mysterious mythological beings said to inhabit Australia is short and hairy. This creature, if that's what it is, goes by many different names in different parts of the country, including but not restricted to *dinderi, kuritjah, winambuu, junjudee* and *tjangara*.

In the late nineteenth century, the explorer and writer Ernest Favenc published a story titled 'A Haunt of the Jinkarras. A Story of Central Australia'. Favenc had lived in the bush and gained some familiarity with First Nations traditions. In his work of fiction, he described these cave dwelling beings as '. . . a crowd of the most hideous beings I ever saw . . . As well as we could make out in the murky light, they were human beings . . . they had long arms, shaggy heads of hair, small twinkling eyes, and were very low of stature.'

The bold ruby-seeking colonials of Favenc's boys' own adventure story capture one of the beings,

> a young man about two or three and twenty, hardly five feet high at the outside, lean, and with thin legs and long arms. He was trembling all over, and the perspiration dripped from him. He had scarcely any forehead, and a shaggy mass of hair crowned his head, and grew a long way down his spine. His eyes were small, red and bloodshot . . .

They discover that the young man has a tail. He also smells very bad, a feature sometimes ascribed to hairy folk in real-life sightings.

Outside the world of fiction, many people have heard about and seen similar beings. Around 1901, young Henry Methven was alone in his campsite near Jervis Bay, New South Wales. As he busied himself 'I looked around, the Hairy Man was standing right behind me. He was only about . . . two or three foot . . . a handsome little fellow . . . he had a long straight nose and he was the colour of a real full-blood . . . dark and coppery . . . everything about the little bloke . . . seemed to be human.'

Henry further described the 'handsome little fellow' as strongly built, with a short neck, hair on the back of the hands and on the head and body. Henry fled, straight into a clump of stinging nettles. But next day, he and his companions tracked the hairy man for some time and saw that he had five toes, just like humans.

The hairy folk are credited with different characteristics in different traditions. They may be malevolent, as in Favenc's yarn; they may be protective, helping lost or sick children; or they may be childlike themselves, playing mischievous, but harmless, tricks on humans and sometimes following them for a taste of honey. They might also be a bit of both. These uncertain attributes and their stature have led some to interpret them as a kind of bush fairy, though this is an imposed interpretation stemming from British traditions.

Other explanations of the hairy people are that they are the survivors of another, possibly earlier, group of humans who made it to Australia from Africa via the islands of South-East Asia. Discoveries of small hominids on the island of Flores and elsewhere are nowadays linked with the myths.

Do the small hairy folk exist? Researchers are divided on the issue, but a great many people have given credible accounts of seeing or even encountering them. Gayndah in Queensland is reportedly a hotspot for sightings, but numerous others have been recorded since settlement, continuing up to the present day.

At just over 1 metre tall, Lizzy Woods was the last matriarch of the Dyirbal (Jirrbal) rainforest people of Queensland. In 2007, at the age of 105, she recollected that 'I was born in the rainforest. I grew up chasing kangaroo and picking berries off the trees. I belong here. This is my land. The pygmy tribe— that is my mob. And this is the place I have chosen to die.'

MARK OF THE WITCH

If you were suffering from piles (haemorrhoids) in nineteenth century Tasmania, you could have consulted William Allison. Depending on what sort of piles you had, Allison would consult the printed almanac in which he kept his accounts and also his secret recipes. For 'blind', or outward-growing, piles he would prescribe hog's lard rubbed between two sheets of lead, the resulting 'ointment' to be rubbed on the affected parts. Allison had written 'proved' beneath this one, a venerable proof of the medicine's efficacy.

William Allison was one of several 'cunning men', or folk doctors, known to be operating in Tasmania at that time. Cunning men and 'wise women' were the bearers of old knowledge of cures and magic who had provided medical and magical services to the country folk of Britain and elsewhere for centuries. Sometimes they were called and treated as witches, so usually found it wise to keep their knowledge secret and to cloak it with a shroud of mystery.

As well as providing cures for ailments of humans and animals, their skills might include fortune telling; locating lost property and people; casting horoscopes; and manufacturing charms and spells related to matters of love, revenge and release from someone else's evil spells. They might also advise on such magical traditions as placing old shoes or dead cats in chimneys, beneath floorboards, in roof cavities and other weak points through which evil might enter to afflict a household. Many of these 'ritual concealments' have been found in Tasmania and elsewhere in New South Wales, Victoria and Queensland.

Tasmania has other mysteries that are only now coming to light. Scratched into the walls and doors of colonial stables, granaries and other buildings are some unusual patterns. One of these is a daisy wheel or hexafoil design; another is a series of concentric circles with a dot in their centre; while a third is described as 'an enigmatic mark resembling the board used in the ancient game of three men's morris'. It turns out that these signs, sometimes known as 'witches' marks', are ancient symbols usually found on or near doors, windows and other access points of old buildings.

The exact meaning of these marks is unclear, but experts agree that they are meant to ward off evil and ensure good rather than bad luck. They, and others with a similar purpose, have been located in old buildings near Hobart, New Norfolk, Lewisham and Richmond. They have also been found in Victoria, on Norfolk Island and in Western Australia.

Marks of this kind are well documented in the ancient world and continued to be used on buildings in Britain, the United States of America and Australia until well into the nineteenth century, and even the twentieth. In some cases, symbols were smoked onto ceilings with candle flames. Although mysterious to most, these marks are part of the clandestine traditions of folk magic, transported to Australia in the minds of some who had been initiated into the secrets, like William Allison.

More recent finds of this kind in Victoria suggest that signs found at different locations might be the work of one person. Perhaps someone like William Allison, hired surreptitiously to mark dwellings and workplaces with signs to keep evil and accidents away from those who worked in them. Misadventures and accidents, particularly fires, were frequent in colonial buildings, especially in workplaces such as stables and mills. With no form of insurance or medical cover, these could be devastating financially and physically. Belief in the ability of symbols to avert these might be described as superstition, but for those without much else to rely on it was better than nothing. Cunning folk with the wisdom to perform such magic were probably in great demand in these times and places.

One cunning woman has also been identified in Victoria, but there is little to no documentation of such people, except in the occasional court case, in the chance survival of William Allison's almanac or in the enigmatic markings now being found on colonial buildings around the country.

Engraved by John Skinner Prout, Old Whaling Station *depicts the whale processing station on Schouten Island in Tasmania, which he visited in 1864. Five years prior, Mate Robert 'Bob' Marney and his crew of five men had harpooned a whale and disappeared without a trace despite clear weather conditions, knowledge of the coast and landmarks in sight.*

2

STRANGE SEAS

THE *FLYING DUTCHMAN* DOWN UNDER

The legend is first recorded in 1790, but it was already old in sailors' lore. Undoubtedly the most famous nautical legend of all, the enigmatic tale of the *Flying Dutchman* is known around the world. And the spectral sailing ship has been sighted everywhere in the world, including in Australian waters.

At first, the story was a short yarn about a distressed Dutch ship seeking safe harbour at the Cape of Good Hope during a raging storm. A pilot to guide the vessel to safety was not available and the ship was lost with all her crew. Ever since then, the glowing apparition has been seen during stormy weather. Sighting the *Flying Dutchman* was considered to be an omen of doom.

The Cape of Good Hope was a regular port of call for ships on the Australian run from Europe and although the legend was initially a Dutch story and largely restricted to sailors, it flowed into the broader community in the late eighteenth century. One of the earliest accounts is that of the 'Prince of Pickpockets', George Barrington, on his way to serve a sentence in Australia in 1795. Barrington's version of the story is a little more elaborate than the basic legend (though he was a notorious confidence trickster with a silver tongue):

> . . . it seems that some years since a Dutch man-of-war was lost off the Cape, and every soul on board perished; her consort weathered the gale, and arrived soon after at the Cape. Having refitted, and returning to Europe, they were assailed by a violent tempest nearly in the same latitude. In the night watch some of the people saw, or imagined they saw, a vessel standing for them under a press of sail, as though she would run them down: one in particular affirmed it was the ship that had foundered in the former gale, and that it must certainly be her, or the apparition of her; but on its clearing up, the object, a dark thick cloud, disappeared. Nothing could do away the idea of this phenomenon on the minds of the sailors; and, on their relating the circumstances when they arrived in port, the story spread like wild-fire, and the supposed phantom was called the Flying Dutchman.

Barrington did not see the apparition, but he met a sailor who did. About 2 a.m. he was woken by the boatswain 'with evident signs of terror and dismay in his countenance' and begging for a drink of spirits. The man claimed to be 'damnably scarified' because he had just seen:

> the Flying Dutchman coming right down upon us, with everything set—I know 'twas she—I cou'd see all her lower-deck ports up, and the lights fore and aft, as if cleared for action. Now as how, d'ye see, I am sure no mortal ship could bear her low-deck ports up and not founder in this here weather. Why, the sea runs mountains high. It must certainly be the ghost of that there Dutchman, that foundered in this latitude, and which, I have heard say, always appears in this here quarter, in hard gales of wind.

After a few deep draughts, the boatswain 'grew a little composed', admitting that he was prone to seeing ghosts. Barrington went on deck with him to see for himself but 'it had cleared up, the moon shining very bright, and not a cloud to be seen; though, by what I could learn from the rest of the people who were on deck, it had been very cloudy about half an hour before, of course I easily divined what kind of phantom had so alarmed my messmate'.

A more respectable figure who did see the *Flying Dutchman* in Australian waters was no less a personage than Prince George of Wales, destined to be King George V. Sometime before dawn on 11 July 1881, while travelling through Bass Strait, the prince (or his brother travelling with him) recorded:

> At 4 a.m. the *Flying Dutchman* crossed our bows. A strange red light as of a phantom ship all aglow, in the midst of which light the masts, spars and sails of a brig 200 yards distant stood out in strong relief as she came up on the port bow. The look-out man on the forecastle reported her as close as on the port bow, where also the officer of the watch from the bridge clearly saw her, as did also the quarterdeck midshipman, who was sent forward at once to the forecastle; but on arriving there was no vestige nor any sign whatever of any material ship was to be seen either near or right away to the horizon, the night being clear and the sea calm. Thirteen persons altogether saw her . . .

Just over six hours later, the sailor who had first reported seeing the *Flying Dutchman* fell to his death from the foretopmast and 'was smashed to atoms'.

Another Australian connection with the *Flying Dutchman* comes from John Boyle O'Reilly, the famous Irish rebel. While being transported with his fellow Fenians to Western Australia in 1867, O'Reilly wrote a poem for the ship's newspaper. The poem uses the *Flying Dutchman* tale to give expression to

O'Reilly's forebodings at what was going to be a long exile from his homeland:

> They'll never reach their destined port
> They'll see their homes no more,
> They who see the Flying Dutchman
> Never, never reach the shore.

Since then the legend has grown, gathering more detail and depth through endless accounts, books, films and artworks that feed from it. The *Flying Dutchman* soon fused with another piece of world folklore known as the 'Wandering Jew'. This is said to be a man who refused to help Christ bear the burden of the cross as he struggled towards his crucifixion. In a bit of Old Testament revenge, the man was condemned to wander the Earth forever in eternal life. In the *Flying Dutchman* version, the captain of a Dutch merchantman attempting to enter Table Bay was frustrated by a change in the wind. The captain swore to be eternally damned if he did not enter the bay and that he would sail these waters until Judgement Day. He did not and he does.

In another version it is said that the crew of the Dutch ship committed some atrocious crime and are condemned to never enter a port and must voyage onwards until their penance is done. This echoes a theme of Coleridge's famous poem, *The Rime of the Ancient Mariner* (1797–98). A few years later the arch-romancer Walter Scott made the *Flying Dutchman* a pirate ship, in which guise the tale may be most familiar to modern audiences in the *Pirates of the Caribbean* movies.

THE DEADWATER WRECK

Could there be a pre-colonial Dutch, or even Spanish, ship beneath the mud of the area known as the 'Deadwater'? With a name like that, you'd certainly like to think so! The Deadwater is in Wonnerup Inlet, Western Australia, a boggy lowland of shifting sands and confusing watercourses often battered by fierce storms. These have led to considerable reshaping of the terrain and helped the growth of the Deadwater wreck mystery. By any measure, this one is a beauty. As well as the possibility of a pre-colonial mishap, there is mention of treasure along with smuggling and even murder.

According to one of the early pioneers of the region, a John McGibbon, the wreck was visible when he first saw it in 1834. Speculation at the time and since was that it was an old Dutch East India Company ship blown very far off course and wrecked by a storm, possibly as early as the seventeenth century. The wreck was reported by a number of others, like McGibbon—who in 1876 was recalling his childhood—often in retrospect. It was definitely there in the 1870s, though by the 1890s was reportedly sinking into the surrounding mud. By the early twentieth century:

> The ship was there all right, though not very much of her was above the surrounding swamp. At low tide we clambered aboard, the deck appeared to be intact, though all the hatches were full of mud, which had sifted in, tide after tide, and now probably filled every hollow space.

By then, the legend was firmly embedded in local folklore and had grown some new branches. One was a lost treasure yarn. In 1855, entrepreneur John Hurford was murdered by his wife and her lover. The story went that they were after the treasure Hurford had taken from the ship. In fact, they were after the considerable wealth he had amassed from work and speculation. They were both hanged.

For a good few years before settlement, the south-west coast of Western Australia was the haunt of sealers, whalers and even a pirate usually known as Black Jack Anderson. These desperadoes were notorious for ill-treating First Nations peoples and generally behaving like real pirates did: very unpleasantly. When settlement brought potential markets to the area, their boats were useful for smuggling rum and tobacco. These activities formed another romantic backdrop to the story of the Deadwater wreck.

Some researchers have suggested that the wreck could be one of a few Dutch East India Company craft that went missing on their way from the Cape to what is now Jakarta, Indonesia, but was then called Batavia. The Dutch had a strong presence in the islands to our north, based on their discovery of a route across the Indian Ocean through the roaring forties. When in sight of what we now call Australia, their ships turned directly north and made a straight run along the coast to Batavia. Navigation in those days was very hit and miss, so it was easy to miscalculate and literally crash into rocks along the west coast. Most did not, but several known to have left the Cape in the seventeenth century have not been seen since. One of these could possibly have become the Deadwater wreck.

But where was it? Many people have searched for it since the last sightings without success.

And what was it? Was there really a large, possibly Dutch or Spanish ship wrecked on these shores at such an early date? Or was the wreckage people were seeing in the dunes and mud just the shattered remnants of an old whaling boat?

It seems that the answer could be 'both'.

Between 2005 and 2015, a team of maritime archaeologists surveyed the area where the wreck had been reported. They conducted a thorough search of historical weather and other records and used metal detection and other archaeological techniques to understand the effect of natural forces and discover a possible location for any pre-colonial wreck. They found not one, not two, but three possible hidden wrecks. One of these was already well documented: a longboat belonging to the French Baudin expedition of 1801.

. . . but not that of the wreck in the Wonnerup Deadwater, nor that of the Vasse Estuary wreck. Both the wrecks of unknown origin were known locally as Deadwater Wreck. This has led to great confusion over the years. Both wrecks lay in areas of deadwater (absence of current). In an attempt to avoid further confusion, we have given the popular name to the wreck in the Wonnerup Deadwater.

In reaching this apparent resolution of the mystery, the report cited evidence that pointed to the possibility of Dutch shipwreck survivors living with local First Nations communities. Some seemingly Dutch words are spoken in the local dialect and tradition also mentions white men living in the area long before European settlement in the 1830s.

Further research will be required to settle this but, as the report concludes: 'Until that time the mystery and the speculation will doubtless live on.'

Other early Dutch wrecks are believed to lie along the rugged Western Australian coast. The Abrolhos Islands are only a few hours by sea from the popular holiday location of Geraldton. Spearfishing there in 1966, veteran shipwreck hunter Hugh Edwards picked up an elephant tusk from the seabed. It could only have come from a Dutch East Indiaman that disappeared 300 years ago. The *Aagtekerke* left the Cape of Good Hope for Batavia, modern-day Jakarta, and was never seen again. As well as a load of elephant tusks, she was carrying a hefty cargo of silver coins thought to be worth many millions of dollars today. If they can be found. Hugh is still looking, though any treasure found would be the property of the federal government. Solving the mystery, rather than claiming the money, is what drives many treasure hunters.

THE LOST WHALEMEN

In 1961 the historian Lloyd Robson visited St John's Home for the Aged in New Town, Hobart, Tasmania. Like a few other historians and folklorists of the period, he was seeking out old Australian folk songs in the well-founded belief that many would die out with the generations that carried them. In the retirement home he interviewed and recorded Mr J.H. Davies, a veteran of the Tasmanian whaling industry, then aged 88. Davies went whaling as a teenager and over the course of his adult life had seen and heard a thing or two, as they say. Among his stock of old songs was a whaling ballad about a mysterious tragedy that took place off the Tasmanian coast more than a century before Lloyd Robson turned on his tape recorder.

The Tasmanian whaling trade was established with shore-based operations in 1805 and expanded rapidly in the 1820s. From 1828 to 1838 it is thought that almost 3000 southern right whales were harpooned by Tasmanian whalers. From the 1840s whale numbers declined and it was necessary to change to deep-sea whaling. By 1849 the Hobart whaling fleet boasted 34 ships and whalemen from around the world worked in the industry. The fishery declined from the late 1870s due partly to overfishing. The last deep-sea whaler out of Tasmania, the *Helen*, returned home in 1900, effectively ending the Tasmanian trade.

Whaling with handheld harpoons was a dirty and dangerous business with many disasters and high, but usually explainable, fatalities. That was not the case with this event. On 5 November 1859 the brig *Grecian* sighted whales off South West Cape. Mate Robert 'Bob' Marney and 'his boat's crew' of five men were lowered into the sea. They gave chase and harpooned the whale. The small boat was dragged by the whale until nightfall, when the *Grecian* lost sight of it. When the *Grecian* returned to home port over three weeks later, the local paper carried a report:

The whaling brig Grecian came in and anchored in the South West Passage last evening. Captain Clarke reports that all his endeavors to find the boats crew which missed the vessel while killing a whale, on the evening of the 5th, have been ineffectual; he has still, however, hopes of their safety as Marney, the Chief Officer, who had charge of the boat, was well acquainted with the coast, off which they were only about twenty-five miles distant, and just before sundown Mount Hemskirk, situated a little to the north-ward of Macquarie Harbour, was plainly visible.

During the two succeeding days the weather was fine and the wind for the coast was fair. A vigorous search with the boats and ship has been kept up ever since the occurrence, and Port Davey has been visited, but not Macquarie Harbour, in consequence of the wind having veered round to the north west, before it was determined to stand in for the land . . . The Grecian has 22 tuns sperm oil . . .

For some unknown reason, it seems Marney and his men did not cut themselves free of the harpooned whale. Were they all thrown into the cold sea as their boat capsized? Or, Moby Dick-like, were they so entangled in their ropes that when the whale dived they were dragged beneath the waves? Perhaps they were simply adrift? It was not unknown for whaleboats to be stranded for days before being picked up. The mother of the boat steerer, John McFarlane, chartered a private search vessel but nothing was ever found.

The loss of six men from a small community was a deep shock that resulted in a ballad documenting the incident, based closely on a broadside usually known as 'Lady Franklin's Lament'. That song commemorated another mystery, the loss of Sir John Franklin and his crew in their famously ill-fated attempt to find the Arctic Northwest Passage from 1845. Franklin had been a not very popular lieutenant-governor of Tasmania from 1837 to 1843, though Lady Franklin was widely liked and respected for her good works. Although Bob Marney was lost some years before Mr Davies was born, he knew some of the men who had served with Marney on the *Grecian* and from whom he presumably learned the song, which seems to have been quite popular in Tasmania.

Far out-ward bound, far o'er the deep,
Slung in my hammock I fell asleep,
I had a dream which I thought was true,
Concerning Marney and his boat's crew.

With all his crew he sailed away,
Lost in the darkness one stormy day*
Off yon green island out far from here,
Where we lost Marney and his boat's gear.

There's Captain Kennedy of Hobart-town,
There's Captain Reynolds of high renown,
There's Captain Robertson and many, many more,
They've long been cruising Macquarie shore.

They cruised east and they cruised west,
Round the sou'-west cape where they thought best.
No tale or tiding could they see or hear,
Concerning Marney or his boat's gear.

In Research Bay where the black whale blow,
The sad tale of Marney they all do know,
They say he's gone like a many many more,
He left his home to return no more.

As we draw nearer to Hobart shore,
I saw a fair maid in deep replore, [sic]
She was sobbing, sighing, saying pity me,
I've lost my brother, poor Bob Marney.

[2 lines missing]
I've lost my brother, no more to see,
I've lost my brother, poor Bob Marney.

*Hypothetical reconstruction of part lines missing from
original recording.

The 'Captain Reynolds of high renown' was probably Michael Reynolds, born in Hobart in 1830. Reynolds went whaling in the Pacific at the age of sixteen. He later became captain of a whaler, though if the song is accurate he would have been a very young captain in 1853. It seems more likely that folk memory has inserted his name into the song long after the originating events faded into the past, leaving only the faintest traces in an old ballad.

The whalemen who died with Bob Marney were John McFarlane, John Gray, Joseph Kemp, George Jackson and Joseph Walton.

THE SPECTRE OF ARMIT ISLAND

As well as the sometimes odd characters who have made their homes along the Great Barrier Reef, there are one or two fine ghost stories floating around the area. One of the best is the spectre of Armit Island in the Whitsunday Islands where a man named Heron took up a lease of the island from the Queensland government in the 1890s. He lived alone, collecting wild seeds and plants that drifted in from far off places. Passing yachts and other boats called in from time to time and during a conversation with one sailor who asked Heron how he managed to live in such isolation, he replied that he had company: 'a sailor'.

There was no sight of any other human on the island, as later visitors confirmed, and Heron's statement might have been put down to the ravings of an eccentric hermit. Except that some years later, a Captain Gorringe camped on the island for a week or so and Heron told him about the first time he had seen his phantom companion:

He had not been long on the island, he said, when, disturbed by something he could not remember, he rose late at night. He walked out of his hut, and as he did so there came a shrill cry of unmistakable agony from the scrubby-slopes of the island. Soon afterwards the silent watcher saw the figure of a sailor come from the scrub, pass through the stunted oaks, and walk to the water's edge.

Heron thought the apparition was real and called out but received no answer. Dressed in a short jacket with buttons and the three-quarter-length trousers worn by sailors centuries earlier, the figure marched straight down the beach and disappeared into the sea. Afterwards, Heron often heard the agonised screams and witnessed the same night-time march of the sailor into the surf.

Gorringe did not see the ghost himself. But Charles Anderson did when anchored off the island in 1908 on his cutter, *Faith*:

> 'It was a misty-looking figure,' Anderson said, 'and there was something about it which immediately convinced me that it was not the figure of a living man. It did not walk so much as float a few inches above the sand. The phantom came and went so quickly that I did not have time to examine it properly, but my impression was that the sailor clothes on the ghostly figure were those of the seventeenth century.'

The journalist Frank Reid ('Bill Bowyang') claimed to have seen and heard the ghost while camping on the island in the 1930s. He described it as 'a shadowy figure dressed after the fashion of a "sailor of Nelson's days". The face was that of a man of between 35 and 40 years of age . . . and the eyes stared straight ahead and never glanced in the direction of the camping party. The phantom appeared to be wafted along rather than to walk.'

Fantasy? Delusion? An unusually long-lasting hoax? And where would an ancient mariner come from? Captain Cook didn't lose any of his crew along that coast. At least, he didn't note it in his journal. Of course, the fabled Spanish have been mentioned as a possibility. Despite an absence of historical evidence, the legend of the Armit Island spectre can still be heard along the reef today.

THE HEADLESS ANGEL

The sailing ship *Torrens* was fortunate to reach its destination in February 1899. She limped into Adelaide harbor without a foretopmast, jib boom and bowsprit. Her foremast was also badly damaged and her 'graceful cut-water bow jagged and patched'.

Captain Falkland Angel reported that his ship had smashed into an iceberg almost a month before, some 40 kilometres south-west of the Crozet Islands, around 46 degrees South in the Indian Ocean. Lifebelts were issued in fear that the *Torrens* would founder. She hit the iceberg once more, then grazed the ice as the crew tried desperately to get clear. Just as the stricken vessel was coming around for a fourth and almost certainly fatal collision with the berg, it floated away. It was, as the nautically knowledgeable types of Adelaide confirmed on inspecting the wreckage, 'a marvellous escape'. Captain and crew were commended on their professionalism by the relieved passengers.

The *Torrens* misadventure caused no human casualties, but the damage to the ship included the loss of her female figurehead, a wooden statue that many sailing ships carried beneath their bowsprits. An ancient tradition, adorning ships with female figures was thought to protect them and those aboard from harm, in accordance with the mariners' belief that stormy seas could be calmed by the female breast. Sailors were notoriously superstitious and regarded the figureheads of their ships as vital good luck charms. Even as late as 1899, the loss of the figurehead would have been disturbing for the crew.

It might also have been disturbing for the captain. The figurehead on the *Torrens*, last of the great clippers to ferry wool and passengers between London and Adelaide, was said to have been modelled on his sister Flores, daughter of the ship's first captain, Henry Robert Angel. Emily, as she was known, launched the Sunderland-built vessel in 1875.

The accident was only one of a number of mishaps suffered by the *Torrens* after Angel senior relinquished his original command in 1890. A Captain Cope took over for some years, during which the aspiring writer, Joseph Conrad, served aboard as Chief Officer from 1891 to 1893. He later wrote of the ship's seaworthiness: 'A ship of brilliant qualities—the way the ship had of letting big seas slip under her did one's heart good to watch. It resembled so much an exhibition of intelligent grace and unerring skill that it could fascinate even the least seaman-like of our passengers.' The Angel family involvement with the ship ended in 1906 when the *Torrens* was sold and, four years later, broken.

But that was not the end of the story.

In 1973, members of the Australian National Antarctic Research Expedition (ANARE) were carrying out scientific fieldwork on Macquarie Island, midway between New Zealand and Antarctica. They noticed a large pile of driftwood in a mudhole and eventually managed to drag it out. It was a life-size female ship's figurehead, missing its head. Over the next two years, ANARE members managed to drag the 140 kilogram weight back to their base station. At one point, the prize was almost lost again when the rope attaching her to a helicopter broke and the statue disappeared into the foliage. But she was recovered and, after much strenuous effort, reached the station. From there, she was shipped to the Melbourne warehouse of ANARE and forgotten for many years until she was sent to the Queen Victoria Museum and Art Gallery in Launceston for much-needed conservation work.

It would not be until shipwreck researcher Glyn Roberts came upon an account of the *Torrens* accident that a likely connection was made. Could this be the headless figure of Flores Angel? If so, how did it come to be on a remote subantarctic island?

Roberts got hold of the original plans for the *Torrens*. They showed a figurehead painted in white and gold, similar to the one discovered on the island. He made some calculations based on the circumference of the Earth at the point between where the *Torrens* hit the iceberg and Macquarie Island. His estimates suggested that the figurehead would need to have floated eastwards for more than 7300 kilometers to end up where the ANARE members found her.

Impossible!

Not so. Using figures and research on the global ocean flow known as the Antarctic Circumpolar Current, Roberts concluded that the figure could have reached Macquarie in as little as eighteen months. Not only that, but it might have floated around the world on the circumpolar current, a voyage that would take about eight to ten years. It was even possible that the decapitated lady had traversed the world as many as seven times by the time she was found, 74 years after being torn from beneath the bowsprit of the *Torrens*.

But there are still some unanswered questions. Inquiries to the Queen Victoria Museum and Art Gallery in 2018 confirmed that the headless lady is still safely in their keeping. Though whether or not she is the figurehead of the *Torrens*, we may never know.

THE MYSTERY OF THE *MADAGASCAR*

Outside the secretive world of treasure hunters, the disappearance of the *Madagascar* is not widely known today. But in the 1850s, the fate of the Blackwall frigate and her valuable cargo was headline news and remained of great public interest until well towards the end of the last century. Some are still interested in the story.

The appeal of the story at the time was amplified by a link with an audacious and violent gold escort robbery at McIvor goldfield (Heathcote, Victoria) in July 1853. After an exchange of gunfire that wounded several of the robbers, they made their escape to Melbourne with more than 2000 ounces (57 kilograms) of gold and £700 in cash. Several of the robbers boarded or attempted to board the *Madagascar*, due to sail for London via Cape Horn. Police tracked them down and made arrests, though it seems that one of the gang might have eluded capture and sailed with the *Madagascar* when she eventually left port.

As well as whatever the elusive robber might have been carrying, and the probably large number of well-heeled diggers among the passengers, the *Madagascar* was transporting 60,000 ounces (1.7 tonnes) of gold dust and a large cargo of wool. This hoard, along with the cargo, the crew, the passengers and the ship that carried them, has never been seen again.

By the time it was obvious the *Madagascar* had come to grief, the rumours began and have never stopped. She was sunk in a bad storm around the notorious Cape Horn, or splintered by icefloes. There was a mutiny. The ship and the treasure were taken by pirates. Sightings of the lost ship were made around the world, all unsubstantiated. Nearly twenty years later a man on his death bed confessed to knowing who had murdered the *Madagascar*'s captain.

The sensational possibilities of these speculations were quickly picked up by writers and journalists and became the basis of many fictions. Novels and stories about the events were published—one in France—within a few years of the disappearance. They continued to be published, along with frequent newspaper articles, throughout the rest of the century and into the 1920s. The writer of *Hawaii* and other well-known works on the Pacific, James A. Michener, picked up the tale again in the 1980s.

All of these writers advanced various theories about the mystery and added details, real or not, to the story. In some, the death-bed confessor became a female passenger who was raped by mutineers and was too ashamed to tell until her death. Even the 'boys' own' aviator, Biggles, was attached to the story in the 1940s.

More recently, a case has been made for the *Madagascar* falling prey to William 'Bully' Hayes, notorious trader, blackbirder, fraudster and alleged child rapist of the Pacific Ocean. American-born Hayes had an ongoing relationship with Australia, possibly visiting first in the early 1850s. He was charged with indecent assault of a young woman aboard his stolen ship, the *Ellenita*, in 1860, only one of many accusations of paedophilia made throughout his life. Hayes escaped this charge but went to Darlinghurst gaol for debt. After some theatrical experiences he sailed for New Zealand where, among other things, he ran a pub, married again and operated nefariously. In 1866 he entered the blackbirding trade, bringing South Sea Islanders to Queensland for indentured work mainly in the sugar industry.

Hayes later made himself obnoxious in the Caroline Islands and the Philippines, washing up again in San Francisco. From here he embarked on the yacht *Lotus* with a woman and a small crew. There was repeated trouble between Hayes and the cook that ended with Hayes being killed and thrown overboard. No one was ever charged with this crime and the man believed to have done the deed was treated as a hero. It has been said that the killing was sparked by a desire of the crew to obtain the treasure Hayes was believed to have buried in 1874 on an island in what is now known as the Federated States of Micronesia.

Bully Hayes was described by one of his many biographers as 'notorious in every Pacific port' and appears in several sea shanties from the days of sail as a harsh villainous master. The seizure of the *Madagascar* and murder of the captain and others aboard would have been extreme behaviour, even for him, but not completely unbelievable, though it would have been very early in his ill-starred career. Mostly forgotten today, Hayes was a larger-than-life character and one whose exploits, real and otherwise, have been much romanticised by writers, filmmakers and journalists.

Whatever Bully Hayes had to do, or not, with the disappearance of the *Madagascar*, it remains one of the many mysteries of Australia's offshore domain, as does the fate of the treasure aboard. People have been looking for that ever since she disappeared. In 2014, a treasure hunter claimed to have found the wreck on a French Polynesian atoll 1500 kilometres south-east of Tahiti. Artefacts were retrieved but no treasure.

Hmm.

AUSTRALIA'S *TITANIC*

Claude G. Sawyer had a dream. Several dreams, in fact, though none of them were sweet.

Sawyer, an engineer by trade, was one of several hundred passengers aboard the *Waratah*, travelling from Sydney to England via Cape Town, South Africa, in 1909. He was a frequent sea voyager, journeying in some style aboard the Blue Anchor Line's large luxury liner with an option to disembark, or not, at Cape Town. It did not take long for him to begin wondering about the stability of the ship. She seemed top heavy and was slow to correct after rolling. His bathwater once slid away from him at a 45 degree angle as the ship listed.

Sawyer then had the same nightmare three times in one night. A figure appeared to him carrying a sword in his left hand and a bloody cloth in the other. The apparition pushed the cloth straight at Sawyer's face. After this unsettling experience, Sawyer decided to get off the ship early in Durban. He planned to catch another vessel from there. Later, he telegraphed his wife to let her know that he thought the *Waratah* was top heavy and that he had booked an alternative passage to Cape Town. He even tried, unsuccessfully, to convince some of his fellow passengers to leave with him. While he waited in Durban, he had another dream in which a large ship was sunk in rough seas by a giant wave. Sawyer's dreams and misgivings saved his life.

Versions of this story, which Sawyer gave to the subsequent inquiry, have been told and retold many times over the century or so since the *Waratah* vanished without trace, some time after 27 July. The liner was definitely sighted by another ship after leaving Durban and possibly by several others, though weather conditions were deteriorating rapidly and it was difficult to make out the identity of a vessel without radio in the blackness of the ocean night.

Like the *Titanic*, which was lost three years later, *Waratah* was said to be unsinkable, so it was some days before concern in Cape Town elevated to fear and a search began. The weather turned bad again and nothing was found. A few days later the Australian parliament received a cable saying that a ship that might be *Waratah* was making its way slowly for Durban. But the jubilation was short-lived; it was another ship. Further searches were made without success and *Waratah* was listed as missing by Lloyd's in December that year.

Speculation about the fate of the *Waratah* and those aboard fastened quickly on the instability noted by Sawyer and other passengers. At that period, passenger ships were often designed to allow for long, slow rolling, which most passengers, unknowledgeable about nautical design, found more comfortable than the jerkier but safer motion of a properly balanced craft. Could the ill-fated vessel have been hit by an unusually powerful wave and never recovered? There was a bad storm, sometimes described as a cyclone, in the region at the time.

A couple of linked possibilities were suggested. Perhaps her cargo of a thousand tons of lead concentrate had shifted, probably due to storm activity? That might have been enough to fatally unbalance the vessel. Whirlpools are not unknown along those coasts. Was she sucked deep beneath the waves by one of these creations of wind and current?

Sailors aboard another ship in the area around the time *Waratah* disappeared reported seeing two bright flashes on the horizon. It was suggested that the dust from the coal she carried to fuel her boilers had ignited, causing an explosion that sank her.

Most of these possibilities did not account for the total absence of wreckage or bodies. The inquiry was further frustrated in reaching a conclusion by the testimonies of past crew and passengers. While some agreed with Sawyer, just as many recalled that the *Waratah* was an acceptably stable ship and there was no evidence to suggest any flaws in her design or construction. As the *Waratah*'s last voyage was only the second she had taken, this evidence, too, was inconclusive.

The Board of Trade inquiry made a few observations about the Blue Anchor Line's internal safety processes but was unable to reach any firm decision about the end of the *Waratah*. Underinsured, as most shipowners were, and suffering a public relations disaster, the consequences of the disaster bankrupted the company.

Many people have searched for the *Waratah* since then. How could a 141 metre liner of more than 9000 tonnes vanish into the ocean without verifiable trace? One avid seeker, Emlyn Brown, spent over twenty years searching. He finally gave up in 2004, declaring: 'I've exhausted all the options. I now have no idea where to look.'

WRAITH OF THE *KØBENHAVN*

She was the largest sailing ship in the world. The *København* (*Copenhagen*) was launched in 1921, her 131 metre steel hull supporting five masts towering nearly twenty stories into the winds that would bear the barque twice round the world before her still inexplicable disappearance *en route* for Melbourne.

The *København* carried some cargo, but was primarily a training vessel for young sailors between fifteen and twenty years of age seeking an officer's ticket. Her voyages provided an opportunity for seasoned mariners to teach young men the many skills they would need to make a career in sail, still a serious option in Scandinavian countries at that time.

On her tenth voyage, the *København* sailed from Northern Jutland bound for Buenos Aires with a cargo of cement and chalk. Aboard was the experienced Captain Hans Andersen together with 26 crew and 45 cadets from many of Denmark's leading families. Unloading at Buenos Aires, the ship was unable to find another cargo for Australia and so Andersen decided to set sail without one. Now with a crew of only fifteen, they set a course to Adelaide (then on to Melbourne) eleven days before Christmas, a trip expected to take just under seven weeks. On 22 December the *København* signalled 'all is well' to a passing Norwegian steamer around 1500 kilometres from the island of Tristan da Cunha.

Captain Andersen was known not to make much use of radio and often went for long periods without signalling. In those days, marine radios had a very limited range. The Danish East Asiatic Company, which owned the ship, was not unduly concerned when they had no word. But as the weeks slipped by and there was no sound from their magnificent vessel, nor any sight of her, they became increasingly alarmed. The Australian press echoed Danish fears for sons, brothers, fathers and uncles. 'Where is the Kobenhavn?', asked the *Adelaide Advertiser* in mid-March, initiating a lengthy chronicle of newspaper articles in the Australian press and around the world.

A search vessel was sent to Tristan da Cunha. A large sailing ship with a broken foremast had been sighted in late January. With her sails only partly set and low in the water, the drifting vessel showed no signs of life. Locals were unable to reach her because of bad weather but had found no wreckage and thought she must have passed by the island. With the assistance of a small Australian interstate steamer, the *Junee*, the search continued for some months, but without result. At one point it was surmised that wreckage might drift to the Western Australian coast. A plane was chartered to fly from Fremantle to North West Cape, but again nothing was found. The Danish government declared the *København*, her captain, crew and cadets lost. Another mighty ship joined the untold others foundered in the world's ocean deeps.

But then the sightings began. Over the next few years Chilean fishermen reported a five-masted ship in their waters. Sailors aboard an Argentinian freighter saw what they called a 'phantom ship' fitting the *København*'s description as they fought a gale. Other sightings came from Easter Island and the coast of Peru. It was also reported that a ship's stern section with the name *København* had washed up on a Western Australian beach.

And then they found the bottle. In 1934, the son of Argentina's president visited the United States telling a strange story. Men from a whaler working off Bouvet Island in the South Atlantic had found a sealed bottle containing a 'log' or diary of a surviving cadet of the *København*. The log told a grim story. The *København* struck an iceberg. There was no option for those aboard but to take to the lifeboats. In the distance they saw their fine ship crushed between two icebergs. The diary ended with, 'It is snowing and a gale blows. I realise our fate. This sea has taken us beyond the limits of this world.'

Whatever the authenticity of this now missing document, the story fitted the predominant theory about the disappearance of the *København*: like the *Titanic*, victim to a drifting iceberg. The following year another grim find appeared to provide further support for this explanation. It was reported that the remains of a ship's boat with seven skeletons had been found on the south-west coast of Africa, over 600 kilometres north of the city of Swakopmund in South West Africa (now Namibia). Nautical experts ridiculed the suggestion that this might be a boat from the *København*: 'It is a far-fetched theory, absolutely without justification,' said Captain Davis, Victorian Director of Navigation.

Other speculations abounded. The *København* might have encountered a tsunami. As her holds were empty and she sailed only in ballast she might have capsized in bad weather. Rumours, theories and searches for the lost barque have continued ever since. In 2012 divers found a wreck on Tristan da Cunha that some believe might be the missing ship. The Danish government and the East Asiatic Company were reportedly taking the suggestion seriously enough to establish the truth of this possibility. But nothing has since been reported and, today, the fate of the *København* and her crew is regarded as one of the world's greatest unsolved maritime mysteries.

THE FATE OF *PATANELA*

The radio call received at the Sydney Maritime Radio Centre in the early hours of 8 November 1988 was nothing unusual. Sailing boats often needed to tack far out into the Pacific to access Sydney Harbour. Ken Jones, skipper of the 19 metre steel schooner *Patanela*, said the boat was out of fuel and might need assistance when entering the harbour later that morning.

But almost an hour later, something had changed. *Patanela* called again asking for weather information and, according to some accounts, directions for Moruya, a coastal town several hundred kilometres south of Sydney. A very drastic change of course, especially for a boat running out of diesel.

No more was ever heard from the *Patanela* or the four people aboard. A buoy bearing the name *Patanela* was found at Terrigal six months later, though was probably not from the boat in question. A message in an empty rum bottle was discovered on a beach near Eucla in 2007. Dated almost two weeks before the vanishing, the note gave the *Patanela*'s position and read: 'Hi there. Out here in the lonely Southern Ocean and thought we would give away a free holiday in the Whitsunday Islands in north Queensland, Australia. Our ship is travelling from Fremantle, Western Aust, to Queensland to work as a charter vessel.'

The note was signed by John Blissett, one of the crew members. Otherwise, no trace has ever been found.

What happened? The schooner was a high-end craft that had weathered round-the-world passages and Antarctic voyages. She had watertight compartments and was fitted with all the latest navigational and safety gear.

The *Patanela* was owned by wealthy Perth businessman Alan Nicol and, it seems, another person. Exactly who owned the boat is one of the unclear elements of this mystery. Whatever Nicol's exact ownership of the vessel was, he had been aboard the yacht when she left Fremantle. He went ashore to attend to business matters back in Perth. Another passenger, the daughter of Ken and his wife Noreen, left the boat later, leaving Ken, Noreen, John Blissett and Michael Calvin to voyage onwards to whatever fate they met.

A few days before the schooner disappeared, Michael Calvin made a radio telephone call to his father but was abruptly cut off before he could say more than 'G'day, Dad'. Was it a technical fault or an omen of something more sinister? Calvin did not call again.

Officials found nothing in the backgrounds of the missing to suggest anything criminal or otherwise suspect. Ken Jones was an experienced sailor while Calvin and Blissett were a couple of young sailing enthusiasts keen to crew in return for a free trip and some sea time. They had also been promised the use of the boat for a charter service in the Whitsundays.

The weather at the time and place of the disappearance was fine. There are no known submerged rocks or other hazards. No other shipping was thought to be in the area. It should have been plain sailing.

Was there some kind of catastrophic accident? If so, why was no wreckage ever found? A search was mounted but soon called off. The police pointed out that although the messages from the *Patanela* were allegedly from a position outside Botany Bay, they could have been hundreds of kilometres away. Perhaps the *Panatela* and those aboard had been the victims of piracy and kidnap?

After some jurisdictional issues were settled, the Australian Federal Police took over the case in early 1989. A national and international investigation was established under the name 'Operation Lilac'. Led by Detective Superintendent Ed Tyrie, the investigation had its work cut out. There were hundreds of sightings of the *Patanela* by yachties and others around the world. Theories again abounded. A collision with a Russian submarine or floating container. Uncharted reefs. Drug dealers hijacked the boat and used it elsewhere for smuggling.

After three years, nothing was found to explain the disappearance. The coroner concluded from the scant evidence available that the *Patanela* had foundered sometime after 1.57 a.m. 'on 8 November 1988 in the Tasman Sea off Sydney Heads'. What caused the boat to sink he could not say, but the crew members were dead.

Sailors and authorities have remained baffled by the case ever since. The *Patanela* has joined the long list of vanished vessels that now sail only in tales of mystery and loss.

FINDING *ENDEAVOUR*

There's something odd going on with the search for Captain Cook's famous ship.

The *Endeavour* carried Lieutenant James Cook and his companions around the world between 1768 and 1771. As well as claiming the land we now call Australia in the name of the British Crown, the 30-or-so metre *Endeavour* made many significant discoveries and its fabled group of curious scientists carried out some important research tasks. This voyage, together with others made by Cook, confirmed him as arguably the greatest ocean navigator the world has ever known. That is some claim when you consider that others who might lay claim to that honour include Christopher Columbus, Ferdinand Magellan and Vasco da Gama.

Since its first circumnavigation, *Endeavour* has become almost as famous as Cook himself, with researchers having many unanswered questions about the humble Whitby collier that made one of history's most celebrated voyages. One of the mysteries associated with Cook and his ship is how a vessel built for England's coastal coal-carrying trade was able to cross and recross the world. Undoubtedly, the seamanship of Cook and his crew is a large part of the answer to that question. But whatever qualities their ship possessed must also have been important. What were they?

And where was *Endeavour*? The Royal Navy had quietly disposed of Cook's ship and she sailed into the twilight world of vessels past their use-by date. But her name became burnished with greater and greater fame over time. A River Thames wreck was falsely touted to sightseers as the remnants of *Endeavour*. Relics associated with the ship are exhibited in museums around the world and several replicas have been built. Maritime archaeologists, historians and treasure hunters have been searching for her remains for many years, not because *Endeavour* is thought to have any treasures in her hold but because of her fame and that of her captain.

After the worn-out *Endeavour* returned to England, she was used to transport naval goods to and from the Falkland Islands, then sold into private shipping interests. Under the name *Lord Sandwich* she took part in the American Revolution as a troop transport and prison ship. In 1778 she was scuttled with another dozen or so ships at the entry to Newport Harbour, Rhode Island. *Endeavour* was now part of an underwater blockade against the attacking French, allied at that time with the American forces. It was not until 1993 that a local maritime archaeology group, the Rhode Island Marine Archaeology Project (RIMAP), rediscovered the wrecks. It was not known until 1999 that *Endeavour* was among them.

Previously, another wreck at Newport had been identified as Cook's ship. Her name was *La Liberté*. Sections of this ship were displayed around the world as relics of *Endeavour* and one sliver even went into space with the *Apollo 15* mission in 1971; one of NASA's space shuttles also bore the name. It is now thought that this ship was, in fact, the *Resolution*, the ship Cook sailed on his second and third voyages of discovery. If proven, it would be an enormous historical coincidence for two such famous ships sailed by the great James Cook to be lying a few kilometres away from each other.

But difficult ocean conditions and funding problems have hampered confirmation of these likelihoods. *Endeavour* has been reported 'rediscovered' at least six times since 1999. Such is the hunger to know for certain where Cook's ship lies that whenever the research group makes an announcement about progress in their search, the world's media immediately trumpet that the ship has been found. Researchers have been progressively and painstakingly narrowing down the options for which of the many wrecks is actually *Endeavour*. They are close, but not there yet.

Hopefully, now in conjunction with the Australian National Maritime Museum, progress will be made and the mystery of *Endeavour*—and of *Resolution*—may finally be resolved, along with those intriguing questions about her design and amazing seagoing capabilities.

THE VANISHING WRECKS OF WAR

In 2016, divers in the Java Sea were astonished to find that the very large wreck surveyed fourteen years earlier had completely disappeared. The only remaining trace of where the 6545 tonne *De Ruyter* once rested was an enormous impression in the ocean floor.

At least six more World War II warships have also vanished over recent years. Others also show signs of attack from the 'metal pirates', including the cruiser *Houston*. Divers, professional and recreational, salvage professionals, scientists and historians were baffled. How could these enormous structures simply disappear and who was making it happen?

The Java Sea, running between what are now the Indonesian islands of Java and Sulawesi and the country of Malaysia, was the scene of mighty naval confrontations in 1942. The Imperial Japanese Navy was arrayed against combined Australian, Dutch, British and American forces seeking to stem the enemy advance through south Asia and, it was feared, to Australia.

Three Dutch ships were sunk, two British ships and one American submarine were lost in various actions.

These were not small ships. The *De Ruyter* measured over 560 feet (170 metres), while the British *Exeter* was almost 540 feet (165 metres) long and another well over 322 feet (98 metres) in length. Being heavily armoured warships, these vessels are a treasure trove for illegal salvagers. As well as the steel, brass, bronze and even aluminium fittings, shafts, propellors and other nautical equipment can also be worth a great deal of money in the international scrap market.

Further afield, other wartime wrecks off Malaysia and Thailand have been targeted. As well as continuing to be the property of the countries to which these wrecks belong, they are war graves. Grave robbers who interfere with the wrecks are committing international crimes. There are also ethical and emotional issues deeply disturbing to many. The governments of the countries involved, as well as Australia, are concerned about these activities, as is the Indonesian government in whose waters the wrecks—or the little that is left of them—lie. So are the descendants of those who died in the battle.

There is a great deal of speculation about exactly how the robbers are carrying out their operations. The usual mode of operation for plundering wrecks involves small groups of local fishermen or divers taking a few bits and pieces. The even more serious stealing of larger sections of hull usually leaves a trail of rusting rivets, bolts and other items on the sea floor. What makes the more recent activity especially baffling is that none of these bits and pieces remain behind. The giant ships have completely disappeared. How could that be?

Salvage experts can only guess. A very large barge and crane using a giant grappling claw or a powerful industrial magnet is one explanation. But even then, no known salvage equipment is that powerful. Explosives or an undersea wrecking ball are also possible, but all these techniques leave telltale fragments on the sea floor, as well as some sort of ghostly metal skeleton behind. These big ships have totally vanished.

Who could have such enormous and advanced equipment? And why did no one witness what must have been intensive, loud and lengthy activity above the removed wrecks? Suspicions have been raised that a national government is the most likely source of such sophisticated and expensive apparatus, possibly posing as a research craft of some kind. This aspect of the mystery is not likely to be resolved any time soon, despite sophisticated satellite tracking technology that can pinpoint potentially illegal activity on the sea surface.

It is all about money, of course. But there may also be a more sinister reason for plundering these war graves. The steel bodies of the sunken ships were smelted before the world went nuclear. Unlike post-1945 ships, the carcases of these wrecks are free of radioactivity, making them prized for medical steel but especially for military purposes in the present.

'Yankee Ned' (Edward Mosby) with his grandchildren in the Torres Strait,
shortly before his death in 1911. An American 'of uncertain origins
and background', he managed to make his fortune and become a
benevolent patriarch of Masig Island. But he buried all his pearls
and didn't tell anyone where to find them before he died . . .

3

LOST TREASURES

YAMADA NAGAMASA'S HOARD

As far as history is concerned, no seventeenth century Japanese pirates ever visited Australia. But a persistent tradition has it that Yamada Nagamasa not only sailed to Magnetic Island near Cape York Peninsula but also buried his treasure there.

Yamada's story is colourful enough even without buried treasure. Born in Suruga province in 1590, he followed the merchant trade into South-East Asia, establishing his base in the Japanese colony of Siam (now Thailand), attacking Dutch shipping and rising through the ranks among the *Nihonmachi* (expatriate and locally born Japanese). The *Nihonmachi* both traded and provided warriors for the Siamese army and a bodyguard for the king and Yamada rose to become the leader of the Japanese in Siam.

In 1628 the ruling monarch died and a ruthless new ruler took the throne. Yamada remained loyal to the forces of the old king and so became a political liability. He was sent to take back control of a rebel southern province and to be its governor. Yamada succeeded in this task and by 1630 the province was back under royal control, though the heroic warrior was wounded in the battle. While recuperating he was poisoned in unexplained circumstances, but almost certainly on the orders of the new king of Siam. The *Nihonmachi* were attacked and driven from the country. The Japanese emperor was outraged by these events and, in spite of the value of trade and the eventual return of the *Nihonmachi* to Siam, contact between the two countries faded away and was not renewed for another 250 years.

From this blend of politics, trade, violence and national pride, the legend of the great, if ultimately unsuccessful, warrior Yamada Nagamasa evolved in Japan where there is a strong cult of tragic heroes. He is celebrated in literature, film, manga comics and a theme park. Throughout the country, festivals in his name are regularly held and he is regarded as a culture hero of the Japanese people.

But did he bury his treasure on Magnetic Island?

The earliest reference for this possibility seems to occur in a poetically overwritten and undated tourist guide put out on behalf of the Queensland government, probably in the late 1930s. In extolling the delights of Cairns, the author writes:

> In imagination I seem to see phantom vessels which sailed these coral waters in the far off alkaringa [sic] times. Proas, junks, sampans from China Seas and Arafura; the gallant gentleman pirate, Yamada Nagamasa, sailing for Seiyo—the 'Coral Land of the South'; perhaps early Dutch navigators and Spanish and Portugese [sic] captains ... It is recorded that sea-rovers from the East and the Old World visited these northern waters long before the 'Endeavour' sailed past the Bay on Trinity Sunday, 1770.

Evocatively romantic, no mention of treasure though. But as the Queensland coast does have a few authentic treasure finds as well as a good many legends, why not one more? Often the two are inseparable.

In the 1890s pastoralist John Jardine stumbled across half a ton of silver doubloons and pieces of eight in the bones of an ancient wreck on a reef in Albany Passage. He had some of his lucky find made into a silver plate that he used to serve special guests. Despite there being no evidence that the Spanish ever made it as far south as Australia, the belief quickly grew that the wreck must have been one of that nation's galleons. Other yarns of mysterious old wrecks, such as the one sighted but subsequently lost beneath the sands of Stradbroke Island, play into the same mythology.

The belief that a seventeenth century Japanese pirate sailed the long distance from his usual places of pillage and plunder to bury his takings on an island in northern Australia is certainly difficult to credit. Even if he happened to be sailing in that direction he would have encountered many more islands suitable for hiding his hoard. And it would have taken him a long time to get to Australia and back again to Siam or Japan. According to the historical details of Yamada's life, sketchy though they are, he was pretty well continually occupied in freebooting, political intriguing and fighting battles. How he would have fitted an Australian sojourn into such a busy schedule is difficult to imagine. He was only 40 years old when he died.

TREASURE OF THE *GILT DRAGON*

In 1656 a cargo of 78,600 florins was a great deal of money. All those silver coins were in the hold of the Dutch East India Company's almost new *Vergulde Draeck* (*Gilt Dragon*), voyaging from Texel in the Netherlands to the company's stronghold in Batavia. Six weeks out of the Cape the ship, with more than 190 passengers and crew, sailed straight into a reef off the Western Australian coast, a little north of the Moore River.

The shock of the grounding destroyed the ship almost instantly. A few items of wreckage washed up, including one of the ship's small boats. The 70 or so survivors who managed to escape the wreck eventually gathered together to take stock of their dire situation. It was decided that the understeersman and six crew would sail the small boat to Batavia, a voyage of nearly 3000 kilometres, in search of rescue. The remaining survivors would try to repair what was left of the other ship's boat and hope for rescue.

The understeersman duly sailed with the hopes of many in his navigator's hands. In an amazing feat of seamanship and almost certainly good luck, the sailors in the *Vergulde Draeck*'s boat did succeed in reaching Batavia after 40 days at sea. The Company immediately despatched two search vessels to rescue the survivors and the money. The rescuers were instructed that once the people were safely aboard the two ships they should 'try to recover in the most careful way, whether diving or otherwise, if it is possible, firstly the cash and then as much as is practicable and possible of the cargo, the guns and what else is particularly valuable'.

This attempt came to nothing and another eleven men were lost in the process. They went ashore to search the bushland beyond the beach near where they thought the *Draeck* was wrecked and were never seen again. Another expedition the following year also failed and it was not until early in 1658 that a third attempt succeeded in locating the wreckage. The expected items were found—oak beams, a keg, buckets and chests. But no survivors. Nor was there any sign of them.

One of the sailors with the rescue expedition was Englishman Abraham Leeman, a remarkable sailor who is also thought to have been with the stricken *Vergulde Draeck* and may have been one of the six men who sailed with the bad news to Batavia. In the journal that he kept of the rescue voyage, Leeman wrote that they found 'no footprints nor any place where people had lived'. There was one curious find that has been the subject of ongoing controversy to the present day: Leeman noted that 'a number of pieces of planking had been put up in a circle with their ends upwards'.

Still puzzling over the purpose of this structure, the rescuers searched north and south for the survivors, but found nothing but a few more items from the stricken ship. Eventually, the captain gave up the search and callously left Leeman and thirteen men behind on an island to fend for themselves. After an epic voyage in a small open boat, Leeman and only a few others finally managed to get back to Batavia. Their criminally negligent captain was punished and, as far as the Dutch East India Company was concerned, the fate of the *Vergulde Draeck* survivors and her golden cargo faded into the past. But not the mystery.

Soon after continuing European settlement was established on Western Australia's Swan River in 1829, Aboriginal people came bringing old items of European origin. Sections of mast and domestic equipment were found in 1890. A cache of silver coins was found north of Cape Leschenault in 1931. The inevitable treasure maps began turning up and by the 1950s the availability of scuba equipment saw modern wreck hunters begin a series of searches for the wreck. It was officially found in 1963, though it seems that previous attempts had been made to access the wreck.

Now the hunt was on. Attempts were made to excavate a sand dune with machinery and dynamite, creating an eighteen metre crater with nothing at the bottom but more sand. Professional archaeologists were able to make a survey of the site in 1972, reporting remains of the cargo, ballast, tools, armaments and implements. Little mention is made of the treasure. A few items are held by the National Museum of Australia, others with the maritime collections of the Western Australian Museum. Artefacts and coins possibly from the wreck turn up on the internet from time to time. The exact circumstances of the 1963 discovery and of subsequent events remain contentious in archaeological and treasure-hunting circles.

As well as the enduring lure of sunken treasure, there is the more important mystery of the fate of those who survived the tragedy. While it is known that a large group of men made it to the beach, it is not impossible that one, even a few, of those left aboard the wreck may have survived, perhaps blown south on a spar by the strong current. The discovery of old Dutch coins, almost certainly from the *Vergulde Draeck*, at a significant distance south of the wreck gives some support to this possibility. On the other hand, a group of the beach survivors may have made their way south in search of help. Speculations like these, together with expeditions and the assiduous work of a small group of researchers, have generated an intriguing mix of history, artefacts and folklore.

In 2015 two letters purportedly written by the survivors and carried to Batavia in the escaping boat appeared on a Facebook page. How and where the letters were discovered was not stated but, if genuine, they reported the circumstances of the *Draeck*'s destruction and confirmation that the survivors were in good enough shape to pen an account of their ordeal. Of course, it throws no further light on what happened to them after their understeersman set sail for Batavia. Speculations about their fate continue today and it has recently been claimed that traces of a survivor settlement have been found 100 kilometres north of Perth. So far, no hard evidence of this claim has been produced and most experts remain sceptical.

THAT CURSED SHORE

Mystery still surrounds the massacre and eating of at least 60 people in Whangaroa Harbour in northern New Zealand.

After transporting a cargo of convicts to Sydney Cove in 1809, the *Boyd* under Captain John Thompson sailed from Sydney in October that year. Aboard were around 70 passengers and crew, including a number of Maori, one a chief's son named Te Ara. Thompson was keen to obtain some kauri spears to add to his cargo of seal skins, coal, lumber and whale oil. Te Ara recommended Whangaroa, where his people lived and where he assured Thompson there were excellent stands of kauri.

The *Boyd* moored and Te Ara went to greet his kin after a long absence. The Maori came aboard the ship and relations were cordial at first, until Thompson took a small boat party ashore to search for spears. They never returned. The Whangaroa Maori clubbed and axed them all to death. The Maori then rowed out to the *Boyd* and began to massacre those aboard, dismembering the victims while a few survivors watched in horror from the rigging.

At the end, only five of those aboard the ship escaped the butchery, aided by Te Pahi, a visiting Maori chief from the Bay of Islands apparently shocked at the scene. One survivor was later killed, leaving Ann Morley and her baby, two-year-old Betsey Broughton and cabin boy Thom Davies in dangerous captivity.

What caused such brutal events?

At some point before the *Boyd* reached Whangaroa, Te Ara was lashed to a capstan and either flogged or threatened this punishment by Captain Thompson for his refusal to work his passage. He protested that he was a chief's son and should not be so basely punished but was mocked by the sailors and denied food. This was a loss of face among his people that triggered an obligation to take revenge. A dreadful vengeance it was.

According to the rescuers under Alexander Berry who arrived at the scene in December, there was evidence of mass cannibalism. As Berry later wrote: 'The horrid feasting on human flesh which followed would be too shocking for description.' They also found the charred remains of the *Boyd*, apparently blown up when the Maori tried unsuccessfully to make use of the muskets and gunpowder aboard. The flames ignited the whale oil and the ship quickly burned and sank, a number of Maori, including Te Ara's father, dying in the conflagration.

Assisted by Maori from the Bay of Islands, Berry secured the safe return of the four survivors as well as the government despatches and private letters carried by the *Boyd*. Betsey was in a poor condition, crying 'Mamma, my mamma.' After threatening the killers with a murder trial in Europe Berry relented, avoiding further bloodshed, though so great were tensions in the region that a planned mission settlement was postponed for several years.

Berry took the remaining four survivors on his ship. They were bound for the Cape of Good Hope but suffered storm damage and eventually ended up in Lima, Peru. Here

Mrs Morley died. Davies went to England aboard another ship and the two children went with Berry to Rio de Janeiro and then to Sydney.

Meanwhile, news of the massacre, cannibalism and capture of the survivors fuelled darker emotions. Men from a small fleet of whalers attacked Te Pahi and his people. This seems to have been a complete misunderstanding of the massacre as by most accounts Te Pahi had tried to help the Europeans. Berry may have confused the similar names of the two chiefs in his account of what had happened. Up to 60 Maori and one whaler died in this misguided act of revenge. Te Pahi then attacked the Whangaroa Maori and died from wounds dealt in battle.

In later life, Thom Davies returned to New South Wales where he worked for Berry, but he drowned on an expedition to the Shoalhaven River with Berry in 1822. Betsey Broughton married well, living until 1891. Mrs Morley's daughter eventually ran a school in Sydney.

As the story of the *Boyd* massacre became more widely known in Britain and beyond, it encouraged both shock and humour. The grisly tale of blood, betrayal, cannibalism and survival fuelled the growth of a 'savage natives' stereotype that would become the stock in trade of rip-roaring adventures and South Seas island concoctions for decades to come. Pamphlets appeared warning people against migrating to such dangerous places, one referring to New Zealand as 'that cursed shore'. Popular comic songs such as 'The King of the Cannibal Islands' were based on this and other colonial encounters, reflecting European attempts to process such dramatic cultural and social differences through absurdity:

Oh, have you heard the news of late,
About a mighty king so great?
If you have not, 'tis in my pate—
      The King of the Cannibal Islands.
He was so tall—near six feet six.
He had a head like Mister Nick's,

His palace was like Dirty Dick's,
'Twas built of mud for want of bricks,
And his name was Poonoowingkewang,
Flibeedee flobeedee-buskeebang;
And a lot of Indians swore they'd hang
    The King of the Cannibal Islands.
        Hokee pokee wonkee fum,.
        Puttee po pee kaihula cum,
        Tongaree, wougaree, ching ring wum,.
            The King of the Cannibal Islands.
This mighty king had, in one hut,
Seventy wives as black as soot,
And thirty of a double smut—
    The King of the Cannibal Islands.
So just one hundred wives he had,
And every week he was a dad,
Upon my word, it was too bad,
For his smutty dears soon drove him mad;
There was Hungkee Monkee, short and tall,
With Tuzzee Muzzee, and Keekoo Pall,
And some of them swore they would have all
    The King of the Cannibal Islands
        Hokee pokee, &c.
One day the king invited most
All of his subjects to a roast,
For half his wives gave up the ghost,
    The King of the Cannibal Islands.
Of fifty wives he was bereft,
And so he had but fifty left,
He said with them he would make shift,
So for a gorge all set off swift.
The fifty dead ones were roasted soon,
And all demolished before the noon,
And a lot of chiefs vowed to have soon
    The King of the Cannibal Islands.
        Hokee pokee, &c.

When they had done, and the bones pick'd clean,
They all began to dance, I ween;
The fifty wives slipped out unseen,
    From the King of the Cannibal Islands.
He turning round, soon missed them all,
So for his wives began to bawl,
But not one answered to his call,
He sprung out through the muddy wall;
Then into the woods he went with grief.
And found each queen 'long with a chief,
And swore he'd Macadamise every thief,
    The King of the Cannibal Islands.
    Hokee pokee, &c.
He sent for all his guards with knives,
To put an end to all their lives,
The fifty chiefs and fifty wives—
    The King of the Cannibal Islands.
These cannibal slaveys then begun
Carving their heads off, one by one;
And the king he laughed to see the fun,
Then jumped into bed when all was done;
And every night when he's asleep.
His headless wives and chiefs all creep,
And roll upon him in a heap,
    The King of the Cannibal Islands.
    Hokee pokee,&c.

Today, the remains and relics of the *Boyd* still lie in Whangaroa Harbour. Archaeological surveys have revealed splinters of hull, copper pins and lumps of coal scattered on the sea floor. Visitors to the area later reported seeing Maori children wearing gold coins as necklaces. Despite this and a Maori legend that there was gold and silver aboard the ship, no one seems to have found any.

THE *HOPE* TREASURE

Tasmania's Bruny Island is beautiful, but it is also dangerous to shipping. In the early colonial era, several vessels were wrecked there with great loss of life. Around four o'clock in the morning of 29 April 1827, the trader *Hope* ground into sand 7 feet (2 metres) below her 15 foot (4.5 metre) keel. She was stranded and at the mercy of a high sea. The *Hobart Colonial Times* described the scene:

> The moment she struck, the consternation and terror became general; and the scene is described as truly terrific—the Captain raving at the Pilot like a man distracted, the latter standing in mute dismay—females just left their beds—the sailors not knowing which way to turn, to relieve the creaking vessel, which was expected to go to pieces every moment, as she already leaked like a sieve—the heavy surf rolling over her, adding horror to the scene—while the dismal half-hour guns of distress seemed to sound the death-knell of all on board.

Next morning, two whaleboats arrived at the rapidly deteriorating wreck. Attempts were made to haul *Hope* off the sand, without success, and one of the whaleboats was lost. The other returned to Hobart with the news and a sloop was sent to recover as much of the cargo as possible before *Hope* sank. The crew manned the pumps full time as the rudder was lost and the sea stove in part of the stern. All passengers were taken off, together with much of the cargo. But not all of it.

Hope was said to be carrying the pay chest for the Hobart garrison, allegedly over £3000 worth of gold and silver coins. Among the passengers on the ship were two soldiers. According to one version of the legend, they somehow managed to secure the chest and bury it in the dunes, from where they planned to later recover it. But the soldiers had no chance to retrieve their trove because they were transferred to India. One died there and the other returned to England.

At this point in the story the obligatory treasure map turns up. The returned soldier provided a rough sketch of where the treasure was buried to an Irish farmer. He sold up his farm and took passage to Van Diemen's Land, eventually reaching Kellys Point, three miles of open sea away from what is now known as Hope Beach after the wrecking. The newcomer had a heavy metal box among his luggage and was not forthcoming when questioned about it. He was later observed wandering around, claiming that he was searching for 'hone stones' used for sharpening metal blades. No one believed him and the police were called in. The man was asked to open the box but only two phials full of unknown liquid were found inside. A snakebite cure, he claimed.

With no evidence of wrongdoing, the police left the man to continue whatever he was doing. He disappeared shortly after. But eighteen months later he was back again, supposedly with a yet more detailed map, and went to another location, Bligh('s) Point. Here, he searched and searched. Eventually, he ran out of funds and, as he had found nothing, he was forced to go to Hobart and find work as a labourer.

So, perhaps the missing money is still hidden somewhere in the sands? Not if another version of the story is true. In this telling, the money was loaded onto one of the whaleboats that had reached the stricken *Hope* first. In the panic and chaos nobody noticed. It is said that the whalemen buried it somewhere and later returned to recover their loot. If so, they would have lived happily ever after, as the treasure would today be worth more than two million dollars.

Are there any verifiable facts in this yarn? Not too many. The *Hope* certainly foundered in April 1827. After that, the records are scarce. There was at least one soldier of the 40th Regiment of Foot aboard the *Hope*. His name was Ensign Barcley (variously spelled) and the regiment was indeed transferred to Bombay the following year. After that, the trail goes cold.

But perhaps an enterprising family history researcher could track the ensign down, just to see if any clues to the whereabouts of this tantalising treasure just might turn up.

FATAL MYSTERIES OF THE *GENERAL GRANT*

Sailing from Boston to Melbourne late in 1865 the 1000 tonne barque *General Grant* lost a man overboard in a gale. The young William Sanguily and others among the crew thought this was an ill omen. Their ship reached Melbourne without further incident then loaded for London. But then, 'by one of those coincidences, which sailors dread, we took aboard part of a cargo that had been intended for the steamer *London*. This ill-fated vessel had sunk in the Bay of Biscay on her voyage out, and there were many gloomy prophecies that no freight of hers would reach London in any ship.'

The superstitious sailors also noticed that the rats had left the *General Grant*, a sure sign of doom in the lore of the sea. Nevertheless, the *General Grant* set sail for England on 4 May 1866 with a load of around 80 passengers, including men, women and children returning home from the diggings and crew. Among the wool and hides in the hold was the unwelcome but hugely valuable cargo—4000 ounces (113 kilograms) of gold.

After days of good running, the ship was blown westward towards the subantarctic Auckland Islands. Several days of thick fog eventually lifted and land was sighted, but later the breeze died. Despite the efforts of the captain and crew, around one o'clock in the morning of 14 May the *General Grant* smashed into the rocky shores of the main Auckland Island. She was forced further and further into the pitch darkness of a large sea cave. Crewman Joseph Jewell described the scene:

> . . . such a night of horror I think was never experienced
> by human beings as we passed in the cave for seven long
> hours. It was so dark that you could not see your fingers
> before your eyes, and there we were with falling spars and

large stones tumbling from the roof of the cave (some of which went through the deck), and so we remained until daylight.

The helpless crew and passengers huddled at the stern of the ship, still free of the cavern slowly sucking in their vessel. At daylight the mizzen top gallant mast collapsed through the ship's hull and she began to sink.

The scene at this moment was one of such utter misery as few men ever see, and fewer still survive to tell of. Every sea washed over the stern and swept the deck. The longboat was crammed with all who could gain a foothold. It was partly filled with water, and several poor creatures lying in the bilge were crowded down and drowned before she was clear of the ship. Women clinging to their children, and crazy men to their gold, were seen washing to and fro as the water invaded the upper deck.

One wretch saw his wife and two children driven by him in this way without making an effort to save them, while the last man who got aboard nearly lost his life trying to persuade the mother to be saved without her children.

The boats were launched into a swelling sea but only a few were able to reach them, most being trapped aboard the *General Grant*. The lucky few watched helplessly as men, women and children were washed away and the ship disappeared beneath the heaving water, her captain waving farewell from what was left of the rigging as he went down with his ship.

The two boats with their fifteen survivors, including one woman, spent two miserable nights and days in search of a place to camp. They had little food, few supplies and no water. Their clothes were inadequate for the climate and some were without shoes. A landing was eventually made at a place known as Sarah's Bosom on the ominously named Disappointment Island. Here they confronted the possibility of cannibalism if they were unable to make a fire. Fortunately, they were. Albatross and shellfish made a welcome stew. From that time the fire was never allowed to go out.

The survivors split into two groups, existing as best they could in huts erected by earlier shipwreck survivors and a failed colony. They suffered greatly. There was dysentery, cold and a form of scurvy caused by their survival diet. Passing ships were sighted, but they were unable to attract their attention. They decided to prepare one of the boats for a desperate attempt reach the South Island of New Zealand, almost 500 kilometres away. Four men volunteered to sail her and they left on 22 January 1867, but without a chart or compass they would need to be both clever and lucky to reach safety.

Eleven souls watched their four companions depart. James Teer, (Frederick) Patrick Caughey, Nicholas Allen and David Ashworth had all been passengers aboard the ill-fated ship. Aaron Hayman, Cornelius Drew, William Ferguson, William Sanguily (known as 'Yankee Jack') and David McClelland were all sailors, as was Joseph Jewell, who was accompanied by his wife, Mary.

They waited hopefully. The weeks passed with no sign of rescue.

The anxious waiting which ensued told more severely on us than all the privation. The feverish excitement of hope caused a cessation of labour one day, and blank despair rendered us helpless the next. One man would accuse the unhappy crew of deserting us, and curse their selfishness. Another would, sobbing, deplore their cruel fate, and realise the noble men who ventured on a hopeless task.

After six weeks they gave up their companions for dead. Despair and depression were balanced by the need to find ways to stay alive. They moved to another island and built a substantial house using materials left over from an abandoned Maori settlement. They learned to capture and kill the wild pigs and goats that roamed the island and began domesticating them.

Life was maintained but it was monotonous and hard, rescue constantly in everyone's mind. They prepared signal fires, used Cape Hens as messenger birds, forced written pleas for help into seal bladders which were then inflated and set afloat. Scraps of wood were carved with information for potential rescuers and cast into the sea. They made small boats of wood and metal with sails of zinc on which was scratched:

Ship General Grant wrecked on Auckland Isles 14 May, 1866; 10 survivors to date. Want relief.

As autumn chilled the air even more their situation seemed hopeless, Sanguily recalled.

> ... we were sorely afflicted with scurvy, or, as whalers call it, 'the cobbler'. The entire party was attacked, and it was only later that we realized how severely our ankle and knee joints were stiffened, and the flesh so swollen that the imprint of a finger would remain for an hour or more. We had heard that the remedy for scurvy was to bury a man all but the head. This we tried in several cases, but it did no good. In closing our mouths our teeth would, on meeting, project straight out, flattened against each other. General weakness and despondency, with a longing for vegetables, was our torment. Severe exercise seemed to be the only remedy. This was our most trying time.

David McClelland, the oldest member of the group, cut his hand on a scrap of copper. The hand became infected and he passed away: 'All cripples, we bore him to his grave.' Who would last the longest, they all wondered?

In November 1867 a sail was seen. They rushed to light the signal fire but the ship passed without seeing the desperate and despondent survivors. Two days later another sail appeared.

This time, some of the survivors leapt into their remaining boat and 'pulled with might and main' for the brig *Amherst*:

> The boat reached the strange vessel, and though our savage appearance at first alarmed the crew, they received us on board. Then were we made welcome to all they could spare. The Amherst, Captain Gilroy, of Invercarghill [sic], manned by Maoris, and bound on a sealing voyage, was the means of our rescue. Captain Gilroy beat up between the islands and anchored off the huts. We were all taken aboard, and treated in the most hospitable manner. No Persian monarch ever enjoyed such a treat as we when tobacco and tea were set before us.

The survivors remained with the *Amherst* for two months and eventually landed at Invercargill in January 1868. A private subscription was taken to send the *Amherst* out in search of the boat launched with such high hopes a year before. The search failed. The men in her may have made the wrong guess about the direction of New Zealand from Disappointment Island and sailed west to their deaths in thousands of kilometres of empty ocean.

The ten survivors of the wreck moved on with their lives. Some of the gold sunk with the *General Grant* belonged to Joseph Jewell. His life was saved but his fortune lost. He eventually became a stationmaster on the Victorian railways. Fortunately, Mary was able to make a great deal of money giving lectures about their survival epic. Unable to have children, in later life they were able to become parents through a surrogate arrangement.

Patrick Caughey returned to Ireland and, perhaps ironically, went into the insurance industry. He was known as a storyteller, often regaling listeners with yarns of his adventures whether they wanted to hear them or not.

'Yankee Jack' was from the eminent French–Cuban family of Sanguily Garrite. He returned to Boston to follow a less adventurous but safer career as a shopkeeper, later marrying an Australian. He and his wife returned to Sydney, where she gave birth to several children.

A few months after the survivors of the *General Grant* were safely back in New Zealand, the first salvage attempt put to sea. Accompanying the expedition was survivor James Teer. He led them to the 'cave of death' where the barque had gone down but the waves were too powerful. They failed to find the wreck, as did the next few attempts in 1870. The first of these was accompanied by another survivor, David Ashworth. He disappeared with five others lost in a whaleboat as they tried to find the fatal cave.

At least a further ten expeditions are known to have searched for the *General Grant*'s sunken gold. Coins, cannon balls and a range of miscellaneous artefacts have been recovered, probably from a number of the ships wrecked on these bleak islands. But, they say, no one has come across the 4000 ounces of gold and, despite all of these attempts, the *General Grant* herself has not been located.

LOST AND FOUND IN THE TORRES STRAIT

The Torres Strait Islands between Australia's north and Papua New Guinea are a trove of lost treasure tales and the mysteries that inevitably go with them. But not all Torres Strait treasures are lost.

In 1897, reports reached Brisbane of a hoard of copper ingots found by pearl-shell divers in two fathoms of water off 'Marbiac Island' (properly Mabuiag, also formerly known as Jervis Island). The ingots were spread out on the sea floor in a long line, suggesting that they had been jettisoned by a ship trying to right itself after running into trouble. But there was no wreckage other than a rusted old cannon. Local inhabitants had no knowledge or oral traditions of a wreck in the area, leading to speculation that the copper had once been part of the cargo of a Spanish treasure ship sailing from

South America to the Philippines. Islanders sold their finds to a local trader, reportedly doing very well from the proceeds and making enough to buy much-needed food and to build a church for their community.

Where did the copper ingots come from? Was it indeed a Spanish treasure ship or some other vessel? No one knew until 2006 when two more copper ingots were brought up near Mabuiag. At first, it was thought that the ingots were gold, perhaps evidence of the many lost bullion yarns that are heard throughout the Strait, particularly the 'golden loaves' said in local lore to lie off Mabuiag.

Disappointing though it would turn out for the finder, scientists tested the ingots, did their research and solved the mystery. The copper was probably from Chile and was being transported to India aboard the *Hercules*. Built in Calcutta (Kolkata), the 424 ton (430 tonne) teak ship was only eight years old when she anchored in rough weather on the Orman Reefs in June 1822. But her anchors could not hold against wind and tide. Near sunset, one of the ship's officers, John Lawrie, later recalled: '. . . the vessel struck with fearful violence upon a sunken coral rock, and, so sudden, and terrible was the shock, that the man seated upon the fore top sail yard—as a look out—was instantly thrown from his place, and dashed upon deck, where, after a few moments of excruciating agony, he breathed his last.'

The *Hercules* was dragged along, smashing into sand and rock. A boat was launched to tow her out of trouble, but the sailors became exhausted trying unsuccessfully to haul their ship to safety. As they desperately rowed against wind and tide, the men in the little boat came upon what was left of an old wreck. 'This proved a most unfortunate occurrence indeed, for it tended to confirm the men's worst fears, and they now became still more obstinate, and morose.' They refused to take further orders until the officer felled one man with the rudder tiller and drew a pistol on the rest. Just as he was ordering the men to take up their oars again, a large piece of their ship was ripped away and fell across the bow of the small boat. Forced to quickly cooperate to remove the danger, the men returned to their duty, their officer wisely rewarding them with a tot of rum. They spent the rest of the night on a sandbar, returning compliantly to their ship at daybreak.

After ten days of effort and always in fear of the Torres Strait Islanders who, they had been told, were cannibals, *Hercules* was successfully refloated, but only after throwing many of the 600 copper ingots she carried overboard.

And the cannon? It remains a puzzle. An English anthropologist visiting the island in the late 1890s examined and photographed an object believed to be the one retrieved 70 years earlier. It is thought that it might have belonged to one of a number of ships wrecked around Mabuiag before the 1820s—but not a Spanish treasure ship.

BUSHRANGING BOOTY

Where did the bushrangers bury their loot? Tales of hidden bushranger booty are a never-ending source of intrigue and fascination. They are taken seriously by some intrepid prospectors who have always searched for these fabled troves. Are they just legends? Maybe. But how would we know if any of these treasures had been located, or not?

Mystery has long surrounded the whereabouts of gold stolen in the Eugowra Rocks robbery of 1862. The Forbes gold escort left for Sydney on Sunday, 15 June. Sergeant James Condell was in charge and told the story in a report to the Inspector-General of Police:

> ... About 5 o'clock p.m., we were attacked by a party from twelve to fifteen armed men, dressed in red jumpers, red caps, and blackened faces. The road being blocked up with several drays, so that we had to pass close to a rock, where they were concealed, and as the coach was passing, six or seven men fired into the coach, and then drew back.

Then six or seven others fired. We then returned the fire; two of the horses got wounded and started off with the coach, capsizing it, and turning the escort out. I received four bullets through the coat, one entering my left side. Senior Constable Moran received two balls, one which wounded him in the groin. The coachman receiving also two bullets, but was not hurt.

The bushrangers dragged the gold storage boxes out, along with the mail bags also carried by the coach, and they opened up some of the letters looking for cheques. Condell had a good idea who the leader of the gang might be: 'The bushrangers were commanded by one man, who gave them orders to fire and load. I believe it to have been the voice of Gardiner, as I know his voice well . . . I cannot identify any of them with the exception of the voice I heard.'

Condell and two of the escort party escaped to raise the alarm and the chase, which got under way around four o'clock the next morning. Two blacktrackers and some local settlers found the empty gold boxes at the cold remains of the robbers' camp.

As Sergeant Condell told the tale, the robbers were great in number and he fought gallantly against them, just managing to escape to raise the alarm. In folklore, Sergeant Condell is remembered in a ballad as 'cowardly hearted', he being one of the policemen who shot Gardiner gang member Ben Hall dead, allegedly while he slept.

But whatever the sergeant's actions might or might not have been at Eugowra Rocks, he was right about Gardiner being the leader of the gang. The bushranger quickly disappeared, eventually turning up in Queensland where he was betrayed by his mistress and arrested in 1864. He was tried, found guilty and sentenced to life imprisonment, though after ten years or so of agitation from his family and other interests he was exiled, ending up in the United States of America, where he died, probably in the 1880s or, according to another story, possibly early in the twentieth century.

But only some of the gold from the robbery was ever recovered. Where did Frank stash it? Legend has it that he buried it somewhere around Wheogo station and the nearby Weddin Mountain Range. It wasn't long before hopeful treasure hunters began looking.

Locals will still tell you the tale of a couple of Canadians or Americans who arrived out of the blue around 1914 with a very keen interest in the geography of the country round about. They were said to have been seen digging in various spots. One day, they were gone as suddenly as they had arrived, leaving a very large hole on Wheoga Hill. It is sometimes said that they were Gardiner's sons, following up directions given by their father before his death or, perhaps, afterwards in a secret note of some kind? No one knows, which just makes it even more intriguing.

Another hoard of gold acquired through bushranging is said to still lie hidden in the bush. Frederick Ward, the New England bushranger known as 'Captain Thunderbolt', was said to have been a man of simple tastes. Over an unusually long criminal career he carried out some profitable robberies until 1870, when he was gunned down by a police constable. He is said to have secreted much of his loot somewhere in the very large area across which he is thought to have robbed, north from the Hunter Valley to Queensland and west from Tamworth to Bourke. A lot of ground to cover with a metal detector.

YANKEE NED'S PEARLS

In 1871, a man of uncertain origins and background turned up in the Torres Strait. He was American, possibly a Civil War veteran, and also on the run. As a sailor on board an American naval ship moored at Sydney, he had a disagreement with an officer. It ended with the officer being tied up at gunpoint and the sailor, Edward Mosby (Moresby), travelling fast and far. In the north, the deserter came to learn the main trades of the Strait's islands, *bêche-de-mer* or trepang hunting and pearling, and eventually he set up his own business with a partner on Masig, then known to Europeans as Yorke Island.

At that time the islands between Australia and New Guinea formed something of a maritime frontier with little regulation and a constant flow of blow-ins seeking to make their fortunes. What they usually found was hard work, despair and the grog. But Edward Mosby was of a different character. Possibly fearing lawful retribution for his violent attack on a ship's officer, he had come to stay.

'Yankee Ned', as Mosby would be known on the island and beyond, became a member of an island community that at first rejected him as an unwanted interloper. But he later married Ulood, a First Nations woman known as 'Queenie'. Together they had four sons who played a continuing role in the family business and in island affairs. There are various stories about Ned's role in relations between the Masig islanders and the people of Mer (Murray Island). Some say that there was an attack on Masig by the famously fearsome Mer islanders and Ned organised the villagers into an effective defence force that thoroughly, and permanently, trounced the attackers.

Another story has it that the relations between the two island groups were more about trade than fighting. If so, Ned would have played a significant role here as he quickly became the main trader on Masig. Unlike most of the companies operating in the Strait, Ned set up a cooperative system with the local divers. This gave them a share of the profits instead of the usual meagre wage, allowing them to rent or even buy their own boats and so potentially gain economic independence. He was also responsible for building houses and public works and introducing horses and cattle to the island economy. Perhaps most usefully, Ned brought western education, personally paying for a schoolteacher to be resident on the island.

Through these good works and his trading enterprises, the runaway sailor became wealthy and was regarded by most as a benevolent patriarch who had earned his place in the community—'In York [sic] Island "Yankee Ned's" word was law, and very good law, too'. He was, of course, no saint. He was often involved in conflicts with the government related to the pearling and *bêche-de-mer* business and was a heavy drinker.

Towards the end of his life, Ned's leg became infected from an untended coral cut. It had to be amputated, putting an end to his active career. The business was run by his sons while the old man sat on the verandah of the roomy two-storey home he had built in a grove of coconut palms and watched the passing shipping. He was also in the habit of counting out his pearls. As the story goes, Ned was engaged in this satisfying activity one day when he noticed that he was being closely observed by one of the Japanese divers on the island. Seized by the fear that others coveted his wealth, he took action. Ned gathered up his considerable stash of lustrous pearls and buried them on the island.

But when the old man died in 1911, he had apparently neglected to tell anyone just where he stashed his treasure. 'Yankee Ned' died in the local hospital and took his secret with him, becoming another of the many treasure tales of the Torres Strait.

GIPPSLAND GOLD

If someone hasn't yet done it, this tale should be turned into a thriller. And a movie.

The story begins in an ordinary way with the robbery of 5000 gold sovereigns in 1877. Aboard the *Avoca*, the vessel's Norwegian carpenter planned a daring and clever heist. The name he went by was Martin Weiberg (sometimes Wyberg or Wiberg, though his real name was Olsen), an enterprising man whose criminal activities gave rise to an enduring Gippsland legend.

Weiberg discovered the existence of the sovereigns and managed to have a duplicate key made for the strongbox lock. When he knew he would not be disturbed, he opened the box, removed the sovereigns and replaced them with metal bolts. With his carpentry skills, he was then able to reseal the box so precisely that it did not appear to have been opened. The now much lighter chest was then transferred to a steamer bound for Ceylon, modern-day Sri Lanka. Of course, when it arrived, the robbery was discovered and the police began their investigation.

They didn't get very far. They concentrated on the *Avoca* and her crew but found nothing. Around this time, Ned Kelly was shooting three policemen dead at Stringybark Creek. This dreadful news filled the press and it seems that even such a spectacular gold robbery was relegated to the middle pages of newspapers and perhaps the 'pending' tray of the police. With the hunt for the Kellys going on in the foreground, Weiberg was able to remain in the background. He continued to work and live aboard the *Avoca*, hoping to avoid raising any suspicions. Five months after the disappearance of the sovereigns, and now married, he took up a selection on the Tarwin River, east of Inverloch, Victoria.

But Weiberg had not waited long enough to start enjoying his ill-gotten gains. Someone tipped off the police and detectives headed to Gippsland for a serious chat. They apparently bumped into their suspect on the road. He was 'very much surprised, but offered no resistance. He was at once searched and a number of sovereigns found upon him. After securing their suspect in the Griffith Point lock-up, the three officers proceeded to Weiberg's hut.'

When the police searched the house Weiberg had built for his family they found some of the missing coins neatly hidden in what was described as 'a large carpenter's plane'. The cunning carpenter had constructed a barrel in which he had concealed around 250 coins. All up, around 320 coins were recovered at Weiberg's home, with over 1000 from other sources.

Weiberg was held in custody for more than a month and grilled for the names of the accomplice he would have needed to transport the enormous cache of coins from the *Avoca* to wherever they were first stashed. He eventually confessed to the crime and named the *Avoca*'s first officer as his partner in crime, a claim that was eventually proved to be false. Before this was determined, police returned with their man to the area. Weiberg had agreed to show them where he had sunk a kettle full of sovereigns, but during the search for the cache he managed to escape into the bush. He hid out for five months, during which time he took on an accomplice who helped him shift money to Melbourne to buy a boat. He was recaptured in May 1879 and subsequently sentenced to five years hard labour.

During that time no progress was made in locating the missing sovereigns. Of course, tongues wagged and the legend of the lost gold sovereigns grew and grew. The tale received a big boost in 1883. On his release from prison Weiberg went to Hobart, where he bought a yacht in partnership with his brother. He sailed it to Gippsland's Waratah Bay, where he moored. He went ashore in a small boat to visit his family, who were still living in the area and, it is assumed, to retrieve another one of his many plants of gold. While returning from the visit, he was caught in a bad squall and his skiff capsized. The mastermind of the *Avoca* bullion heist disappeared, presumed drowned.

But, once again, that was not the end of the story. Despite a large search, the body was never found, prompting widespread belief that he had somehow faked his death to shake the police off his trail. Locals reported seeing lights on one of the uninhabited Glennie Group islands, fuelling further speculation on the thief's survival. There was even an alleged sighting of him years later in Europe and he was also reported to be the owner of a hotel in Sweden. Perhaps he had successfully fooled the police and escaped to live the rest of his life in the luxury that a great many gold sovereigns could fund?

People were still puzzling over these events in the 1890s when a skeleton was found at Waratah Bay. A small section from the back of the skull was missing. Most thought it was Weiberg's—but then who had murdered him?

Twenty years later, another of Weiberg's stashes was found in an old tree. It contained 75 coins. By now, many people were keenly searching for the lost sovereigns. While the exact total is difficult to pin down and some may have been misappropriated, almost 1800 sovereigns are said to have been retrieved from whatever sources. Where are the rest?

Many people believe that most of them are concealed somewhere in the Gippsland area. Various locations are favoured, including Tullaree homestead, location of another famous mystery of the twentieth century and since (see The Lady of the Swamp). Optimistic searchers with metal detectors are still looking for the glowing mint coins. On the other hand, Weiberg spent a lot of money in his attempts to buy boats and, once out of jail, he had to live. Maybe he did have the rest with him in the small boat lost to the waves and managed to fake his disappearance. Perhaps he was then killed by his still unknown partner or partners in crime? Or he drowned, dragged down by the dead weight of his stolen sovereigns.

THE MOTHER SHIPTON NUGGET

The man rushing across London's Trafalgar Square early in the morning of 30 August 1906 was trying to catch the last bus home. As he ran, he called out to some nearby policemen. He had just heard the sound of a window smashing in the Orient Steam Navigation Company offices nearby. When the police arrived they found shattered glass and nothing else. The two valuable gold lumps—pieces of a once larger nugget—that had been displayed there were gone. The oddly named Mother Shipton nugget has not been seen since.

The Mother Shipton lead or mine was part of the Temora (New South Wales) gold rush of the 1880s. The reef on which the mine was founded was discovered in September 1881:

On last Wednesday afternoon (14th Sept. 1881) the town was electrified out of its chronic state of dullness into quite a fever of excitement by the news that some extraordinary rich stone had been struck at Upper Temora and until a late hour in the evening curious spectators gathered round where the specimens had been found . . .

'Mother Shipton's Prophecies' was a collection of predictions said to have been made around the end of the fifteenth century by Ursula Southeil (variously spelled) of Knaresborough, Yorkshire. Among her tips for future wonders were horseless carriages, aircraft and submarines. At least, the predictions could be interpreted in these ways, or just about any other. Despite their vagueness, the prophecies were immensely popular in Britain and in Australia.

Mother Shipton also foresaw the end of the world. At least, she did by 1862 when yet another edition was published, this one inserting a rhyme that was not in the original.

> The world at an end shall come
> In eighteen hundred and eighty-one.

Most people were unaware that this new prediction was a fake and so popular were the prophecies that, as the year proceeded, the public became increasingly nervous that the world might end. But the owners of the Temora claim were not among the gullible, it seems, and defiantly named their asset after the seer.

The reef was estimated to go 1000 ounces (28 kilograms) of gold to the ton, an immensely rich yield. As the inevitable attempts at claim jumping and legal manoeuvres over ownership proceeded, the mine continued to produce astonishing finds. Most amazing of all were the pieces of nugget blasted out of the mine just a few days after the earlier excitement:

> They are three in number, and the gold is almost as plentiful in them as the quartz. But the quantity of gold is not so attractive as the peculiar forms which the gold has assumed. These are very striking, and they include the very rare feature, in specimens of the kind, of gold crystals or octahedrons.

The New South Wales mines department shrewdly purchased the three pieces of gold, not for the government coffers but for promoting the colony to intending migrants. The nugget, as the pieces were called, went around the world, amazing crowds at displays and exhibitions of all kinds. At the 1886 Colonial and Indian Exhibition in London, the smallest piece of the nugget was offered to and graciously accepted by Her Majesty Queen Victoria. By the time it disappeared in London, the nugget had been in New Zealand and Chicago, then back to England for the International Exhibition of Mining and Metallurgy at the Crystal Palace. The *Kalgoorlie Western Argus* enthused:

Apart from their intrinsic value, the lumps of gold have been considered among the Colony's finest advertising assets. Since they were exhibited in Trafalgar Square the emigration returns have shown a decided increase. For the first two weeks in August, thirty-one new settlers went out to New South Wales, but for the past fortnight the figures stand at eighty-one . . .

But now they were gone. Hoping to salvage them from melting down, the insurance company offered a large reward for the return of the two pieces 'but little hope is entertained of their recovery'.

By then, the Temora rush and the Mother Shipton mine had been long forgotten. However prospectors are eternally hopeful and in 1919 the much-depleted town of Temora was excited by reports that rich gold had been found around the old mine and the madness began once more. Were these the events predicted in the famous prophecies? Among her other cryptic predictions Mother Shipton had a couple about gold:

Gold shall be found, and found
In a land that's not now known . . .
The world upside down shall be,
And gold be found at the root of tree . . .

Perhaps there is something to these famous prophecies after all?

NO TRACE OF THE MACE

According to the outraged *Argus* newspaper it was 'the most extraordinary robbery ever heard of in the colonies, probably indeed without parallel in the constitutional history of the world'. In a further piece of overexcited journalism, the theft was described as the work of a 'sacrilegious hand' and compared with criminal attempts on the crown jewels, no less.

The missing object was the ceremonial Mace of the Victorian Parliament, symbolic of the Legislative Assembly's Speaker's authority. Basically an elaborate stick or staff, the Mace was hollow, decorated with silver and sported a Maltese cross in its headpiece with the Victorian and English coats of arms engraved. The bling was secured in an oak box one night in October 1891. It has been missing ever since. The circumstances of its disappearance and of its whereabouts have become one of Melbourne's favourite mysteries.

As the scene of the crime was Parliament House, police were rapidly on the job. They quickly discounted a professional criminal as no valuable plate had been taken. And, despite popular belief, the monetary value of the Mace was small, its silver components worth only £40. Various individuals connected to the parliament in some way were at first suspected, though soon cleared.

But, if so, where was the 'bauble', as the Mace was often disrespectfully called?

One story was that the Mace had ended up in a brothel at some point during the night it disappeared but had then vanished again. A few years later, it was suggested that the Mace had not left the brothel at all but remained there to be used for unspecified but decidedly improper proceedings. There was a furore, as they say. Officially straitlaced Victorian society of the time reacted loudly to the possibilities inherent in this raunchy scenario.

Being politicians, there was, of course, an inquiry. The inquiry rejected the suggestion that the Mace had ended up in a brothel and also raised a brief hope that the case might be solved with some sensational new evidence.

A tram driver came forward to testify that he had seen a man running from the back gate of parliament on the night in question with a long, thin, brown-paper parcel. The man jumped on a passing tram and the witness heard a metallic sound from the parcel as it was stood on the tram floor. Not only that, but the helpful tram driver knew the man. It was Parliament House's electrical engineer, Thomas Jeffery.

Police smartly interviewed Jeffery, who denied it all, though not very convincingly, changing his story and giving detectives good reason to like him as their top suspect. But they couldn't prove anything against him and the Mace remained missing.

In 2013 a letter, allegedly written years earlier by Thomas Jeffery's son, turned up. It suggested that the robbery was a practical joke. Some Members were in the habit of partying on in the House after late-night sittings. They had partied a little too hard and conceived the drunken scheme of carrying their trophy away to one of the high-class houses of ill repute around Little Lon, then Melbourne's red-light district. Sobering up but unable to sneak the Mace back to its proper place without revealing their crime, the miscreants hired a couple of city crims to dump it in the Maribyrnong River near the Colonial Sugar Refinery. It might still be there. Or not.

In 2001, the parliament of Victoria offered a $50,000 reward for the return of the Mace, or even pieces of it. So far, no one has returned the Mace. Its fate is unknown. Perhaps in the river. Perhaps broken up and melted down for the small but still spendable amount of silver it contained. Or maybe it is lying in someone's garden shed, wrapped in a dusty cloth, hung with cobwebs and completely forgotten.

*These three Austrian girls wait for their rations at the Molonglo
Internment Camp outside Canberra, which had been 'secretly' built in
under ten weeks in early 1918. The expected 'several thousand enemy
nationals' were never sent, so instead 150 families were transferred in
from other Australian camps and created a thriving community for
a few months before World War I ended and the camp closed.*

4

RIDDLES OF WAR

LOST IN CELTIC WOOD

The place marked on their field map as 'Celtic Wood' was mostly shattered stumps when the 'Terrible Tenth' attacked. It was early October 1917, just one small action in the fighting that would later be known as the Battle of Passchendaele. Raised in South Australia, the 10th Battalion of the Australian Imperial Force (AIF) had orders to fight fiercely for half an hour, giving the Germans the impression that a major attack was being made on them at this point. This was a feint. The real action was to their north.

The soldiers did as they were ordered. They had carried out an earlier attack on this position, which was deemed a success, though the Germans were still in command of their lines and had taken the opportunity to reinforce them with more machine guns. The men of the Tenth advanced at dawn with a rolling barrage of artillery before them to further suggest that this was a full-frontal attack. Not only was the barrage ineffective, but when the attackers reached the enemy trenches they realised they were outnumbered two to one.

There was fierce fighting in the wood and the battalion commander later reported: 'A desperate hand encounter followed, in which heavy casualties were inflicted upon the enemy.' But then the German artillery began, cutting the Australians off in their rear just as German reinforcements arrived. The leader of the group, Lieutenant Frank Scott, was last seen 'trying to fight his way out with his revolver'. When it was over, the commander was 'only able to account for 14 unwounded members of the party'. What happened to the rest became what was once described as 'the greatest mystery for the AIF in WW1'.

Military units have been going missing since ancient times. The most famous is probably the Roman Ninth Legion, which apparently vanished into the mists of what is now Scotland around AD 120. Another Roman legion is thought to have disappeared in what is now China in 53 BC.

There are other lost military unit legends, but the best-known modern mystery also took place in World War I, at Gallipoli. Here, the 1/5th Battalion of the Norfolk Regiment (also once known as the 'Sandringhams'), was seen advancing against the Turks on 12 August 1915. It was later claimed that the company of more than 200 men disappeared into a cloud of smoke. Sir Ian Hamilton, overall commander of the Dardanelles campaign, himself reported that 'nothing more was ever seen or heard of any of them. They charged into the forest and were lost to sight or sound. Not one of them ever came back.'

As with the lost Norfolks story, the mystery of Celtic Wood deepened over time. And, like all legends, it grew into a larger perplexity that troubled the generation that lived through the Great War and also those who came after. What had happened to the men of the Tenth? Almost total casualties, even on the Western Front, were rare. Were the Australians taken prisoner? There were no reports of the Celtic Wood action in German documents. Had the enemy massacred them, perhaps in revenge for casualties they suffered earlier, and tried to cover up the atrocity? Or had something mysterious happened in the blighted wood? Rumours circulated that the Australians simply melted into a mist, remarkably similar to the fates associated with the Norfolks and the Roman Ninth Legion.

Those with an interest in the Great War have long puzzled over these events. What happened, or did not happen, in Celtic Wood was still undetermined at the beginning of the twenty-first century. It was not until researchers Robert Kearney and Christopher Henschke diligently combed the available records that the likely fate of the missing soldiers was revealed.

The seed of the mystery was buried in the battalion commander's statement about the survivors of the action. Eighty-five men went into the wood, but the commander only counted fourteen 'unwounded' survivors. This was subsequently misread to mean that seventy-one soldiers had disappeared, an enormous casualty rate. What the records actually show is that there were more than fourteen survivors, but the remainder of the soldiers unaccounted for, around thirty-seven, died in the battle.

Subsequent shelling of the area reduced the bodies to bloodied mud, explaining why no remains of the dead were ever found. The fighting moved on. The Germans withdrew a week later and the larger action, of which Celtic Wood was but a small part, failed to secure more than one Belgian village.

THE YOUNGEST ANZAC

Little Walter Dunn, or 'Charlie Chaplin' as he was known to his comrades, is said to have been the youngest Anzac. He certainly had something of the mystery tramp about him, so the story goes. Or perhaps, more accurately, the many stories about him.

In October 1914, at the age of thirteen years, Walter decided to go and fight the war just then getting underway in Europe. He stowed away on a troopship bound for Egypt, was discovered when the ship arrived and adopted by the Light Horse as a mascot. He was then made a bugler, an official rank that meant he was entitled to whatever benefits were due to all soldiers of the AIF.

The boy went to Gallipoli, where he was wounded in the arm. After spending time in England for recuperation he was then sent to the Western Front, where he fought in the battles of Bullecourt and Armentieres. After surviving three years of active service abroad, Walter returned to South Australia as a civilian. Uncomfortable with civilian life, he enlisted again and was preparing to return to the front when the war ended in November 1918.

This was actually a late refinement of Walter's adventures in the AIF. The first version appeared in April 1916, with some radically different details:

> Walter Dunn, aged 14, otherwise known as 'Charlie Chaplin,' stowed away with the 1st Canadian Contingent, staying with them at Salisbury and Shorncliffe, in England, and smuggled himself with the contingent to France, where he had many adventures, including a compound fracture of the left arm. He saw several battles and was in the fighting at Loos. When he heard there was an army at Salonika, he took the train to Marseilles, found troops embarking, stowed away, reached Salonika, and has now attached himself to an Army Service Corps camp. Dunn is a great favorite with everyone, and makes himself really useful. His father is an officer in Princess Patricia's Light Infantry.

Yet another telling account was published later the same year. In this version, Walter was now sixteen years and three months of age. He had been born in Canada and came to Australia with his parents around about 1905. The family lived in Melbourne, but his mother died in 1912, followed by his father two years later. Walter reached the war, not from Canada but as a stowaway on a ship from Australia to Colombo in what is now Sri Lanka. From there he managed to reach Egypt and then join the Light Horse.

In fact, he reached Gallipoli, not as a Light Horse member but by stowing away on one of the transports to be present at the now famous landings from 25 April 1915. He worked with the Army Medical Corps. After four months on Gallipoli he went back to Alexandria and then, in company with a bunch of British soldiers, stowed away again to Salonika, where he was part of a service corps. He returned to Alexandria, teamed up with a sergeant who was absent without leave and went to Cairo, where they were both apprehended.

Now Walter joined the New Zealand Rifles, fighting with them in the desert for a while. Then it was off to Marseilles as a stowaway, from where he served with the 21st Battalion AIF at Armentieres (although the 21st does not appear to have been at Armentieres). He was then sent to England, where 'he again decamped', wanting to take a look at Salisbury Plain, presumably to see the enormous military facilities spread across it. No doubt completely fed up with Walter, the army put him on a steamer and he arrived back in Melbourne in late September 1916.

When he signed up once again in South Australia he was, at last, probably eighteen years of age, though only just over five foot (152 centimetres) and weighing 48 kilograms. During this short period of service, Walter was frequently absent without leave and his conduct was considered by the army to be 'bad'.

What happened to Walter after his discharge? He claimed that a woman in Adelaide wished to adopt him and, if that process was successful, he would go and live with her. Perhaps he did.

Whichever version of Walter's stories we care to credit, his war service and associated exploits were remarkable, especially for one so young. Surely such a bold and resourceful boy would make an impact in later life? But no further trace of the 'youngest Anzac' has yet been found. He seems to have disappeared as suddenly as he began stowing his way across the world 'to see things', as he put it.

THE SECRET WATCHERS

Who was Reginald Hockings and why did he receive an Order of the British Empire (OBE) in 1920? People were generally pleased for him but must have wondered what the northern Australia pearl trader had done to receive such an imperial honour. The answer was 'top secret'.

Born in 1868, Reginald Hockings was a Brisbane man who went into the pearling business in 1898. With his business partner, he built up a trade through Torres Strait and into what were then the Dutch East Indies (now Indonesia). He prospered, and by the time World War I began was a well-respected businessman with excellent connections to the Dutch, then in control of much of the area where his luggers were mostly engaged. The Netherlands remained neutral during the war but Germany, also having considerable interests in the East Indies, in the Pacific islands and in China, was declared an enemy. Australia's first engagement of the war was against the German radio base at Bita Paka near Kabakaul, not far from Rabaul, in 1914. Naval encounters between German and Australian vessels went on throughout the war.

As a civilian, Hockings was not involved in these hostilities. But his skills, operating facilities and contacts in the Dutch colonial administration became valuable assets to the Australian Commonwealth Naval Board. Why? The story is a convoluted tale from the murky annals of the 'Great Game', the espionage activities of the great powers towards the end of the nineteenth and the beginning of the twentieth centuries.

Germany operated extensive networks of agents in the United States before and especially during World War I. Their intention there, as it was wherever they conducted espionage, was to undermine the imperial power of Great Britain and to win the Great War that began in 1914. Although America was neutral in the first three years of the war, the country supplied large amounts of arms to the British and their allies in Europe. On 30 July 1916, an enormous explosion in New Jersey was heard as far away as Maryland and Philadelphia. Over a million pounds of explosives awaiting shipment from Black Tom Island detonated with a force equal to an earthquake measuring 5.5 on the Richter scale. It was then the largest man-made explosion in history. German agents had managed to penetrate the docks where the explosives were stored while awaiting shipment to Britain, plant their charges and flee.

As well as being an ancillary combat zone for the European war, America was also a convenient place for German agents to purchase weapons for use in parts of the world where they wished to destabilise the British. At that time, there was nowhere more important to Britain than India. There, a number of nationalist groups opposed to the occupation of their country took to violence to achieve their aim of independence. With the enthusiastic cooperation of Germany and a group of Irish–American nationalists, arms were purchased for shipment to the Indian rebels from the American west coast.

The most feasible way for ships to reach the subcontinent from the Pacific Ocean was via South-East Asia. Through their own counterespionage activities, the British and the Americans were aware of these plans and alerted the Australian government to the need for surveillance of the passage to the Indian Ocean. Desperately short of ships, the Australian Navy recruited Reginald Hockings. With his radio-equipped fleet of luggers diving for pearl shell and *bêche-de-mer* all through Torres Strait, the East Indies and the Malay Archipelago (more or less those places now known to us as Malaysia and Singapore), Hockings was ideally placed to provide a surveillance fleet to keep an eye on foreign shipping. With his mostly Malay pearling crews, Hockings did just that throughout the war, sending coded reports gathered by his luggers and relayed via the mothership, *Wanetta*, to the naval authorities.

In the US, the ship that was supposed to be carrying the arms, *Maverick*, had in fact been unable to load them. Commanded by German sailors, and so technically at war with Australia, she had been diverted to Java, where a German agent was to get rid of the incriminating vessel. Instead, *Maverick* was impounded by the Dutch and her crew imprisoned. A sensational five-month trial of more than 100 conspirators, including German consular staff, was held in San Francisco.

One of the accused assassinated the ringleader in court and was himself gunned down by a United States marshall. A group of Indian nationalists was eventually indicted for military conspiracy against Britain, though American public opinion saved them from being extradited to face British justice in their home country.

While the work of Hockings and his employees was not armed combat, the high stakes involved meant that it was dangerous. As well as maritime surveillance, it involved creating a network of informants among Dutch officials, police and anyone likely to have information. In the process, they uncovered a previously unsuspected German spy operating in the region. Running these successful covert efforts gained Hockings his OBE. He also managed to have his two chief assistants, Tommy Loban and Batcho Mingo, given Australian residency. As the White Australia policy was well and truly in operation at this time, this was a considerable achievement.

FINDING THE LOST SUBMARINE

A World War I submarine disaster initiated an enduring mystery that has still not been fully solved.

In September 1914, *AE1* was part of a fleet of Australian naval vessels operating in what was then German New Guinea. War had recently been declared and it was necessary to locate and engage German naval shipping. *AE1*'s sister submarine, *AE2*, was also part of the fleet. Aboard the *AE2* was Stoker Petty Officer Henry 'Harry' Kinder, who in later life wrote down his recollections of what happened, recording that 'on 14th September 1914, *AE1* went out, accompanied by a destroyer, on what was to be her last journey. Little we thought, when laughing and joking with the crew just before she left, that it was the last time that we were going to see them.'

AE1 was due back with the fleet in Rabaul harbour by 6 p.m., when 'some of us went onto the parent ship, as it was the custom for any crews of boats lying in harbour to watch any submarines coming in off duty. As it was just on six, everyone was watching a point a mile or more away where we would get the first sight of *AE1*.'

The sailors waited. Six o'clock came and went. Still they waited: 'We guessed that something had happened but no-one liked to voice an opinion as to what it was. At last we saw the destroyer come around the point full speed. Our worst fears were confirmed when she signalled the flagship asking if *AE1* had returned.'

The crew of the destroyer reported that around 4.30 p.m. *AE1*, running on the surface, turned for harbour. Through a megaphone, the captain of the destroyer told *AE1* that he would take his ship around one side of a small island while the submarine headed straight back to harbour. With his faster vessel, he would catch up with *AE1* before she got there. But, on rounding the island, the captain of the destroyer saw no submarine. He assumed she had headed straight back without waiting and so made for Rabaul.

All the destroyers immediately began to search, but apart from a small oil slick no other trace of the submarine was ever found. Harry Kinder expressed the general puzzlement:

> It was hard to say what had happened to her to cause her sudden disappearance, as so many things can cause a submarine to sink. Rumours went around regarding her sinking but none were ever proved. So she remains, to this day, one of the mysteries of the war. It was fully believed that it was through some cause in the boat and not by the enemy that she went down.

The rumours Kinder mentioned were that a German warship, disguised as a merchant trader, had attacked and sunk *AE1*, but there were no indications of battle or other evidence to support this theory. The submariners' assessment of the disaster was probably the most accurate. *AE1* had been plagued with problems since her launching in England in 1914. But even then, for a submarine to suddenly disappear without trace, along with her crew of 35 officers and men, was difficult to comprehend. 'A sad and terrible end,' Henry Kinder concluded. The men of *AE1* and *AE2* had been together for up to three years and many had mates on the lost submarine.

After the eventual discovery of the cruiser *Sydney*'s last resting place in 2008 (see 'There'll always be a *Sydney*'), the fate of *AE1* remained the most perplexing in Australian naval wartime history. Many searches were made in the decades after her loss, but wherever searchers looked, even after extensive studies of the surrounding waters and with increasingly sophisticated technology, *AE1* remained lost. Even the famous French scuba diver Jacques Cousteau tried to locate the wreck in 1990.

In 1976 Royal Australian Navy officer Commander John Foster convinced the navy to allow a sidescan sonar search of the suspected area, with promising results. Unfortunately, these could not be followed up at the time. Foster was instrumental in having several subsequent searches carried out, again with tantalising clues but no result. Finally, in December 2017, a search funded by the Australian government and a range of other sponsors located *AE1* in 300 metres of water near the Duke of York Islands.

After 103 years, the lost submarine had at last been found. But the mystery of her loss persists. *AE1* is mostly in one piece on the ocean floor and a subsequent survey found that the rear torpedo tube was fully open. To what extent this may have contributed to the loss of the submarine and exactly what were the causes of the disaster are questions still under examination. The wreckage of *AE1* is a war grave and the Australian government has declined to publicise its exact location.

THE MOLONGLO MYSTERY

Under the heading of 'The Molongolo [sic] Mystery' the *Labor News* of Sydney, New South Wales, revealed a secret to its readers early in 1919. The paper stated that a 'solemn veil of official secrecy has been lifted and we are at last free to discuss the question of a town of mystery which some time ago was erected on the banks of the Molongolo [sic] River within the Federal Capital area'. By then, though, not only was the secret well and truly out but this covert community—the Molonglo Internment Camp—was losing most of its residents.

The rapid construction of extensive accommodation for more than 3000 World War I German and Austrian internees from the Middle East is now almost forgotten. But in 1918, as the war came to an end, 'the name Molonglo Camp connoted an atmosphere of mystery and romantic enterprise, of strenuous endeavour, of willing and successful co-operation, and of wartime sacrifice', claimed an informant in 1940.

This not very clandestine construction began on 'a certain day, early in the year 1918, upon which a secret cablegram was received from the British Government, asking whether suitable arrangements could be made to accommodate several thousand enemy nationals who were to be removed from the Far East and interned'. Despite a ridiculously short timeframe and a major shortage of resources, equipment and labour, the Commonwealth Public Works Branch accepted the challenge.

Canberra's population was very small then and there was no shortage of available land. The Public Works Branch found a 250 acre (100 hectare) site on a hill along the Molonglo River.

The plans called for living spaces for over 500 families, together with shops for meat and bread, a school, teachers' residence, hospital, military and guard facilities, a fire station, stables and a dedicated railway loop and station. It was a major residential development 'contained in 40 tenement blocks of uniform design, each containing two separate parallel buildings returned at each end and thus enclosing a small internal square in which bathrooms, laundries, and conveniences for the block were placed'.

Building firms from Sydney were contracted and the massive operation got underway. Everything had to be done from scratch, beginning with surveying the site, digging the stump holes for the buildings and fixing the prefabricated frames. The army of carpenters made a deafening racket as they hammered and sawed through over 7000 cubic metres of timber. Major works involving several rivers delivered water to the camp through more than ten miles (17 kilometres) of piping. A dedicated sewage works was installed and over 50 miles (80 kilometres) of wiring ran from a new electrical substation.

An army of tradesmen and labourers was needed. Twelve hundred had to be fed, watered and accommodated in tents to have the camp up and running and ready to receive its residents. Although the facility was called a 'camp', it was meant to be a prison. Guard towers had to be built and surveillance lights installed. All this, and more, was accomplished in less than ten weeks.

But as everyone was justifiably patting each other on the back the political situation changed. The thousands of Middle East internees never arrived. The wonderful project on the banks of the Molonglo River was suddenly an enormous and expensive white elephant. It did house a few hundred people detained internally from Australia and also from South-East Asia and the Pacific, but they were not there for long as the war ended in November 1918.

A few months earlier, a Norwegian diplomat was asked to inspect Australia's internment camps in response to rumours that internees were being poorly housed and treated. At Molonglo, he found a generally happy community of 'enemy aliens'. Inmates could play tennis, engage in cultural activities and go on walks in an 'elevated beautiful position'. Children were being schooled and internees 'ate as well as the guards and officers in charge'.

Soon after the war's end, most of the Molonglo camp inmates were sent back to their countries of nationality, even some who had never lived in those countries. Much of the land and its improvements were sold, though the remainder was still in use into the 1950s as accommodation for workers building the growing city of Canberra. Today, nearly all traces have disappeared, though the remnants of the military buildings remain on grounds now occupied by a local arts facility in the suburb of Fyshwick.

WHY CAMP X?

In mid-1942, Camp Tabragalba was established on a Queensland cattle property of that name. It was to be a site mainly for training personnel in anti-aircraft operations. But it wasn't long before, under the codename 'Camp X', it became the home of much more covert activities.

Early the following year, Camp X became a base for the Allied Intelligence Bureau (AIB), whose job was to gather intelligence in the south-west Pacific region. Within its organisational structure, the AIB included Z Special Unit (sometimes known as 'Z Force'), M Special Unit, the Coastwatchers, a Dutch intelligence outfit and, from 1943, the Philippines Regional Section (PRS). Very few knew of the existence of these groups and even today their activities, with the exception of the well-publicised Z Special Unit, remain opaque. For good reason. Together, these were the basic 'dirty tricks' departments of Australia's war in the Pacific.

The raid on Japanese shipping in Singapore harbour carried out by the ex-fishing boat *Krait* has become a much-lauded legend. In September 1943, a few men with limpet mines managed to paddle folding canoes right into the Japanese stronghold, place their charges and escape, sinking or damaging six, possibly seven, ships in the process. Z Special Unit tried it again in 1944, but this larger raid was a failure, with the loss of all personnel.

The Coastwatchers had been in existence since the 1920s. The small but valuable network observed and reported on enemy activities. It was originally confined to Australian mainland coasts, but after the outbreak of World War II it also stationed operatives in New Guinea (now Papua New Guinea) and the Solomon Islands. From 1942, Rupert Long, Director of Naval Intelligence, was primarily responsible for upgrading and expanding the group under the name M Special Unit to deal with the new challenges posed by Japanese expansion in the Pacific and to Australia's north. M Special Unit was a joint Australian, British, Dutch and New Zealand operation and also had American participation. The unit specialised in operating behind enemy lines. The consequences of capture were often lethal, most infamously the beheading of Sergeant Leonard Siffleet by samurai sword.

As the allies sought to re-establish command of the Pacific from 1943, a number of American units dedicated to infiltrating Filipinos into the Japanese-held Philippines were located at Camp X. These men were trained in radio operation, cryptography and speaking Japanese and were transported behind enemy lines for intelligence gathering and aiding the Filipino resistance.

Not all members of M Special Unit were engaged in active field operations. Many were needed to receive and relay the information transmitted back to Australia by the field operatives. In 2001, an unidentified man who worked with M Special Unit as a teletype operator on the Moluccan (Maluku) island of Morotai recalled his experiences. He spent his shifts in a tent with six Americans whose names he did not know. The tent was surrounded with barbed wire and guards. His job was to type coded messages into the teletype machine and receive coded messages from those working behind enemy lines. He had no idea of the meaning or significance of the messages. The secrecy continued into the afterwork arrangements and neither he nor those he shared quarters with knew each other's names. When the war ended, the teletypist took part in arranging the records generated by all this activity. The paperwork was divided into two categories: one for the Australians and one for the Americans.

By that time, the United States Army had long since taken over the running of Camp X, which was now a considerable military establishment of 38 buildings. As well as barracks, latrines, kitchens, a laundry and administration buildings necessary to house possibly up to 1000 men, there was a butcher shop, an aid post and a lime and straw hut. The inventory of buildings also lists a gas chamber.

How did the cattle property known as 'Tabragalba' come to be renamed Camp X, if only for a few years? There was another wartime Camp X in Ontario, Canada, also dedicated to covert operations training. Although this operation had links with British intelligence, it was designed mostly for Canadian and American forces. It seems likely that the Australian facility was named for the secret radio frequency used by the Coastwatchers—'X'.

DIAMOND JACK

As Japanese forces advanced through Java in 1942, Royal Dutch Indies Airways pilot Ivan Smirnov was given the task of flying Dutch residents of Bandung to what they hoped would be the safety of Broome. Just as the DC-3 Dakota was about to taxi to the runway, an airport official ran onto the tarmac with a brown paper package, telling Smirnov it was to be delivered to the Commonwealth Bank as soon as possible after he landed. With the possibility of encountering Japanese Zero fighters on his mind, Smirnov paid little attention to the last-minute package and took off towards Broome with his eleven passengers and crew.

Approaching Broome, Smirnov's radio operator received a message telling him that the airfield was safe 'for the time being'. Not long after, the Japanese destroyed it and most of the planes on the ground. And now Smirnov had his own problems. Three Zero fighters appeared and attacked the passenger plane. Using the skills that had served him well as a Russian war ace more than twenty years before, Smirnov climbed, dived and turned. But with the limited manoeuvrability of a commercial aircraft he could not shake off the attackers. He was wounded several times and the left-side engine caught fire.

A fatal crash into the Indian Ocean seemed inevitable, yet Smirnov was able to bring the DC-3 down on the beach at Carnot Bay, steering what was left of his burning plane into the surf to douse the flames. As they all struggled out of the wreckage the Zeroes strafed them again, wounding several passengers. Stranded, with few medical supplies and little food or water, the small group did what they could to survive, finding a few items in the plane and using the parachutes for a tent. Over the next few hot days, several, including a baby, died. They were buried in the same wet sand that saved the survivors when another Japanese plane later bombed them. The ordeal ended when those left alive were rescued by people from Beagle Bay.

But the brown-paper package was missing. And now the story becomes very murky.

Some weeks after the survivors of the crash had been rescued, a 'weatherbeaten' beachcomber, dugong hunter and adventurer sailed to the crash site in his lugger. Ferreting through what was left, 40-something Jack (John) Palmer found a sea-sodden package. There was a red seal on it and inside was a leather wallet. Later, anchored in Beagle Bay, he opened the wallet and discovered millions of pounds worth of 'white stones', diamonds from a Bandung jeweller, the property of several wealthy Dutch families. He shared a few out to his two mates, who disposed of them as they saw fit, injecting an unprecedented new currency into the remote Kimberley economy. Diamonds began to be used to buy tobacco and other of the few products and services that were available. Some were buried, some turned up in tree branches and in waterways. Jack still had the lion's share, worth, in today's money, somewhere around ten million dollars.

But there was a war on and it had come very definitely to northern Australia, so Jack turned up in Broome wanting to join the army. When interviewed, he handed a set of salt and pepper cellars full of jewels to an astonished Major Gibson, telling him that the rest washed away in the surf. Gibson didn't believe the adventurer but enlisted him anyway and posted him to the remote Gantheaume Point to look out for the Japanese.

Palmer's contact with authority set the wheels of government, the army, the police and the Commonwealth Bank in motion. He and his two mates were arrested. The army took the beachcomber back to Carnot Bay to search for the diamonds he said were lost in the sea. They found none.

Around the Kimberley, diamonds were appearing everywhere. Children were even using them to play marbles. But news that the police were looking for those with the precious stones in their possession spooked the locals, who jettisoned them as quickly as possible. There are stories of diamonds being dropped down unsewered lavatories and probably emptied out with the nightsoil. The 'officer in charge of native affairs' at Broome came across three caches that were reported to be worth more than £100,000.

Jack and his companions were taken to court for stealing. Pilot Smirnov, recovered from his wounds and the ordeal of the crash, was called as a witness. His evidence was eagerly anticipated, but he could not say much about the diamonds beyond the fact that they were lost in the crash and following events. Later, he would write in his memoirs that he was approached by a man representing himself as a director of the Commonwealth Bank:

'Is there something you want to hand over to me?' he asked me with some urgency. 'To hand over to you?' I replied rather clumsily. 'The packet which they gave you in Bandung. Where is the packet?'

Slowly it dawned on me. 'Lost in the battle,' I said, simply. I told him in brief words the history of our emergency . . . the banker appeared as white as a sheet. 'Well, what was in the packet?' I asked him with interest. I wondered in this same minute that I had not asked myself this question earlier.

He then said in sombre tones: 'Nothing particular, nothing more than a few diamonds which had a value of 500,000 guilders.' I was absolutely taken aback.

In his court evidence, Jack said he at first intended to sell the stones but, on hearing that there would be a reward for their finding, decided to hand them in: 'The military got all the diamonds I had in my possession except the few I gave to Robinson and Mulgrue. They were lucky to get what they did, for if I had known as much then as I do now the military would not have got any of them.'

Despite a determined and testy Crown case against the three men, there was little solid evidence. Jack and his mates were acquitted by a jury in May 1943 and then Jack went back to fighting the war. Smirnov later went to America, where he continued his adventurous life, marrying an heiress and eventually retiring to the pleasure island of Majorca, where he died in the 1950s.

But in the Kimberley, the diamonds continued to weave their spell. Jack Palmer was even more of an identity around the country, living in noticeably better style than before the war. He had various businesses and was known as what used to be called a 'ladies' man'. Rumours persisted up to his last days in Broome hospital in 1958. Here, quite a few people had contact with him, including medical staff and a priest. He was asked by some if he really did have the rest of the diamonds, but all they could get from the wily Jack was 'nudge, nudge—wink, wink'. The dying adventurer made broad hints but gave nothing away.

All his visitors and carers later reported that Jack kept a small case under his sick bed. He was said to have checked the case every night, locked it and slept with it firmly under his pillow. Vera Dann, working at the hospital, spoke with Jack in his last hours. He asked her to be his 'caretaker' and to look after the case. But, she recalls, 'he died overnight, and the next day there is no suitcase, no nothing . . .'. Others confirmed the disappearance of the case or bag.

The passing of 'Diamond Jack', as he was known locally, only deepened the mystery of the missing diamonds. Speculation continues to this day, as does interest in the story. The Kingdom of the Netherlands has supported a number of related activities and in 2012 co-published a memorial booklet on the Broome attack and the diamonds.

That same year, the tale took a new twist. Letters written by Norman Keys, one of the downed Dakota's rescuers, came to light. They contained assertions that Smirnov did know that he was carrying a fortune in jewels. Keys recalled: 'When I arrived the four survivors were in a pretty bad way and Captain Smirnov appeared to me to be delirious and kept repeating that he had to get back to the aircraft to pick up the diamonds.'

Did Smirnov know about the jewels or not? What did Diamond Jack have in the locked case? Where did it go? Whatever the answers to these questions might be, it is estimated that probably two-thirds of the original consignment are still missing.

THE BROOK ISLANDS EXPERIMENTS

One morning in late 1942, Corporal Patterson Charles Mills of the 6 Transportation and Movements Office RAAF was roused out of bed early. He was stationed at Townsville, Queensland, along with other Australian and American troops. A small group of these men were taken to a deserted beach north of the city where they loaded a cargo of 44 gallon drums onto a barge. They were to deliver the drums, which were very light in weight, to a small island while being closely observed by a group of very high-ranking Australian and American officers.

The drums were duly delivered to the island, but on the return voyage the barge unaccountably ran out of fuel. The men drifted for several days, apparently without any attempt being made to search for them. They were lucky to be spotted and picked up by a corvette. The *Bowen* took them back to Townsville and landed them. The rescued men were still not of any interest to the authorities, it seems, as there was no one to greet them or provide any medical attention they might have needed. Then they were split up. Corporal Mills often wondered if their potentially lethal situation had been deliberately arranged for some unknown military reason.

Mystery and ignorance were very much the tenor of events on this part of the coast during the last few years of World War II. Beginning in January 1944, a series of secret tests were carried out on the Brook Islands, and other islands, with some related activity on the mainland, including field trials in the rainforest at Innisfail. The tests were designed to study the effects of various chemical weapons, including mustard 'gas' (not technically a gas), on humans.

Under various names, the Australian Chemical Warfare Research and Experimental Section was formed in New South Wales in 1942 and eventually relocated to Innisfail in December 1943 for research in tropical climates. It was a diverse unit of Australian, British and American civilian scientists, military and supporting personnel drawn from various services, including the Australian Women's Army Service and Australian Army Medical Women's Service. Their job was to carry out trials on chemical weaponry to find methods to counteract their effects on troops affected by them. This inevitably involved human guinea pigs.

Volunteer army personnel were involved in experiments like that described by Gunner John Henry Roche in December 1944. He and others, without protective equipment other than standard respirators and wearing only army uniforms without underwear, had been required to walk through rainforest bombed with mustard gas by American Beaufort bombers three days before. The aim of the trial was to see how mustard gas might still burn them after a few days. Anyone who was burnt or blistered was hospitalised while various experimental treatments were tried on them.

The aim of the test was to see how long soldiers could continue to operate while affected by the gas. Roche slipped in a pool of oily black residue and developed badly burned buttocks and upper thighs. An experimental ointment was applied to his clothing and he managed to maintain his route marches over several days, keeping his contaminated uniform on. He was finally transferred to the research unit's section of Innisfail Hospital, where 'each day they would measure the size of the burns and extract some of the liquid. They also got us to swallow a long rubber tube and took 10 cc's of gastric juices off the stomach. They put it in a test-tube and it used to finish up looking like a rainbow in the test-tube.'

Discharged after a couple of weeks, Roche was still suffering nausea, loss of interest in food and pain if he ate any. But Gunner Roche was a tough character. He went back to his unit and later volunteered to take part in more mustard gas trials.

As with most mysteries, there were rumours. The most outrageous is that 50 American convicts were promised their freedom in return for taking part in the tests. Unfortunately, none lived through the experience to claim their liberty. This has been strenuously denied by the government and by relevant experts but, like all such factoids, it lingers.

These activities were closely guarded secrets. The participant soldiers were not told their purpose, but it is likely they were related to the clearing of Japanese troops from Pacific islands as the Americans and their allies reclaimed the region on their way to Tokyo. Whether the allies feared the Japanese might use chemical weapons or they planned to use them on the Japanese remains a tantalising question.

There has been ongoing controversy about the tests, as well as claims of ongoing health issues among volunteers. Questions were asked, and partly answered, in federal parliament as veterans of the tests sought to advance their health claims. In a worrying reprise of the World War II tests, the defoliant known as 'Agent Orange' was also tested at Innisfail early in the Vietnam War period.

'THERE'LL ALWAYS BE A *SYDNEY*'

These words were spoken by a member or members of the Australian War Cabinet on 1 December 1941. That same day, Prime Minister John Curtin announced that the Australian light cruiser *Sydney* (II) had disappeared with all hands almost two weeks earlier, on 19 November. No other details were given, further fuelling the many rumours burning through the wartime population.

Sydney was a celebrated vessel with an honourable record of service. The 645 sailors and Royal Australian Air Force (RAAF) men aboard, and their families and friends, were proud of their ship and so were the Australian people. Her loss was not only a military disaster but a national tragedy. It was also a mystery that, despite the eventual location of the wreck in 2008, holds as many questions as answers.

What had happened to the *Sydney* and her crew? Where did she lie? Were there any survivors? If so, where were they?

Official answers to these questions, such as they were, satisfied hardly anyone at the time or for years after. Rumour and gossip filled the information void. *Sydney* had been sunk by a Japanese submarine. She was destroyed by a German raider. Her sailors had been machine-gunned in the ocean as they swam desperately for their lives. The survivors had been taken prisoner by the Germans. Or the Japanese. *Sydney* was not at the bottom of the sea but had survived beached on some island—somewhere.

The refusal of the government and the Royal Australian Navy (RAN) to give a definitive position for the action that had taken place between the German raider *Kormoran* and the ill-fated cruiser only made matters worse. It was long suspected, though not finally proven until 2008, that the official bearings given to the public were deliberately distorted to avoid a panic if people learned that a major naval engagement had taken place quite close to the Australian coast. Near enough to be seen from the shore, as oral histories of residents of Port Gregory (Western Australia) taken after the war recount.

But the discovery of *Sydney* did not put an end to the puzzling questions that surround the ship and her loss. How could a relatively lightly armed raider, disguised as a Dutch merchant ship, have so devastatingly destroyed the well-armed *Sydney*, which also had a reconnaissance aircraft aboard? Why did the usually cautious Captain Joseph Burnett allow his ship to come close enough to the raider to allow the Germans to fire the first shots? Interrogations of the surviving *Kormoran* captain and crew produced a stark version of events.

Sydney approached *Kormoran* to around 1200 yards (1100 metres) without, inexplicably, opening fire. But *Kormoran* did, loosing two torpedoes that struck the Australian vessel even as her longer-range guns pounded the raider. *Kormoran* was scuttled six hours later and reported seeing *Sydney* on fire and limping over the horizon to the south-west. Most of the German ship's crew took to the lifeboats and were picked up a few days later and imprisoned.

This satisfied few, especially the next of kin to the many missing. But in those days and in those circumstances, doubts and suspicions were suppressed and it was not until after the war that a gathering cloud of questions began to demand proper answers. At first, individuals, including ex-RAN officers involved in suppressing the true location of the battle, carried out their own inquiries. So did people associated with the next of kin, as well as an increasingly vociferous community of amateur investigators.

Eventually, there were several official inquiries. The most thorough was a commission of inquiry chaired by Justice Terrence Cole established after *Sydney* and *Kormoran* were found very near to where the German sailors claimed they went down. The commission clarified and confirmed other aspects of the German story, though erroneously concluded that *Sydney* was not at action stations when she approached *Kormoran*. We now know she was, though that knowledge only deepens the unfathomable enigma of why she did not fire first.

One possible explanation has been advanced by those studying World War II intelligence records. It is argued that the Germans knew the supposedly secret radio call signs used by Australian ships and that *Kormoran* lured *Sydney* close with one of these. This is supported by the otherwise baffling preparation of the RAAF plane on board *Sydney*, followed by its sudden standing down.

Among other mysteries still seeking resolution is why there was only one known immediate survivor? There was enough time for survivors to launch life rafts but only one body, washed up on Christmas Island and finally recovered in 2006, has ever been found. Forensic examination determined that the sailor was in all probability from the *Sydney*, but as yet he has not been identified and remains the poignant 'Unknown Sailor'.

Some of the remaining questions will never be answered, at least not to the satisfaction of everyone. While the bones of the *Sydney* have been found, the full story of her fate and that of her sailors remains an enigma. Whoever said 'There'll always be a *Sydney*' in the War Cabinet meeting of December 1941 was unarguably correct.

THE HANGED MAN

Could Adelaide be a spy city? The mysterious 'Somerton Man' case of 1948 remains as baffling today as it was then. 'Tamam Shud', as the dead mystery man was sometimes known, may or may not have been a spy, but there were spies aplenty around Australia during the Cold War.

Early in 1963, a man was found hanging from a tree branch on an Adelaide golf course. There was no identification on the body and the death was treated as a suicide, but we now know it was a fatal element of a winding espionage intrigue involving the Australian Security Intelligence Organisation (ASIO), the Russian KGB and a brave single mum.

Kay Marshall was a recently divorced mother working for the British High Commission in New Zealand in the passport processing department. One day a Russian diplomat invited her out to a concert. She reported the incident to her superiors, who identified it as an attempt to recruit Kay as a source of classified information. She was told to play along.

After a few months, the diplomat asked Kay to obtain classified documents for him, which she did and continued to do for almost two years. But the documents she gave the diplomat were all fabricated by New Zealand intelligence to mislead the Russians.

Kay—codename 'Sylvia'—then moved to Sydney, where she was asked to meet a man at Taronga Park Zoo. She was to hold a copy of the Melbourne *Age* newspaper in a certain way and was given passwords to use to confirm the identity of the mystery man. He didn't turn up the first time, nor the second. But on the third attempt a chubby Russian showed up, introducing himself as 'John'.

Of course, Kay was 'wired' and ASIO had covert cameras set up to document the meeting. When they examined the footage they identified 'John' as high-ranking KGB officer Ivan Skripov, and Kay was asked to play along as she had in New Zealand. She was instructed by Skripov in basic spy craft, including invisible ink messages and dead-letter drops. These were deployed as Skripov sought to test her to make sure she was not a double agent. After many meetings he was evidently convinced, because he tasked Kay with a secret mission.

Skripov gave Kay what looked like a hair dryer. In fact, it was a covert communications device. She was to fly to Adelaide to meet a man carrying a black briefcase who would have combed back hair and be wearing spectacles. Once again, ASIO set up a surveillance operation. South Australia was home to the Weapons Research Establishment (WRE) overseeing weapons research at Woomera and elsewhere. The spooks correctly assumed that the package was related to Soviet attempts to steal these closely guarded secrets. They hoped to snare a top Russian spy.

Kay went to the meet outside the Maid and Magpie, as instructed, and waited. And waited. Nothing. She returned the next day at 1 p.m. A young couple were getting married nearby and after a while a taxi brought the photographer. He looked remarkably similar to the man Kay was to meet and carried a black briefcase. He was nervous, constantly scanning the scene for any sign of trouble. Eventually he spotted the ASIO cameras and made off, looking very worried.

The double agent's cover was 'blown', as they say in spy movies. Skripov made increasingly desperate attempts to contact her to reclaim the messaging device. ASIO informed the Menzies government of their findings. On the basis of what ASIO had found out about him, in no small part due to 'Sylvia', Skripov was declared *persona non grata* and expelled from Australia amid much diplomatic tension with Russia. Kay was in great danger and was whisked off to the distant safety of San Francisco.

But what of the man supposed to receive the package in Adelaide?

In 2020, Peter Butt was researching his television documentary on this spy story. He took a close look at the ASIO footage of the abortive Adelaide meet and followed up with some research into immigration archives. There, he was able to identify the hanged man as the mysterious wedding photographer. His name was Stanislaw Kilanski. An expert pathologist reviewed Kilanski's autopsy report and concluded that the bruising around the dead man's jaw and other marks confirmed he had not committed suicide. It seems likely that once Kilanski's true identify was known the Russians feared he would be captured and interrogated, revealing the extent of their espionage operations in Australia.

Kilanski's postwar resettlement and immigration records show he was born in Poland in 1923, had only a primary school education and spoke 'a little' English. He was unmarried, had no relatives in Australia and was a Roman Catholic. Before that, he had been deported to Nazi Germany for forced factory labour in 1942 for 'political reasons'. He was interviewed and medically examined in Germany in 1950 and found to be in good health and approved for resettlement in Australia. He may have been recruited as a Soviet agent before he arrived or afterwards. ASIO had been watching him for some time and photographed him attending a meeting of the Communist Party of Australia in 1956.

The mystery of the hanged man has now been solved. But another question remains unanswered. Was there a mole inside the WRE?

Suspicion fell on Horace Pile, a former RAAF radar technician and fervent communist who had managed to infiltrate the WRE in the role of a technical salesman. 'Horrie' Pile, well known to security forces, had no security pass but was able to have himself escorted into the facility as often as two or three times a week. He had close contact with technicians and other personnel involved with the research of a variety of weapons, some nuclear. Pile was forbidden further access to the WRE and his employer transferred him from Adelaide to Melbourne. Subsequent investigations at the WRE showed that Pile had plenty of opportunity to steal highly sensitive information of great value to the Soviets. For reasons unknown, he was not arrested and died of a heart attack in 1971.

Dead spies tell no tales.

THE MISSING NUCLEAR FILES

The files suddenly disappeared some time towards the end of 2018. A large number of records relating to the British nuclear tests in Australia during the 1950s and '60s were suddenly no longer accessible from the United Kingdom's National Archives. The files were withdrawn from that public collection without notice or consultation and placed in a shadowy repository in the north of Scotland known as 'Nucleus'. This facility holds records of the British nuclear industry and is not open to the public.

Why have over 1700 files available to researchers and the public for decades been withdrawn indefinitely? And what is the Nuclear Decommissioning Authority (NDA), the British government body that authorised the withdrawal?

At the end of World War II, a new war of lies, spies and nuclear secrets began in earnest. The apocalyptic possibilities of the 'atom bomb' had been chillingly but convincingly demonstrated by the nuclear attacks on Hiroshima and Nagasaki. If one country had the 'bomb', others needed it to even up the global balance of power. With Australia's agreement, Britain undertook years of atomic and related testing at Maralinga, the Montebello Islands and Woomera, a known total of twelve major tests and many smaller ones. One of these, a nuclear-armed rocket fired from Woomera to a point just north of Broome, is thought to have scattered radioactive particles to Adelaide, Sydney and Melbourne.

These tests were conducted until 1963 and remained secret for many years, though growing concerns from veterans and First Nations owners of the affected country eventually led to a Royal Commission in 1984–1985. Among the damaging conclusions of the Royal Commission were findings pointing to inadequate protection for many taking part in the tests and the withholding of vital information about the risks of radioactivity from the Australian government.

The Royal Commission also found that the after-effects of the tests lingered at Maralinga, in particular. Various attempts were made to clean up the area but were not completed until 2000 and were not as thorough as they should have been. By then, compensation had been paid to the traditional owners of Maralinga. In 2014 their land was returned, though there are still concerns about the effects of the tests on the Maralinga Tjarutja people and their country. In 2021 it was found that the contamination of the area was worse than previously thought and remained a threat to humans, plants and animals.

The findings of the commission conflicted with the official British accounts of the tests and caused controversy that, despite the passage of years, has not subsided. Many articles, books, films and television documentaries have covered the issues involved, leaving a strong public impression that the full truth about the tests and their consequences has not been revealed. The answers to those questions lie in the records appropriated by the British nuclear authorities.

The NDA was formed in 2005 with the aim of facilitating and managing the cleaning up of Britain's civil—not military—nuclear sites. It has a small staff with a very large budget and is also responsible for a range of nuclear-related activities, including the transportation of nuclear materials within the United Kingdom and internationally. It has its own insurance company to cover its extensive properties, which include offices and nuclear and related facilities.

As well as this extensive spread of interests and activities, the NDA established the Nucleus Archive in 2015 to gather and store the many records of the United Kingdom's civil nuclear industry. These processes began in 2017 and are proceeding today, though 'access to nuclear documents via this facility is not yet available but will become available over time'. In the meantime, documents can be requested through the United Kingdom's Freedom of Information system or under the Environmental Information Regulations.

Historians researching nuclear matters were nonplussed when the Australian-related records were whisked away from open access, where they had been for nearly 40 years, then locked away at Nucleus. They were especially puzzled as to why an authority and archive concerned with the civil nuclear industry would wish to hold files on military nuclear testing. Professor Jon Agar of University College, London, a researcher in this area, tweeted: 'Why not just *copy* the files if the nuclear industry needs them at Nucleus for administrative reasons? Why take them all out of public view?'

Ludwig Leichhardt, about whom John Mann, one of his surveyors, said '[he] would get lost in George Street', is yet considered one of Australia's greatest explorers after traversing 4827 kilometres from Darling Downs to Port Essington. But in his second attempt to cross the top of Australia and then turn south to Perth he and his party disappeared, leaving little trace and much mystery.

5

OUTBACK PUZZLES

THE LOST WELLS OF THE SIMPSON DESERT

Only two people knew the secret of the lost wells. They were Mick McLean, or Irinyili in the fast-fading language of the Wangkangurru people, and his sister, known as Topsy. In the 1960s, they told linguist Luise Hercus what they knew, by which time the Wangkangurru had long departed their ancestral country in the middle of the Simpson Desert.

Spreading over three states and almost 180,000 square kilometres, the vast Simpson is most people's idea of a desert— sandy, bare, hot and very dry. The only permanent water sources are the mikiri, deep but narrow hand-dug wells that supported the Wangkangurru, and those allowed to pass through their land, for at least 5000 years. The Wangkangurru followed a hunter–gatherer life, living on plants, snakes, lizards, birds, kangaroos, bandicoots and whatever else was available to eat. For water they relied on this series of wells.

Just how these wells came to be is not understood, but it seems that the Wangkangurru knew where the small amount of rain that fell in the desert collected. They then dug through the sand, sometimes as deep as seven metres, until they reached a band of clay on which the rainwater was trapped. They were able to maintain their nomadic lifestyle by following a chain of these wells over the course of a year, or until food ran low and they moved on to the next mikiri.

As well as supporting the survival needs of the Wangkangurru, the wells were part of extensive Dreaming tracks or songlines, some of which stretched for hundreds of kilometres and along which First Nations peoples passed, met and traded. A rich layering of stories surrounds the wells, most of it secret. Some aspects of the 'history time', as the Wangkangurru call the creation era often called the Dreamtime, can be told to others.

Not surprisingly in this country, there are strong traditions associated with water. A large group of figures known as the 'rainmakers' are an important part of our First Nations peoples' traditional heritage, as is the story of the Crane-man who planned to possess his daughters-in-law by luring his people into the desert and killing them. But when the people smelled the water in the well, they were transformed into water birds and flew to safety, cursing the well and the Crane-man.

By the time the explorer David Lindsay travelled through the southern and central areas of the Simpson Desert in the 1880s, the Wangkangurru had almost abandoned the wells. Lindsay was guided by Paddy, one of the last Wangkangurru men who knew their location. But soon after, almost all knowledge of the life-giving waters was lost. With nobody to use and maintain them the desert sands soon covered the mikiri and they disappeared. Fortunately, from the threads of traditional lore passed down to them, Mick and Topsy McLean were able to share their learning. With this information, Denis Bartell retraced Lindsay's footsteps almost a hundred years later in the 1980s and was able to rediscover seven of the nine mikiri. But where were the others?

In 2006, a camel expedition chanced upon an unknown mikiri, east of those already known. Further journeys to the location were later made, and in 2019 researcher Mike Smith and a non-profit organisation were invited to survey one of the mikiri. Led by traditional owner and head ranger Don Rowlands and travelling by camel, they found many stone tools and other implements, as well as ancient human remains, confirming the long habitation of the area by the Wangkangurru.

And they discovered what has been described as an oasis. In an area of no or sparse vegetation, they came upon a scattered group of large trees. The mikiri that supported them had also supported the Wangkangurru for thousands of years. The expeditioners found heavy grinding stones, shells, bones and other evidence of long human occupation. Intriguingly, this particular well is not mentioned in any of the traditional songs and stories. There was no evidence of metal on the site, suggesting it had been abandoned for well over a century.

What happened to the people who last used the lost mikiri? They probably 'came in' from the desert, attracted by an easier lifestyle as settlement developed around the desert. There are also stories of a massacre in the area during the 1880s. What did happen, or not, may never be known, but the mystery of the lost wells is slowly being unravelled.

Although the Wangkangurru people no longer have use for the wells, they are a vital part of their cultural heritage. The rediscovery and rehabilitation of the mikiri is not only of historical and anthropological significance, but also affirms the spiritual traditions, stories and legends of the Wangkangurru.

But it also discredits a different kind of story. The notion that the arid vistas of the Simpson Desert were uninhabited was fostered by the early explorers of the area and through the general settler ignorance of First Nations occupation. Not only were the Wangkangurru people living there, but the Simpson is also the traditional home of at least nine other traditional groups, spread across and around what are now the states of Queensland, South Australia and the Northern Territory.

THE STONE FACE

By the time George Grey published his exploration journals in 1841 he was governor of South Australia. Before that he had been a soldier, but in the 1830s he mounted several expeditions into the almost totally unexplored north-west of the country. Some of the things he found there continue to puzzle us today.

Grey was sympathetic to the plight of the Irish peasantry and believed that colonisation would be a way to alleviate the intergenerational suffering in that country. With the approval of the Colonial Office in London, he embarked in 1836 to find suitable land for Irish settlement in Australia's unknown regions.

Grey's first attempt was almost fatal. With no experience of the harsh conditions or of leading groups of people and animals through Aboriginal country, the expedition was a form of moving chaos. Grey suffered a spear wound, nearly died, but struggled on to discover and name the Glenelg River and several mountains in Western Australia.

His second attempt was even more disastrous. Planning to explore north along the coast from Shark Bay, he and his men were wrecked and eventually forced to walk to safety in Perth, a trek of almost 500 kilometres. Amazingly, all but one of them eventually got back.

It was on this expedition that Grey became the first European known to have looked upon the Wandjina figures. His descriptions and drawings of these primal creation and rain-bringing spirits led to some overdramatic interpretations of their origins. Since Grey's time, we have learned much more about these striking images and their deep spiritual significance. Grey would find other Wandjina figures, admire their beauty and puzzle over their meaning. But he also stumbled on another perplexing artwork that seemed unrelated to First Nations beliefs.

After sketching the Wandjina figures, Grey and his companions prepared to move forward:

> when we observed the profile of a human face and head cut out in a sandstone rock which fronted the cave; this rock was so hard that to have removed such a large portion of

it with no better tool than a knife and hatchet made of stone, such as the Australian natives generally possess, would have been a work of very great labour. The head was two feet in length, and sixteen inches in breadth in the broadest part; the depth of the profile increased gradually from the edges where it was nothing, to the centre where it was an inch and a half; the ear was rather badly placed, but otherwise the whole of the work was good, and far superior to what a savage race could be supposed capable of executing. The only proof of antiquity that it bore about it was that all the edges of the cutting were rounded and perfectly smooth, much more so than they could have been from any other cause than long exposure to atmospheric influences.

Grey provided a sketch of the head that is not in the style of Aboriginal art and appears to be the silhouette of a male European.

How did it get there and who created it?

Grey does not seem to have investigated this anomalous discovery any further. In later life he became, as well as governor of South Australia, governor of Cape Colony, South Africa, and of New Zealand (twice). He was knighted in 1848 and died in 1898, being buried in St Paul's Cathedral, London.

It is possible that one or more Europeans were on this part of the Australian mainland long before Grey. Two of the mutineers of the wrecked Dutch East India Company ship *Batavia* were marooned somewhere along that coast in 1629. They are the first Europeans known to have settled in Australia, in their case of necessity.

Wouter Loos and Jan Pelgrom de Bye (also known as Jan van Bemel) were being punished for their part in the vile bloodletting and misery afflicted on the survivors of the *Batavia* by the mad tyrant Jeronimus Cornelisz (Corneliszoon). Most historians agree that the two men were put ashore near the Hutt River, which is far to the south of the Glenelg River where

Grey found the carving. But Loos and Pelgrom, as he is usually called, were provided with a small boat, all the equipment they needed and instructions to get acquainted with the local people. Maybe they did. Pelgrom was only eighteen years of age and was spared the noose because of his youth.

Unknown others may also have been wrecked along that coast. At least four Dutch East India Company ships leaving the Cape never reached their Dutch destination in Batavia (Jakarta), their fates unknown. Other wrecks and vanished survivors are well documented, although much further south than Grey's field of operation.

This is speculative and improbable, but not impossible. We are continually discovering new things about what was once the 'unknown south land', a place wide enough to harbour many secrets.

LEICHHARDT'S LAST QUEST

Ludwig Leichhardt was reckoned by many to have been Australia's greatest explorer. Others have thought otherwise, including one of his surveyors, John Mann, who said that Leichhardt 'would get lost in George Street'.

These dramatically different views sum up the enigmatic nature of Leichhardt himself. On the one hand he was an accomplished scientist and bushman, on the other a possibly delusional visionary whose journeys into the unknown Australian heartlands seemed fired by a spiritual zeal.

Friedrich Wilhelm Ludwig Leichhardt was born in Prussia in 1813. He was well educated and, although he never took a degree, attended universities in Germany, Britain and elsewhere in Europe following his interests in natural sciences, medicine and philosophy. He arrived in Sydney in 1842 with the aim of exploring inland Australia. His first expedition to Port Essington, a journey of almost 5000 kilometres through mostly untrekked country, took place from 1844 to 1845. Despite the loss of several members, one through an Aboriginal attack, the expedition was a great success. The returned explorers were feted as heroes in Sydney and rewarded with significant government and private funds. Leichhardt's achievement and related scientific work would also be celebrated with recognition and awards in France, England and elsewhere, lauding him as a great scientist.

Leichhardt used some of the reward money to pay for an expedition to cross the continent from Darling Downs in the east to the west coast and then south to the Swan River colony, modern-day Perth in Western Australia. This took place from 1846 to 1847 and had only limited success. But Leichhardt was determined to try again and in 1848 he led a very large party of explorers and animals from the Darling Downs seeking a northern route across the top of Australia towards the west coast. The party, including seven men and more than 70 animals, was last seen in early April 1848 as they headed into the oblivion that still shrouds them.

As time went by and no news came from Leichhardt, people began to fear a disaster. Eventually a reward was offered for information and attempts to find Leichhardt and his companions began. Since then, there have been many public and private attempts to locate the missing explorer. He has never been found. Neither have his companions, the stock or any of the vast amount of equipment and supplies the expedition was carrying. Excepting one small metal plate.

The plate was inscribed with Leichhardt's name and the date 1848. It was found in 1900 attached to the burned remains of a rifle lodged in the branches of a boab tree. The Aboriginal stockman who found it said that the tree was marked with an 'L', Leichhardt's characteristic method of blazing his route. The artefact passed through a number of hands, eventually coming into the collection of the National Museum of Australia in 2006. Scientific tests have since been conducted on the plate, confirming its provenance, and scientists believe that further testing with evolving techniques will reveal much more about where the plate had been.

In the meantime, searchers have continued to look for Leichhardt and his men. Extensive journeys into the desert by many people over many years have discovered nothing else. No boab tree marked with an 'L' has been located. No metal equipment, canned food, surveying gear, buckles, other firearms. No bones. Nothing.

What happened to Ludwig Leichhardt and his expedition? And where and when?

There are many theories about this great Australian mystery. Some speculate that there was a mutiny. Others that the expedition members were killed by Aboriginal people, possibly on the Maranoa River, according to the local folklore of Wallumbilla, Queensland. Perhaps they just got lost and starved to death? There is even a legend of a ragged and bearded white man living out his days with the traditional owners of the outback.

If Leichhardt himself placed his rifle in the boab tree, near Sturt Creek just across the Northern Territory and Western Australian border, then he came close to achieving his ambitious quest of crossing Australia from east to west. On the other hand, the rifle may have left his possession thousands of kilometres eastwards and perhaps been passed through First Nations trade routes.

While any of the theories and speculations are feasible, none explains the baffling absence of any remains. The vanishing of Ludwig Leichhardt is truly perplexing. It is an unfinished story that has inspired not only some heroic searches but also great art by Sidney Nolan and great writing in Patrick White's novel *Voss*. Romancing of the mystery began very early with a poem titled 'Leichhardt's Grave: An Elegiac Ode' by the missing man's friend Robert Lynd. Nearly 40 years after Leichhardt's disappearance, Henry Kendall also chimed in with a mini epic

> . . . On the tracts of thirst and furnace—on the dumb, blind, burning plain,
> Where the red earth gapes for moisture, and the wan leaves hiss for rain,

In a land of dry, fierce thunder, did he ever pause and dream
Of the cool green German valley and the singing German
   stream?
When the sun was as a menace, glaring from a sky of brass,
Did he ever rest, in visions, on a lap of German grass?
Past the waste of thorny terrors, did he reach a sphere of
   rills,
In a region yet untravelled, ringed by fair untrodden hills?
Was the spot where last he rested pleasant as an old-world
   lea?
Did the sweet winds come and lull him with the music of
   the sea?
Let us dream so—let us hope so! Haply in a cool green
   glade,
Far beyond the zone of furnace, Leichhardt's sacred shell
   was laid! . . .

The tradition has continued, with a flurry of books, documentaries and ongoing searches. Perhaps the remains of Leichhardt's last quest will be found one day. In the meantime, there is only the tarnished plate from the explorer's rifle to provide tangible evidence of his existence, whatever death he and his companions might have suffered.

THE WAILING WATERHOLE

It begins as a low wailing noise in the night. As the sound creeps closer the volume and pitch intensify to a hideous shrieking. The deafening reverberations die away as suddenly as they begin. Many have fled the terrifying noise of the Wilga Waterhole. They say few ever go back.

Part of the Barcoo River system, the Wilga Waterhole is on Ruthven station, around twenty kilometres from Isisford in the centre of western Queensland. Legend has it that from the time of European settlement the waterhole has been screaming. The story has various twining threads.

The first is the belief that local Aboriginal people considered the spot to be a dangerous place and avoided it. Early speculations about the noise inevitably involved the possibility of the hybrid Aboriginal and European water monster, the bunyip. This strand of the story seems to have trailed away over the decades, probably because no one is known to have been eaten at the waterhole and any self-respecting bunyip needs to devour the odd human.

The next evolution includes yarns about shearers or stockmen camping at the waterhole and being so terrified by the wailing that they ride wildly off into the night seeking shelter and human companionship, something not in great supply in this area then or since. Here's a version by master storyteller Bill Beatty:

> It is on record that more than 50 years ago a couple of shearers, on their way to a station in the Longreach district, camped by this waterhole one fine summer evening. Though it was dry weather, the Wilga Waterhole as usual, was well supplied. After hobbling their horses, and leaving them to graze, the two men made tea over their campfire, ate their damper and salt beef, and smoked and yarned for some hours.
>
> The fire had nearly died down, the men began to yawn, and there was an uncanny stillness.
>
> Suddenly there came a soft, distant wailing that grew rapidly nearer and louder. To the astonished men the cries appeared to be in different keys—devilish, unearthly shrieking, such as no human voices ever uttered. One thing was certain—the screaming, now ringing in their ears at deafening pitch, was coming from the waterhole.
>
> The shearers thought their eardrums would burst, but they were too terrified to move. Then, to their fervent relief, the shrieking diminished in volume until it was merely a weird wailing. Moments later, it ceased utterly, and once more the bush was deathly silent. Throughout it all, not a ripple or movement marked the surface of the lagoon from whence the noises had emanated.

Without waiting for the dawn the shearers caught their horses and rode off.

When the shearers reach the shearing shed and tell their tale they are scoffed at by some. But others have their own yarns about horses being afraid of the waterhole and exhausted cattle being so averse to it that they stampede at sunset.

Bill included this in his popular *Treasury of Australian Folk Tales and Traditions* in 1960, by which time he'd been telling the story in newspapers for quite a few years and is probably largely responsible for its spread. It has since become a staple of online yarning.

As well as these more or less down-to-earth elements, the tradition has a supernatural aspect. It is said that a worker on Ruthven station built a hut for his family near the waterhole. Returning one night, he found his wife in mortal fear and in danger of losing her wits because she had heard the wailing. They moved out. In a local variation, the woman is said to have murdered her infant and the noise from the waterhole is the wailing of her unquiet ghost.

All very far fetched, of course. But a couple of ghost hunters who visited the waterhole in 2004 found the remains of a hut and old stockyards at the site. They also found two 'lonely graves', as the many unmarked resting places in the outback are known. The graves were encircled with handmade wooden stakes that reveal that one is smaller than the other.

After two nights at the waterhole the ghost hunters left without hearing anything other than crickets chirping and waterbirds calling.

LASSETER'S BONES

'Well, I just dug a bloody 'ole an' poured the poor bastard in.'

Bob Buck was describing how he had found and buried the remains of Harold Lasseter in March 1931. The Territorian bushman was hired to search for Lasseter after the prospector became separated from the expedition trying to relocate a rich reef of gold he claimed to have discovered in the MacDonnell Ranges many years before. The project was a disaster from day one and ended with Lasseter's disappearance into the desert. There are still many puzzling questions surrounding the Lasseter legend: some concern the man who buried him and exactly what was buried, and reburied.

Bob Buck was one of the legendary characters of the Northern Territory. Over his 50 years in the outback, he had done it all and seen it all and was only too pleased to tell about his exploits, real and not so. He was admired as a noted liar in a region where the art of yarn spinning has been taken to new heights.

Wisely recruiting Aboriginal men Johnson Breaden, Lion and Billy Button, Bob Buck set out to find the missing prospector. They found remains and items belonging to Lasseter. That should have been the tragic finale of a lengthy saga of delusion, myth and greed, but it turned out to be far from the end of the tale.

Bob Buck's description of 'pouring' the remains into a hole in the ground suggests that Lasseter had died within the two-week period before the search party arrived. Any longer and there would have been no remains to bury, the elements, ants and desert animals having done their work with flesh, blood and bone. But Lasseter's death certificate would state that he died in January that year.

There were other discrepancies and anomalies. Buck and his companions recovered letters, a pistol, a camera and other items, along with the upper half of a set of dentures. The letters were mainly personal and told a sad tale of the prospector's slow death, despite occasional assistance from the local desert people. When Lasseter's 'diary'—more of a notebook—was later discovered in another of his camps, the entries further confused the timing and manner of Lasseter's last days.

There was consternation in official circles about these loose ends and about Buck himself, not a man with much time for maps, paperwork or officialdom in general. The bushman was also oddly reluctant to confirm the finding and disposal of Lasseter's body. When asked to sign a statement for the expedition company to claim insurance on Lasseter's death he refused, saying that 'he could not swear whether the skeleton was that of a white or black man'.

However, Buck had at least come back with evidence of Lasseter's death, including the seemingly peculiar skeletal proof of the dentures. Like most of the other items, these remained, largely forgotten, in official custody for many years. Until 1956.

In that year, the American journalist and writer Lowell Thomas, together with an Australian television producer, arrived in Alice Springs with a film crew to get to the truth of the now world-famous Lasseter story. To reach the grave he hired Nosepeg Tjupurrula. They found the site and promptly dug up the contents of the grave, an illegal act. The Lowell Thomas crew transported what they found back to Alice Springs, where they were again buried. According to Nosepeg Tjupurrula, the skull he saw possessed a full set of dentures. Of course, the dentures that Bob Buck brought back to prove his location of Lasseter had been lost in police custody, so no forensic comparisons were possible.

Further confusion was created by Bob Buck stating that he had initially disinterred Lasseter from a grave made for him by First Nations people before reburying him, a claim confirmed by the traditional occupiers. There is also a possibility that the remains were again dug up and buried yet again after Buck left and before he returned, some months later, with traveller and amateur anthropologist Walter Gill.

Whoever was buried, exhumed and reburied and by whom and wherever these events took place is one of the enduring mysteries of the Lasseter story. A further twist is a folk story that he did not die at all but somehow managed to make it south to Eucla, where he took ship for America. Lasseter may well not have been buried where he died and, as we have seen, even that location has often been confused. Today, someone's remains lie in Alice Springs General (Memorial) Cemetery. The accompanying plaque reads, on the left side:

> Harold Lewis Bell Lasseter. Died in the Petermann Ranges on January 30 1931. His grave was located on December 14th 1957 by an expedition led by Lowell Thomas and Lee Robinson. This is his final resting place.

At the front of the plaque are some words of Theodore Roosevelt:

> It is not the critic who counts, or how the strong man
>   stumbled and fell
> Or where the doer of deeds could have done better.
> The credit belongs to the man who is actually in the arena
> Who knows the great enthusiasms, the great devotion
> And spends himself in a worthy cause.
> If he fails, at least he fails while daring greatly.
> So that he will never be one of those cold and timid souls
> Who know neither victory or defeat.

The riddle of Harold Lasseter's lost reef of gold, his ultimately doomed attempt to find it again and the continuing attempts to locate it have transfixed journalists, television producers and treasure hunters for decades. There is no sign that the story will ever end.

IT'S RAINING FISH!

'It has been raining fish', wrote a correspondent to Victoria's *Mortlake Despatch* newspaper in September 1873. In fact, it had been raining fish at many places for a very long time, not only in Australia but around the world. For centuries, people had been reporting downpours of the 'finny tribe', filling fields, previously dry fields and ponds with writhing, gasping fish. Is such a strange phenomenon possible?

According to the ranks of Australian yarn spinners, it is not only possible but frequent. There was a time when it was hard to avoid falling fish tales from blokes propping up the bar of any outback pub. While the great days of bush lying are probably behind us, there is no shortage of raining fish reports. Winton in Queensland reported fish flapping along a gravel road. The folks at Bernfels station, 70 clicks north-west of Winton, had just had a welcome downpour. The Oakhill family rushed out to have a look. The kids 'were out there in the mud for hours after that, collecting them up and putting them in a container with some water and trying to figure out what they were going to do with these fish', said Tahnee Oakhill. 'They were pretty amazed.'

And so they should have been.

In this case, the anomalous event was easily explained by science. The fish in question were identified as 'spangled perch', an aggressive creature that is able to move across large distances through very small amounts of water. When they get a chance, the antisocial perch are only too happy to take off from their brethren and seek new homes.

It happened again in March 2020. Drought-stricken Yowah, about 1000 kilometres inland from Brisbane, experienced long-looked-for rain from ex–Tropical Cyclone Esther. Locals were convinced the fish had fallen from the sky rather than welling up from the very hot artesian bore or wriggling overland.

Again, the fish were spangled perch—also known endearingly as 'spangled grunters'—and the Queensland Museum ichthyologist thought the fish had been trapped in shrinking waterholes during the drought and been more or less washed out with the rain, swimming to Yowah along flooded wheel ruts or 'little temporary tributaries'. He did allow that fish could actually fall from the sky if they happened to be sucked up by waterspouts or other powerful climatic events, but these were rare.

Rare they are, but perhaps not as unusual as we might think. There are well-documented cases of fish, frogs and other small creatures being picked up by whirling winds of one sort or another and dropped to Earth many miles from their original habitats. Frogs fell with the rain in Kansas City in 1873 and again in Dubuque, Iowa, in 1882, as well as Marksville, Louisiana, in 1947. More recently, frogs fell on Odzaci in north-western Serbia in 2005.

Back in Australia, locals of Lajamanu, on the edge of the Tanami Desert in the Northern Territory, have seen fishy rains in 1974 and in 2004. In that event one reckoned 'fish fell in their hundreds and hundreds all over the place'. It happened yet again in 2010: 'All I can say is that I'm thankful that it didn't rain crocodiles,' said a relieved local after the 2010 event. Fair enough!

So, no mystery here, then? Well, maybe not, but at least nobody in Australia has yet reported the rather large rats that were said to have fallen from the sky during an especially violent storm in Germany in the late seventeenth century, an unsettling event that was depicted in a contemporary drawing.

SEEING THE LIGHTS

Did Professor Pettigrew solve the mystery of the min min lights?

When European settlers first occupied the country around Boulia, Queensland, from the 1860s, strange lights were soon seen flickering, glowing and even moving through the sky. The traditional owners had also witnessed this phenomenon long before then. They called the lights 'min min' and used them as a disciplinary measure for children, a kind of aerial bogeyman approach. Whether it worked any better than the bogeyman in western societies or not, the min min were not considered to be harmful.

Interestingly, Aboriginal peoples' accounts of the lights suggest that they were increasingly observed from the time of European settlement. Certainly, some of the early accounts tell of lights appearing during times of drought stress, as at Winton in 1902 and along the Winton–Boulia road in 1914. Other accounts suggest that sightings of the lights declined around the 1920s and it may not have been until a poem on the subject was published in several newspapers during the 1930s that sightings began to increase.

> Close at hand by lonely Min Min
> There's a bird that's phosphorescent;
> Ev'ry drover says it's dinkum,
> With his hand upon his breast
>
> He will swear it dips its feathers
> In some mixture incandescent
> And its lustre lights the ridges
> Through the darkness of the West
>
> Being curious for knowledge
> I went out investigating;
> 'Twas a night of moonless blackness
> Till I saw that eerie glow
>
> In a misty halo floating
> As I sat there contemplating—
> Then there came a thousand furies
> When the wind began to blow.

Many of these lights have been associated with the assorted graves behind the Min Min Hotel in the Channel country on the road between Winton and Boulia, the most frequently mentioned location for sightings. Built in the 1880s as a Cobb & Co coach stop, the shanty had an unsavoury reputation with some dark mutterings about sudden, unexplained disappearances. The place burned down probably in 1917, the same year in which another early account of the lights was recorded. A stockman riding past the remnants of the burnt-out hotel saw a ball of light rise up from the graves. The light hovered for a moment, then moved towards him. Terrified, he rode hard to the Boulia police station with the light close behind him.

Although the lights are popularly associated with the Min Min Hotel and Boulia, they have been seen in many other parts of the country and are as frequently reported by travellers today as they were by swagmen and others a century or more ago. Many of these reports are credible, leaving no doubt that the lights exist. But what are they?

Romantically supernatural explanations revolve around alleged First Nations stories or the unquiet spirits of those lying behind the old hotel. More scientific approaches refer to 'will-o'-the-wisp', or natural gas emanations from artesian bores or other sources. The possibility of some natural cause, such as phosphorescent fungi, illuminated birds or swarms of fireflies, has also been suggested. Of course, flying saucers are also an explanation favoured by some.

But in 2003, Professor Jack Pettigrew put forward a theory that seems to best account for the min min lights. This explanation depends on the natural phenomenon known as a 'fata morgana', a mirage produced when 'a cold, dense layer of air next to the ground (or sea, or sea ice) carries light far over the horizon to a distant observer without the usual dissipation and radiation, to produce a vivid mirage that baffles and enchants because of its unfamiliar optical properties'. The professor was even able to create a min min light to prove his point. In short, the min min lights are an optical illusion.

Although it was recently endorsed by popular science celebrity Dr Karl, some have pointed to some problems with this theory. The main issue seems to be that the fata morgana phenomenon seems to occur elsewhere mainly in daylight and to produce images of boats, mountains and cities. Proper mirages, not amorphous blobs of sometimes coloured light moving steadily through the sky. However, Professor Pettigrew's scientific paper, based on his field work and the detailed studies of Maureen Kozicka, answers most of these objections.

Still, people may prefer the mystery. Even the professor thought so himself. After intensive research and reaching his conclusions about the ghostly lights he said that 'increased knowledge has certainly not lessened my own wonderment at the phenomenon on those infrequent occasions I've witnessed it'.

A DESERT MIRACLE

How could a man survive in the desert for over 40 days with almost no food or water? Robert Bogucki did, but even he isn't sure how he did it.

Riding a bicycle around Australia in July 1999, the troubled 33-year-old from Alaska took a notion to visit the Great Sandy Desert. With no experience, no desert knowledge and little food and water, his plan was to ride from the Sandfire Roadhouse on the west coast to Fitzroy Crossing, 500 kilometres north-east.

By 26 July, the overoptimistic bicyclist had long ditched his bike and camping equipment and had been in the desert for over two weeks, mostly without food and with little water. His belongings were found that day by tourists travelling the mining survey route known as the Pegasus Track.

Next day, the police and emergency services swung into a well-practised search and rescue routine. People frequently went missing in the desert, including locals who should have known better. Quite a few of them perished. This time, police aircraft, Aboriginal trackers and four-wheel drive vehicles searched for twelve days without result. The police surmised Bogucki had either found his way out of the wilderness or perished in it somewhere. The search was called off.

In America, Bogucki's parents took matters into their own hands. Believing their son was capable of surviving and suspecting that he might not want to be rescued, they hired an American search and rescue company. The Americans duly arrived with tracker dogs and a large group of searchers led by a cigar-smoking 'can-do' character nicknamed 'Gunslinger'. They were not welcomed by locals or the police, who had decided that the missing man was deliberately avoiding discovery.

It was now more than three weeks since Bogucki had gone into the desert. If he was alive, it was vital that all available resources were mobilised to find him. The police and the American rescuers began cooperating on another search in the region where they calculated the missing man was most likely to be. It was a very large area but there was nothing else to go on.

By the time Bogucki had been missing for almost 40 days, the search had attracted the attention of Australian media. Reporters, photographers, camera operators and a television helicopter were now involved, but three days into this search still nothing had been found. It seemed hopeless. But then the media helicopter spotted a blue tarpaulin on the ground. It was covered with Bogucki's discarded clothes, water bottle and Bible, together with notes he had made that, according to the police, were 'the thoughts of a bloke obviously in isolation. It goes all over the place.'

On 23 August, a media crew in a chartered helicopter spotted the missing man in a shallow gorge among a few pools of muddy water in the Edgar Ranges. He was dehydrated, disoriented and emaciated but otherwise in amazingly good health. Despite losing at least twenty kilograms, hospital staff needed only to treat severe sunburn, blistering and scratches. Robert Bogucki's incredible survival epic was over.

Why did he do it?

The great survivor gave several statements about his motivations. He told those treating him in hospital, 'I just wanted to spend a while on my own, just nobody else around, just make peace with God I guess.' Asked if he had found whatever he was searching for in the desert he said that he was not sure what he was seeking: 'I really felt alone, not desperate but just without hope at some point,' he replied.

Whatever Robert Bogucki hoped to learn about himself, God or the universe, his quest had major consequences. The police and state government were angry about the trouble and the enormous cost of finding this apparently self-indulgent and irresponsible tourist. Legal action was threatened, though it never eventuated. Bogucki's parents later made a substantial payment to the state emergency services.

Although the epic was over, speculation about Bogucki's intentions continued. Was he some kind of religious crank? Was he simply crazy? Many believed he had a contract in America to write a book and it had all been a giant publicity stunt.

Ten years later, a journalist who had been at the rescue tracked Bogucki down in his Alaskan forest home and interviewed him. 'I can remember being eighteen years old, and thinking about fasting in the wilderness like Jesus,' Bogucki told him. He said he wanted to escape the modern world and 'all its fakeness' and to 'pay my respects to the creator and be without food, possibly without water, pay attention to this God that I had heard about but never really had any experience with'. He felt a need to emulate the Biblical experience of surviving the wilderness for 40 days and 40 nights and trained himself by fasting and not drinking water.

Asked if he would do it again, Bogucki replied that once was enough. His physical survival was not the miracle, but rather 'the world of emotion, love and eternity that opened up to me'.

THE HAUNTED HOUSE AT HUMPTY DOO

'I have certainly seen a few strange things happening at that house, and the last time I saw a few things flying around.'

Father Tom English was describing his experience in a house in the small Northern Territory town of Humpty Doo. He went on to say, 'This mercurochrome bottle came flying out of the bathroom and there wasn't anybody in the bathroom. It was very strange stuff, I have never seen anything like it.' He blessed the house five times but could not shift the unsettled spirit that seemed to have invaded.

This was just the beginning of the troubled times the residents of the house would suffer over the next few months, and not all from supernatural sources.

It was January 1998. The comfortable four-bedroom bungalow nestled in bush was the picture of banality. Two couples and a male mate were living in the house when another couple with an eleven-month-old daughter moved in. The frightening incidents began almost immediately. Stones fell from the sky or the ceiling. Knives, tools and other objects also fell or were seemingly thrown. And then the messages began to appear on walls or using Scrabble tiles. They read FIRE, SKIN, CAR, HELP and TROY. The inhabitants took this to be a reference to the death of their friend Trouy, so spelled, who had died in a fiery road accident a few months earlier.

It was now that Father English arrived. When he performed his blessings, windows were mysteriously smashed and his Bible and crucifix were thrown around by an unseen force. Other priests also failed to exorcise whatever was troubling the house and its inhabitants.

A television program arrived to cover the amazing story. They paid the inhabitants for access and spent over three weeks documenting the incident, managing to record several examples of apparent haunting. But, after screening the story, the program declared it to be a hoax, the work of the inhabitants. The residents of the Humpty Doo house were not happy and cut off further contact with the program.

Shortly afterwards, some experienced ghost hunters arrived and struck up a more positive relationship with the people in the house. They were able to stay there and witnessed many unexplained incidents, including the frequent disappearance of the crucifix Father English had left in the house. It would suddenly reappear, crashing into a wall. Pistol cartridges materialised from nowhere, pebbles and knives fell or were thrown and mattresses were unaccountably moved.

The residents, traumatised but determined, had now taken to speaking to whatever was haunting them. They swore at it and told it to go away, refusing to believe that it was their dead friend Trouy. They even took to tormenting the spirit by reading psalms from the Bible and generally became used to living with the malicious unknown. But it all became too much in the end and all the residents left the house in May, after almost five months of deeply disturbing and unexplained incidents, intense media scrutiny and what appeared to be a psychic assault.

The story was national news for many weeks. There were the usual suggestions that the events were caused by a poltergeist, the suspect being the one-year-old child. This would be unusual in poltergeist cases as the culprit is usually an adolescent. An Aboriginal curse was mentioned, as well as a curse from the Greek wife of the original owner of the property. He and his family had been forced by their bank to sell out many years before and were reportedly desperate to return to what had been their dream home.

Or was it all a hoax, as many, including the television program, claimed? The ghost hunters paid close attention to this possibility. Their verdict? 'We don't believe hoaxers were at work but if they were they were not only first-rate conjurers but first-class actors as well.'

Nobody knew then what caused the Humpty Doo high jinks, nor does anyone today. It remains one of the most puzzling cases of apparent haunting in Australian history.

HIGHWAYS OF DEATH

The 'Highway of Death' and the 'Horror Stretch' are roads with sinister reputations based on often unsolved murders. The many mysteries of these long roads and the souls lost along them have become a feature of modern Australian life.

Travel is an inherently dangerous undertaking. Away from family, friends and familiar locations, travellers can be at greater risk than they are at home. Sailors were once, and often still are, deeply superstitious, as voyaging was a hazardous undertaking. There is a body of folk belief around journeys that is aimed at warding off possible trouble. Never begin a journey on a Friday, it is said, and many people carry medallions featuring St Christopher, the patron saint of travellers, or have other good luck charms placed in their cars.

There are also plenty of cautionary modern legends about incidents alleged to have happened to those journeying on roads and highways. Corpses on roof racks, hairy-armed hitch-hikers and headless bikies are among the unsettling figures who appear in these yarns. The great Australian emptiness and the vast distances that must be driven through it to reach a limited number of destinations are a fertile environment for the fictions, but also for some grim realities.

The 300 or so kilometre section of highway from Rock-hampton to Mackay in northern Queensland was once known as the 'Horror Stretch' from the number of unsolved murders that occurred along it. One writer early this century used the American term 'badland' to describe the relative isolation of the scrubby floodplain through which the road passes and the generally spooky atmosphere that most travellers experience when they drive the route. Local names serve only to inten-sify the foreboding nature of the area, with landmarks such as Grave Gully, Berserker Range and Charon Point, a reference to the shade who ferried the dead to Hades in ancient Greek mythology.

A series of apparently random and brutal murders during the 1970s added to a dark local history of colonial violence and massacre. A couple were shot dead at Connors River in 1975. Their murderers were caught and imprisoned for life. English tourists as well as Australian travellers have been shot. Sexual assaults, murders and disappearances also scar the area's recent history.

A little further north, the 900 kilometre Flinders Highway between Townsville and Mount Isa is another location of far too many disappearances and murders dating from 1970. Dubbed the 'Highway of Death', twelve people to date are thought to have been murdered or have simply disappeared along the road to or from Charters Towers, just off the highway. The most recent of these cases was in 2018, when Jayden Penno-Tompsett went missing on New Year's Eve on his way to Cairns with a mate. Efforts are still being made to discover what happened to him.

Another often lonely road with a sinister reputation runs from Darwin to Port Augusta. The Stuart Highway was the location of the murder of Peter Falconio and terrorising of Joanne Lees in 2001. Peter Falconio's body has never been found, though a man has been controversially convicted and jailed for the crime. This high-profile incident is only one of many violent ends and vanishings along the road that runs right through the middle of Australia, north to south, once named by the Automobile Association of Australia as 'the most dangerous stretch of highway in the nation'.

Men and women were going missing along this nearly 3000 kilometre artery for at least twenty years before the Falconio case. Some may have wished to disappear, of course, though it seems that most incidents are likely to be foul play of one kind or another. An experienced and well-equipped bushwalker disappeared in 2018. Just a few hours' drive along the highway, Paddy Moriarty and his dog went missing from the hamlet of Larrimah in 2017.

In the last few years, some of the most perplexing missing persons cases have attracted the attention of amateur detectives who return to cold cases, often generating new leads, some of which have led to convictions. There is a strong public interest in these activities, mainly pursued online, helping to keep the disappearances in the public eye and providing some hope for distressed families and loved ones.

THE HOLE FROM SPACE

It was already old when one of the Jaru people's two creation serpents slid out of it. But not as old as was first thought.

Kandimalal, or Wolfe Creek Meteorite Crater in the Tanami Desert, is usually said to be the world's second largest hole created by a meteorite. Its diameter varies from almost a kilometre to a bit less than 900 metres and it is getting on for 200 metres deep, although largely filled by sediment. There may be larger meteor craters, but we can't see them because they have been buried over aeons.

When Kandimalal was first found by geologists in 1947 it was thought to be about 300,000 years old. The iron meteor that made it was around 14,200 tonnes speeding towards the Earth 40 times faster than a high-velocity bullet, around fifteen kilometres a second. When it smashed into the Kimberley sand it pulverised the quartzite in the ground and was itself vaporised into shards and balls, creating a previously unknown mineral now named 'reevesite' after one of the geologists who first spotted the crater during an aerial survey.

One of the space rocks was retrieved and given to a local Atherton museum for display in 2015. Two weeks later the space rock disappeared, stolen by two men who were caught on CCTV. It was another five years before police recovered the artefact in Cairns in late 2020 and returned it to the museum. Who stole the rock, why and what was done with it while it was missing are matters that, so far, remain unexplained. Police hope to be able to tell the story in due course.

Today, Wolfe Creek Meteorite Crater is a dramatic sight in the barren Kimberley landscape two to three hours rough driving from Halls Creek. It rises up out of the plain, its uneven rim slightly out of kilter with the flat surrounding lands, and is the main feature of the Wolfe Creek Crater National Park, taking its name from nearby Wolfe Creek.

Many Australians first heard of the crater when the first *Wolf Creek* film was released in 2005. The chilling murder mystery at the centre of the movie was given a dramatic boost by visuals of the crater. Based on the real-life events of the murders committed by Ivan Milat and Bradley Murdoch, the film was a fictional rendition reset in the Wolfe Creek Crater National Park. The film was a hit, though sometimes criticised for its violence. The archetypal Aussie character of Mick Taylor, frighteningly played by John Jarratt, is revealed to be the incarnation of evil, chilling and thrilling audiences at the same time. *Wolf Creek* was followed by a sequel and a TV series.

The mysteriousness of Wolfe Creek Meteorite Crater is due to its extraterrestrial origin and dramatic appearance in an exotic and remote location, its significance in Jaru tradition and its scientific importance for understanding more about space bodies impacting the planet. Most recently, it is known for its association with, even if only fictionally, some of Australia's most mysterious and chilling murders. In their different ways, these are all attempts to explain and understand something rare in human experience.

The Jaru people also have another story about the crater. According to elder Jack Jugarie, when the evening star and a crescent moon came near to each other the star grew hot and fell to Earth, causing a great explosion of flame and noise. The whole country shook, frightening the people who avoided the place for a long time. But, eventually, they dared approach the site again and saw that the crater was the place where the flaming star reshaped the Earth.

Kandimalal is now thought to be only 120,000 years old, one of seven such relatively recent impact sites in Australia. Scientists calculate that one of these space rocks hits us around every 17,000 years. Fortunately, they only seem to land in the most arid and desolate parts of the country. So far.

WHERE'S THE WATER?

The lack of water has always been a serious issue in the arid continent of Australia. The basic and irreplaceable requirement for the survival of life, locating it, containing it and using it wisely have been constant challenges since European settlement. Much effort and expense—as well as tragedy—went into trying to solve the apparent mystery of Australia's backward-flowing rivers and the existence or not of a fabled inland sea. Eventually these puzzles were solved, but that has not been the end of our water riddles.

In late 2020, scientists reported that over two trillion litres of Murray–Darling River water went missing the previous year.

The water wasn't in Sydney Harbour, because that is enough water to fill the harbour more than four times. So where was it?

The Murray River and its various contributing systems have been controversial since European settlement. Australia's arid nature was broadly realised after the existence of a hypothetical inland sea was disproved and the relatively few river systems were identified as explorers and pioneers became familiar with the interior and the coasts of the continent.

But in recent decades controversy and conflict over the precious waterway has heated up, with environmental concerns complicating widespread unhappiness about the river's flow and the quality of the water that flows through it. The staggering loss was the culmination of yearly declines in flow since 2012. But although we now know what has happened nobody knows why, despite billions being spent on the problem by state and federal governments. The implications of this are potentially grave for agriculture, the environment and the production of one-third of Australia's food.

There are a number of suspects in this whodunnit. The most obvious are those who use the water directly for farming and other activities. A few irrigators have been fined significant amounts for stealing, though it is thought that this crime has decreased in recent years. In any case, water theft alone could not account for anywhere near the missing quantity.

The 'harvesting' of rainwater from floodplains before it can reach the river system is also likely to have a negative effect on the amount of water in the system. Collecting water before it reaches the river is not generally illegal, but scientists have such little information on this that they are unable to measure the extent of the problem, or even if it is one.

Government subsidies for upgrading irrigation works along the river have had an unexpectedly negative result. Before these expensive upgrades and improvements were carried out, a certain amount of water flowed back into the river due to inefficiencies and faults in the methods and equipment being used.

There is no agreement on the exact amount of this loss by increased efficiency, but it could be up to three billion litres a year. While this is worrying, it is not by itself sufficient to explain the mystery.

Increasing annual heat around the basin could be an important factor. Three of the hottest years on record have been recorded in recent times, leading to the suspicion that more water is being lost to evaporation and seepage than envisaged when the much-vaunted Murray–Darling Basin Plan was initiated.

A final twist in the plot is that the water may never have been in the system in the first place. Scientists have suggested that the original modelling of water flows on which the current management plan was based was inaccurate. The overall outcome of this realisation is that the quantity of water expected to flow was overestimated. While this sounds like a 'sigh of relief' moment, it isn't. It means that we need to put even more water back into the rivers to solve the environmental and supply problems that continue to trouble the system.

Inevitably, there is not universal agreement on these findings and debate will continue, possibly forever. Some scientists fear that whatever solutions and methods are adopted to solve the long-term problems of the Murray–Darling Basin will involve finding a very difficult balance between the amount of water to be used for agriculture and the amount needed to sustain associated wetlands, as well as the vital ecosystems on which they rely.

The history of the basin since European settlement and the many attempts to manage it strongly suggest that this will be a deeply fraught decision. In the meantime, the ultimate answer to the mystery of who stole the water is, unfortunately, that we did.

The head lighthouse keeper's quarters on South Solitary Island off
Coff's Harbour, New South Wales, became Lydia Gow's home in 1910.
However, mysteriously she contracted typhoid and died, cut off from
help by stormy seas. Her body was placed in a makeshift casket of
two iron bathtubs soldered together . . . but subsequent lighthouse
occupants swear that Lydia Gow's spirit still inhabits the cottage.

6

MYSTERIOUS PLACES

THE HAUNTED HAWKESBURY

The Hawkesbury River valley was one of the earliest areas to be settled after the foundation of Sydney in 1788. Flowing down to Broken Bay and fed by many tributaries, the valley is filled with creeks, mangrove swamps and some very old and dark tales.

According to a newspaper report of 1928, 'There are men still living who claim to have seen the ghost' linked with the old Greenman's Inn on Mangrove Creek. The apparition took the form of a young woman in her night clothes cradling a newborn baby. She was reportedly seen as often in daylight as at night, though was equally frightening whenever sighted. Toughened timber-getters were said to refuse to return to where they had been joined by the woman. Overnight campers were sent shrieking back up the river when the ghost silently appeared, raising its hand to point at the baby in its arms before disappearing.

As well as the terror induced by this 'weird spectre', there seemed to be no one who could say who the woman had been in life and why she kept appearing over a 50 or more year period. The inn had a sinister reputation as a haunt of gamblers, thieves and worse. It was said that a young man was once staked out on the rocks along the riverbank at low tide, slowly drowning as the waters rose while patrons of the inn looked on and downed their drinks.

The 1928 newspaper account, based on local legend, offered an explanation of sorts:

> The strange death of a girl, barely out of her teens, excited unprecedented interest. She was found dead with a newly born infant in her arms. What became of her body, no one seemed to know. It disappeared before it could be buried. Perhaps, like other corpses, it was weighed down with stones and cast to the sharks.
>
> Although the girl died nearly eighty years ago, the menfolk of the Hawkesbury were never allowed to forget it.
>
> For forty years, her ghost—so the old pioneers of the River will tell you—haunted Mangrove. Dozens of men claim to have seen it, and the remarkable part about the story is the fact that most of these people were once revellers at the Inn.

In 2003, a writer in a local newspaper recalled his grandfather telling him another tale of the ghost of Greenman's Inn. According to this version, a local boatman was paid a guinea to cover the costs of transporting the young woman's body (and, presumably, that of her infant) down the river to Wisemans Ferry, then to Parramatta for burial. But the boatman decided to keep the money and tipped his morbid cargo into the river. Ever since, the boatman told the writer's grandfather, he saw the ghost of the woman each dawn and dusk. Other locals were said to have witnessed a boat with blood red sails appearing from time to time, and at the inn itself bloody prints appeared on the walls and people had witnessed an eerie green light hovering above the well.

Another Hawkesbury River hostelry is also the centre of a smorgasbord of supernatural mysteries. The Wisemans Inn Hotel was the home of Solomon Wiseman, famous for the ferry service he established at that point in the early colonial days. According to local tradition there are stories of ghosts, including:

> women spectres who hurried through the echoing stone rooms and along draughty corridors in trailing gowns, and scared residents swear that they heard the swish, swish of silken dresses as a woman ran to look over the balcony. Sometimes the rustle was accompanied by a scraping of feet and a faint gasping cry like the coughing of a woman with asthma.

It was said that this was the ghost of Wiseman's first wife, whose appearances were attempts to draw attention to treasure hidden in her bedroom. Apparently, the apparitions eventually ceased, but a few years later a box full of gold sovereigns was found hidden under the boards of her bedroom.

Wiseman was also implicated in another yarn in which he refused one of his convicts a permit to go to Sydney to meet his sweetheart. Instead, he had the young man placed in a chain gang. The convict escaped and tried to swim across the river. His leg irons dragged him under, and he was drowned. Visitors to the house reported hearing the clank of chains as the convict's tormented spirit roamed the darkened passageways, presumably seeking vengeance, release or both.

The Howorths were an early pioneer family along the Hawkesbury. Ex-convicts, John and Elizabeth Howorth took up a land grant of 70 acres (28 hectares) near present-day Wilberforce. They cleared the land, established a home and prospered there, together with three sons and two daughters, from 1798.

From 1804, the family suffered the first of an incredible sequence of tragedies. In that year their eleven-year-old son, John, died from snakebite. Two years later, their second son died. Possibly overwhelmed with grief, Elizabeth Howorth vanished. John placed an advertisement in the *Sydney Gazette* imploring her to return, assuring her that 'her imprudence will be pardoned and I promise never to reproach her for any misconduct'. There was never any reply from Elizabeth. Two years later John Howorth died, and by 1811 all the remaining children and John's younger brother, William, were dead.

That might have been the end of a sad pioneer family saga but for the stories that began not long after the death of the last son, Jim Howorth. Locals reported shadowy figures around the now-deserted farm. Then in 1821, children playing on the riverbank near the old Howorth property made a grisly discovery. It was a box weighted down with stones. Inside were the remains of a woman, her hair tied up in a black ribbon.

Memories of the tragic Howorths were rekindled among older residents of the area. Was the skeleton that of Elizabeth Howorth? If so, as seemed likely, had John Howorth murdered his wife and concealed the crime? We will never know the answers to those questions.

THE VICAR'S TALE

Further up the Hawkesbury, the town of Windsor has a respectably mysterious ghost in the Anglican St Matthew's Rectory (or Parsonage). When Reverend Norman Jenkyn 'took charge of the parish', as he put it, early in the twentieth century, the building already had a ghostly reputation. Reflecting on his 30 years living in the building, 'hoary with age', the vicar Jenkyn told his tale:

> When I took charge of the parish a few of the old residents informed me that the Rectory was haunted, and that at the mystic hour spirits walked abroad. They told me that I would soon verify their remarks by personal experience. I was not perturbed by their statements, for, thought I, the Bible itself was full of ghost stories, so I took up my residence in the old house. I had not long to wait for the thrill of the ghostly visit.

One night at about 12.30, while lying in my bed upstairs, I heard distinctly; the drawer of the sideboard in the dining room below open, and then what seemed to me like the turning over of forks and spoons as if someone was searching for a particular one. I was alone in the house. I hastily dressed, and in the dark crept stealthily down the long circular stairway leading to the dining room. I quickly turned the torch on, but found no one. I retired somewhat relieved, yet disappointed, for I was certain that I was about to solve the ghost problem.

Some four weeks later my old housekeeper awoke at about one a.m. and heard similar sounds, and, thinking that I was searching for a knife, called out, 'You will find the cake knife in the right-hand drawer, Sir.' Now I was spending the evening out, and did not return for some hours after, but my housekeeper mentioned the incident to me next morning. I was afraid to tell her that I was not at home when she heard the sounds; for had I informed her she would have packed up and left without a day's notice. My sister came to stay with me, but after one night's experience she decided to return to Sydney by the first train, which left at 5.30 a.m. She has not since been seen within a radius of 5 miles of the old building.

Jenkyn was a bachelor and employed a Japanese man as cook and groom. One evening, shortly before midnight:

he turned excitedly and said 'What's that, Boss?' I drew my breath and listened and quite distinctly we heard the strange sound of someone walking, quickly along the stone-flagged passageway at the back of the hall and placing bricks in position. This went on for 20 minutes, after which we decided to investigate. We walked quickly into the dark passage, but again no one was to be seen.

The cook resigned the next day and went back to Sydney. Yet, 'After he left I still heard the strange sounds, but comforted myself with the admission, "They are only ghosts".'

The Reverend also recalled another strange incident. He woke up between 1 and 2 a.m.:

> and was alarmed at the sound of footsteps on the stairway leading from the hall below to my room, upstairs. Knowing that there was no one else in the house, I determined to wait until the intruder had reached the top step. Slowly, very slowly, but surely, he made the ascent, and stood at last on the landing. I rushed out, timid, but determined to see it through, but, alas, saw nothing. 'Ghosts, I suppose,' I remarked, and went to bed again.

Time after time Jenkyn would go out, locking the front doors securely behind him, 'but found on my return at midnight that the front doors were standing widely open. No other door had been tampered with, and nothing else was disturbed.' Others also had unsettling experiences there, mainly involving the sound of footsteps ascending the 'elegant semi-circular staircase' at the dead of night.

After skilfully spinning these ghostly yarns, Reverend Jenkyn finished with his own adroit accommodation of Christian theology and the mysteries of haunting:

> So I became accustomed to ghosts after 30 years' contact, and to-day I regard them as great company. Of course I am not unmindful of the fact that spirits and ghosts are closely allied—especially if the former are taken within. I am convinced that ghosts or the unseen cloud of witnesses play an important part in the life of man. The visible creation is not the only creation that serves mankind. The things that are seen are temporal, but the things that are unseen are eternal.

Despite these well-formed traditions, nobody has an explanation for these hauntings. It has been suggested that they might be related to the principal chaplain of the colony, Samuel Marsden. He held the first divine service in the Hawkesbury area in the 1790s, consecrated the church at its opening in 1822 and also died at the rectory in 1838. There is certainly a report of someone seeing a ghost there on one dark night around ten o'clock. A local antique dealer encountered Marsden's shade, dressed in his distinctive black garb of a long coat and low-crowned hat. The antique dealer was said to have been ashen-faced and unable to speak for several minutes after the event. If it was Samuel Marsden's spirit it was a long way from the man's eternal home. Marsden is buried in Parramatta, quite a few kilometres from Windsor.

Or perhaps the creepy reputation of the house is related to events that took place when the first stones of the church building were laid in 1817. Governor Macquarie placed a 'holey dollar', the colonial currency he created by removing the centre of a Spanish dollar coin, beneath the corner stone. He tapped the stone three times with a mason's mallet and 'in a very impressive tone of voice, said—"God prosper St. Matthew's Church"'. This old custom, still sometimes practised today when boats are masted or buildings begun, is meant to bring good luck and so avert bad luck.

But, with no respect for such traditions, an unknown thief stole the coin that night. The corner stone was laid once more the next evening and another holey dollar embedded beneath it. A few nights later this second coin was stolen. 'It is supposed that the corner-stone was thrown down each time and the money stolen by some of the indigent convicts employed at the Public Works in the town of Windsor', wrote the exasperated recorder of the parish business in his register.

A CURIOUS CASTLE

There's a spooky black and white photograph of Graham's Castle in the State Library of South Australia. The just-completed Gothic Revival mansion is a four-square, crenellated white box standing alone in sparse, scrubby bushland.

Known as 'Prospect House', it was built in what is now Prospect in 1846–47 by successful Adelaide businessman and canny investor in the Burra copper bonanza John Benjamin Graham. It was said to have 30 rooms and all the trimmings that Graham's fortune could provide and, deliberately, outshone all other private and public residences in Adelaide at the time. Graham soon left for a lavish life abroad and the house was sold in the 1850s. It was owned by various others but was successively demolished from around the 1880s and finally disappeared in 2001, making way for further suburban development.

The mystery of Graham's Castle is a double one. It quickly developed a reputation as a ghost house, but for little or no apparent reason. Most haunted houses have grim tragedies of one kind or another associated with them to form the basis for later spook stories, but not much out of the ordinary seems to have happened there other than the usual deaths of residents in an era when people tended to die in houses rather than hospitals. Nothing especially unusual there. So what is the legend of Graham's Castle?

The Oldham family resided in the mansion in the early 1860s, by which time there were stories of apparitions in the house as a family member recollected many years later:

Mr. Oldham maintains that he recollects quite distinctly that one evening, about dusk, he entered the house and walked up the stairs. On the landing of the first floor he saw his mother in a black dress. He called out to her and ran into her room, but she was not there. That was not so strange, as at the time she was out driving.

On another occasion his stepbrother, who was about fifteen years older, saw the same woman, his stepmother, standing in his room. 'Nothing in the world would ever persuade me that it was not my mother I saw,' he said. No *Wuthering Heights*-style tragedies or traumas here.

There were also said to be strange noises in the night, causing a steady turnover of frightened servants. Subsequent residents also reported 'weird rumblings, knocking and noises in the walls of the service rooms'. In 1938, a writer to the *Chronicle* recalled childhood memories of a family friend who 'lived at the Castle, and . . . After a few nights things began to rattle and lights went out; the ghost began its wanderings, and our friend soon got out of it.' In 1947, a former resident said that she and her friends used to frighten visitors to the house by knocking on the front and back doors, then hiding.

The builder who secured the contract for the main demolition of the property around 1901 recalled twenty or so years later: 'It was generally reported about the neighbourhood that the castle was haunted. I was once almost about to lease the house and paddock, but when I mentioned that matter to my wife she turned it down, and said she would not live in it if they gave it to us rent free, because the house was haunted!' He said that when the workers pulled the place down they discovered that rabbits had made their homes in the walls and that the noise of their rutting was the cause of the sounds, 'which seemed uncanny in the stillness of the night, and caused nervous people to think of ghosts'.

It seems that the mystery of the haunting of the old Gothic structure is a slow accretion of rabbits, a few overactive imaginations and kids playing tricks. Adelaide is rich in ghost stories, so perhaps even one based on such limited haunting found fertile ground. The only evidence of spirits found by the builders who demolished the place was an illicit still for brewing liquor.

SATAN ON DEAD ISLAND

There's no denying that the friendly island of Tasmania has some terrifying tales to tell. With a dark history of dispossession of the original owners, brutal convictism and tough pioneering, 'Tassie' has a certain Gothic feel, projected in its many hauntings and related horrors. Writer and journalist Bill Beatty was of the opinion that 'Tasmania probably has more ghosts to the square mile than any other state in the Commonwealth'. Many of them haunt one of Australia's most feared prisons.

For brooding Gothic atmosphere, the remains of the convict prison at Port Arthur are hard to better. Built from the 1830s, the prison and its many related buildings and sites is said to be the island's most haunted location. The suffering, cruelty and violence experienced by many inmates and warders over the years seems to be embedded in the stone and iron remains of the place, only heightened by the natural beauty in which Port Arthur stands.

Few of the remaining buildings have not reported unexplained lights, strange noises and spooky apparitions. The Model or Separate Prison has some sad tales: William Carter hanged himself with the straps from his hammock. Today, visitors report uncomfortable feelings of anxiety on entering the small stone cell.

The buildings around the prison include a church and parsonage, an asylum and various cottages for housing administrators and the commandant. Charles O'Hara Booth was in charge of Port Arthur from 1833 until 1844. His ghost is sometimes seen standing at the windows of his former residence, surveying his domain of chains while weeping silently. The same building has the ghost of a nanny said to have been responsible for the death of one of the infants in her care. She sits in an old rocking chair in what was her room. Sometimes the chair rocks by itself and strange things happen to the cameras of those who try to take photographs of the chair.

Numerous other phantasms and uncanny events have been recorded at Port Arthur, though one of the most unusual is said to have occurred on the Isle of the Dead, just offshore from the main prison site. Here, Port Arthur's dead were buried: convicts in mostly unidentified graves, free settlers in the usual manner. The graves were dug by convicts, including the colourful Mark Jeffrey, sometime thief, pugilist, fortune teller and killer. After a hard life of crime and violence in England, Mark reached Van Diemen's Land in 1850, later recollecting that 'fifteen years transportation appeared to me equal to being consigned to a living grave'.

Known as 'Big Mark', Jeffrey was six feet (183 centimetres) tall, heavily built and extremely good with his fists, but he claimed to be able to instil such terror that he could kill men without using them. In his memoirs, he described how he inflicted this end on an accomplice he blamed for his sentence, John Hart: 'My gestures and the inflections of my voice made such an impression on Hart that no sooner had I uttered them than his features grew swollen and discoloured, a spasm twisted his lips, and he fell speechless and motionless to the ground like a man stricken with apoplexy.' Three days later, Hart died. With this ability, his menacing physique and a notoriously bad temper, Jeffrey was feared by guards and convicts alike. But there was one entity that terrified Big Mark.

In an attempt to remove the troublesome prisoner from the rest of the Port Arthur population, and at his own request, he was made resident gravedigger on 'Dead Island', as the convicts knew it. He was taken off each Sunday for church and returned on Monday mornings. His only means of communication with the shore was by lighting a signal fire. One night, he lit it.

The unbalanced Mark had been busy digging his own grave on the island. When he finished, he went back to the crude hut in which he lived to eat and sleep. But not for long. That night, Big Mark Jeffrey was visited by the devil. What His Satanic

Majesty said to the violent but pious bruiser Mark did not say, but he was terrified. He ran to the shore and lit the signal fire. When the warders arrived, he begged to be taken off the island and put back into prison.

Mark Jeffrey continued his erratic life of violent crime and defiance of authority, always mixed with a strong sense of his own and others' rights. He ended his days in the Launceston Invalid Depot, where he became a popular inmate and was even given some authority of his own to wield. His obituary summed up this unusual character who:

> brought upon himself every kind of punishment inflicted upon refractory prisoners. His great enemy was his temper, which was of the most violent character, and when aroused he was exceedingly dangerous. He was essentially an egotist—physically and mentally strong but without balance, his animal nature dominating all that was good in him. He desired death, for his life had been a failure.

THE CONCRETE CASKET

Australia has hundreds of lighthouses and most of them seem to be haunted. The tale of Lydia Gow's death at the South Solitary Lighthouse off Coffs Harbour, New South Wales, is not only one of the saddest but also one that still holds some troubling questions.

Lydia (Selina) was the daughter of David and Sarah Gow. Born in 1895, she was around fifteen years old when her father became the principal keeper of the light in 1910. Earlier in his working life David had been a marine engineer, but he decided that his growing family deserved to see him more often so he entered the lighthouse service in 1897.

Life on the island was tough for the Gow family. Rough seas often made it impossible for regular supplies to be delivered and they were forced to live on mutton birds until the next delivery. David introduced rabbits to the island as an alternative source of food during these difficult times. According to family accounts, the six children who then made up the family all hated the life.

In November 1912, the attractive Lydia fell ill with ptomaine, or food, poisoning and also contracted typhoid. The lighthouse signalling equipment was used to send a message to Coffs Harbour requesting urgent medical attention. The weather was bad, with a southerly making it impossible for Mr W.H. Wood to land on the jetty, so the small launch that had braved the seas to bring him to the island put him ashore on the more protected northern side. There was no landing facility here, so Wood had to throw his bag onto the rocks and jump. He made it but ripped out a couple of his fingernails in the process.

When the doctor got to Lydia he knew immediately that she was gravely ill. He had to return to Coffs Harbour and ask for urgent assistance from Sydney. A nurse and a doctor were sent but their ship was delayed for three days in cyclonic weather. When they finally reached the island, Lydia was dead.

South Solitary Island is predominantly rock. With the seas once again prohibiting travel and nowhere to bury Lydia, the family were forced to adapt. Understandably, Sarah Gow did not want her daughter's body to be thrown into the sea. Instead, she was placed in an iron bathtub and covered in powdered lime or concrete, probably both. Another iron bathtub was placed upside down above her and the tubs were then soldered together.

It was several days before the makeshift coffin was able to be taken off the island, but when it was Lydia was buried in Newcastle just two days later. The terse language of death notices painted the scene:

The funeral of Miss Lydia Gow, daughter of Mr. and Mrs. David Gow, of Solitary Island lighthouse, who died on Thursday, from the effects of ptomaine poisoning followed by typhoid fever, took place yesterday afternoon. The remains of the deceased had been brought from Solitary Island by steamer to Newcastle, and the funeral, which was attended by a large number of relatives and friends, moved from the residence of Mr. Robert Gow, Newcastle East. The interment was in the Church of England section of Sandgate Cemetery, where the service was conducted by the Rev. W. J. Ritchie, of St. John's Church, Cook's Hill.

What the death notice doesn't say is that Lydia was almost certainly buried in her concrete and iron casket, a likelihood later confirmed through a reported investigation by the cemetery officials.

After these terrible events, David Gow had to return to the lighthouse to clear out the family belongings and hand over to his replacement. He continued his career in lighthouses, serving on the Barrenjoey and Byron Bay lights.

This might have been another one of the many sad tales associated with the dangers of lighthouse keeping, especially at that time, but there are other uncertainties in this story. One of these is the cause of Lydia's death. One source states that she had ptomaine poisoning, as well as typhoid. Another says that she died of 'Typhoid/Enteric Fever & Haemorrhage perforation'. There is no doubt that she died of typhoid, but how did she contract the deadly disease, usually carried in polluted water and food? And why did no one else in the family contract the disease?

Uncertainties like these may lie at the base of the haunting of the South Solitary Island light. Since at least the 1970s, lighthouse residents and visitors have reported the sound of footsteps in the lighthouse and unexplained interference with kitchen utensils and cutlery. One young resident reported a constant feeling that there was another presence in his room and had the sensation of his hair being tousled. Others have seen shadowy figures flitting around, a photograph of Lydia unaccountably falling from its wall hanging, doors locking and unlocking by themselves and the sounds of sweeping in the passageways.

These unsettling but harmless phenomena are typical of many homely hauntings and the standard fare of ghost stories around the world. Still, when she died, Lydia was old enough to be taking part in the family chores and, as her death certificate states, she was not attending school but engaged in 'domestic duties'.

HERMITS OF THE REEF

Today, the Great Barrier Reef and much of the Queensland coast is settled and a focus of tourism. But in the late nineteenth century it was a favoured haven for drifters and fugitives from the law, jilted lovers and any number of characters with mysterious pasts. One was even said to be a Danish prince.

Harry Envoldt lived by himself on Deliverance Island in North Queensland for 35 years. Rumoured to have been a member of the Danish Royal Family, he never once left the island in all that time. Harry had been wrecked in the Torres Strait and ended up involved in the *bêche-de-mer* and pearling industries before he took himself off to Deliverance Island in 1893.

Here, he survived on vegetables, fish and turtle meat and few people ever visited him. He was said to have feared running out of matches and managed to keep a single fire alight on the island for five years, before a boat called in to the island in 1919. In 1928 he was attacked by a shark as he tended his turtle-curing equipment in the surf. He struggled back to the beach but died there of blood loss. His body was discovered, along with his diary, when a passing pearler came ashore. It's needless to say, perhaps, that he was not a Danish Royal.

Other Reef characters were the subject of legend. One-armed Yorkshireman George 'Yorkey' Lawson lived 25 years on what is now a popular Cairns tourist attraction, Green Island. He was said to have known the notorious 'Bully' Hayes and to have worked as a blackbirder. In 1886 he searched unsuccessfully for a couple of early tourists who took a boat to visit a local wreck and never returned. The distinctive headland known as 'Yorkeys Knob' is named after Lawson. He died in 1907, allowing the council to begin the process of developing the island for tourism.

An unnamed beachcomber lived on Rattlesnake Island, between Cairns and Townsville. The story went that he was once a successful Melbourne businessman who was jilted by a woman. They found his bones in a flat-bottomed boat he had knocked together when he ran out of food and tried to reach the mainland for supplies.

But the most intriguing story of the reef hermits was a mysterious woman who lived on Border Island for five years. The only documentation of this mystery seems to be by writer Frank Reid, who was well versed in the lore and legendry of this part of the country. He told the tale this way in 1932:

When I first heard the story of the female hermit of Border Island, on the northern end of the Barrier Reef, it endowed that wind-swept coral speck with a gleam of romance, and pathos. I have listened to several versions of how the woman came to live there for five years. The one most commonly told by the natives is that a schooner anchored off the island one day and landed on the beach. Among them was a woman with a child. When the vessel was about to sail, the woman began to cry, saying that she had left her baby ashore. The natives say that she was rowed ashore and that, when she went to search for the child, the dinghy pulled back to the schooner. The skipper then sailed away without her . . .

At first the woman became nearly crazed at having been deserted. For a time the natives avoided her, but she found food in fish traps and ate the shellfish eaten by the natives. She built herself a home by standing palm branches in the sand and covering the top with grass. Later she acquired skill in catching birds and became hardened to the life. Knowing the value of pearls she began to collect them, and when she became friendly with the natives she assisted in diving for the lapi shells.

When she had been living on the island for two years her child died. Then the hitherto peaceful nature of the woman changed. She began to bully the natives. On one occasion, when she had been insulted by a burly male, she picked up a spear and buried the point of it in his heart. After this the natives treated her with greater reverence and she became practically the ruler of the island.

One morning, a French whaler anchored off the island and she was taken aboard. When she left she carried with her a fine collection of pearls. When sold they must have returned her a fortune.

Despite the details, even Reid does not seem to have known who this woman was. Another mystery that might one day be explained, or not.

THE GUYRA STONETHROWER

At first, it seemed to be working. Young Minnie Bowen was moved from the family farmhouse in Guyra, New South Wales, to her grandparents' house in Glen Innes. The walls of the Bowen house stopped shaking, unexplained thumps and crashes were no longer heard and stones stopped falling from the sky. For a while.

It was a few weeks into one of the most baffling hauntings ever recorded in Australia. Over two months or so, the country was spellbound by the strange events that began in early April 1921.

The incident began when the Bowens' weatherboard house seemed to come under some sort of psychic attack. Windows were mysteriously broken by stones apparently thrown by no one. Doors and walls shook violently, accompanied by loud noises with no obvious origin. Locals came to help the besieged family, surrounding the house each night in the hope of catching whoever was causing these strange terrifying phenomena. But no human cause could be found and the disturbances continued.

Police came up from Sydney to investigate. They decided that the events were the work of the Bowens' twelve-year-old daughter Minnie. To prove their suspicions correct, they had Minnie sit in her bedroom, seemingly the focus of the disturbances, with the lights on while they watched. A large group of volunteers patrolled around the property.

Right on cue at 9 p.m., there was a loud knock on Minnie's bedroom wall, followed by several thumps that shook the whole house. Minnie reportedly just sat there silently.

The case attracted spiritualists, including a man named Ben Davey (or Davies). After speaking with the Bowens, he learned that Minnie's half-sister, May, had died a few months earlier. He believed that May's spirit was trying to get in touch with Mrs Bowen through Minnie. If the knocking sounds were heard again, he told Minnie to ask if they were made by May. Minnie replied that she could not do that, as May was dead. But Davey persisted:

'Speak, dear. Even if your sister can't speak she might knock again'. I hardly spoke the words before the knock came again. I can tell you my hair stood up on end. But I continued to coax the girl, and about five minutes later a third knock came. Then the little girl crossed and blessed herself, put her hands up in supplication, and said, 'If that's you, May, speak to me'. She was silent a moment and then began to cry. I asked her, 'Did May speak?' She said, 'Yes, May spoke. She said, I can't tell you. The message is for mother'. She then went over and laid her head on her mother's lap, crying. Her mother said, 'Well, tell the gentlemen what she said she told her mother'. 'Tell mother I am in heaven, and quite happy. Tell her it was her prayers which got me here, and I will look after her for the rest of my life.'

Another psychic investigator named Harry Jay Moors also turned up in Guyra. He was acquainted with Sir Arthur Conan Doyle, a man deeply interested in the paranormal. After three days investigating the strange goings-on, including speaking with Minnie, her parents and many locals, Moors supported the Bowens' story and said he was convinced that a poltergeist was to blame.

At that time, poltergeist activity was not as well known as it is today, though the phenomenon had been frequently observed and documented around the world. It usually involves a person approaching or at puberty, a recent tragedy or trauma in or close to the family and unexplained, seemingly supernatural events. The Minnie Bowen case is now considered a textbook example.

After a two-day break from what most were describing as a haunting, the Bowens came home to find that the battens nailed over their broken windows had been smashed and left in a pile on the verandah. The police were still on the job, and a few nights later they lit the whole house up with a spotlight. But even then, a policeman reported being almost hit by two stones hitting the wall where he was standing.

Despite this, the police decided that the whole thing was a gigantic prank perpetrated by the tall, thin and dark-eyed Minnie. Her mother said she was an imaginative child and was described by someone who knew the family as 'not clever'. Despite being unable to substantiate this conclusion, the police reported the mystery solved. 'They suspected that some of the people among the volunteers, who kept a vigil around the house, were "sympathetic" in relation to ghosts.' When questioned, Minnie had also owned up to throwing stones herself on a couple of occasions. That clinched it and the case was filed. But not for long.

Soon after Minnie settled into Glen Innes, her grandparents' home began to shudder and shake, stones fell on the roof and shattered windows. The local police were called out but reached the same conclusion as their Sydney colleagues. It was all mischievous Minnie's doing. Case closed.

But hardly anyone believed this. Plenty of people had witnessed the disturbances while Minnie was doing nothing and, in any case, the noises and shakings were far too loud and violent to be produced by a small girl. After the police constable left to file his report:

> . . . the inmates of the house and the neighbours outside were emphatic in their statements that they heard many noises up till midnight as of stones hitting the walls or the roof. One neighbour, named Mr. Marden, says the noises were like the sounds caused by an axe being struck heavily against the wall. The occupants of the nearest house to Sheltons', named McKillop, a few yards distant, distinctly heard the noises and became greatly concerned. They are threatening to leave the premises if the mysterious noises continue.

It seems that Minnie's grandparents asked her parents to take their daughter back to Guyra, which they did, although fearful that the noises, the shaking and the stonethrower would start again. The Bowens waited. So did everyone else. But the disturbances never returned. People gradually returned to normal and the Bowens later sold the house and moved on.

The case had been a media sensation for several months. It attracted sightseers, cranks and people who wanted to help. A film was even made about it in an attempt to cash in on the public interest and the story was regularly reprised in newspapers and magazines. But no satisfactory explanation has ever been forthcoming. Minnie grew up, married and lived in

Armidale, New South Wales, until her late eighties, when she was reportedly run down by a car and killed.

In a way, the police were correct in their verdict on the Guyra ghost. It was Minnie. But while the paranormal poltergeist explanation is generally preferred to the supernatural haunting yarn, another apparently unrelated oddity occurred in the district. While the 'hauntings' were happening, 87-year-old local Mrs Doran was seen striding over the fields with a potato in each hand. She then walked up a nearby rise and disappeared. The whole district was searched, but she was never found.

THE HOOK ISLAND MONSTER

The Ngaro people of Hook Island in the Whitsundays are thought to have occupied that land for around 10,000 years before first contact with Europeans in 1770. They were a seafaring folk, constructing distinctive bark canoes from which they fished and even caught small whales. The Ngaro suffered the brunt of colonialism and the remnants of what was probably only 100 or so individuals were forcibly moved to a prison on Palm Island or to forced labour in Brampton Island in 1870.

Early in the twentieth century a timber operation was established on Hook Island, followed by a tourism development in conjunction with the declared Whitsunday Islands National Park in 1936. An underwater observatory was constructed in the 1960s as outdoor adventure tourism began to develop. It was during this period that the Hook Island sea monster mystery began on the other side of the world.

In 1958 Robert Le Serrec, a Breton photographer, and his wife, Raymonde, bought one of the last surviving tuna fishing boats. They spent two years renovating it, and with their children sailed off in *Saint-Yves d'Armor* to adventures around the world. They visited Morocco, the Virgin Islands, the Bahamas and Samoa, among other locations, and ended up in the Whitsunday Islands, where the *Saint-Yves d'Armor* was wrecked, fortunately with no casualties. By then, they had been voyaging for nearly five years.

In December 1964, Le Serrec, his family and a friend spent three months on Hook Island. They bought a smaller pleasure boat for local cruising, sightseeing and photographing. As they crossed Stonehaven Bay one day, they saw a very large and peculiar shape on the floor of the lagoon. Le Serrec and his male companion took some photographs and then went into the water to film.

The object was now seen to be around 80 feet (24 metres) long, shaped like a giant tadpole. It was crossed with brown stripes on what looked like smooth skin with no fins or spikes. It appeared to have eyes and what looked to be a gash near the tail. Le Serrec thought the creature was dead, but as he began to film it opened its mouth and came towards him and his friend. They were able to see that it seemed to have no teeth but did not wait around to investigate further. They returned to their boat and the giant tadpole swam away.

Le Serrec wasted no time in selling his still photographs of the creature, first published in the Australian magazine *Everyone* in March 1965. A sea monster mystery was born. The photographs ignited interest around the world. Was it real? If so, what was it? A remnant sea creature from the primal past?

Argument and guesswork have persisted ever since. There was some speculation that the creature might have been an enormous synbranchid, or swamp eel. These exist but are very small. Perhaps it was a selachian, a group of fish to which sharks and rays belong. Someone suggested it might be a deflated skyhook balloon that splashed down in the lagoon.

Or was it all a hoax, just a large sheet of plastic pegged to the sand in the shape of a tadpole?

Apparently Le Serrec's past activities included an attempt in the late 1950s to promote an expedition that would be financially rewarding. The expedition was to find a sea serpent.

In 1967, Le Serrec published *Autour du Monde*, a book of his world sailing adventures with his family. By then, though, most of the many who had taken an interest in the story had concluded that it was a hoax. A number of researchers investigated the photographs and related story in considerable detail and pointed to the way the edges of the beast looked to be weighed down with sand, among other anomalies.

Today, Hook Island is popular for snorkelling, diving, camping and boating. The observatory, always financially struggling, was also hit by cyclone damage and was closed by 2010. It is in a state of decay, though noted on the local heritage register. The tourism promotions for the island emphasise its seclusion and undoubted natural beauty. There seems to be no mention of the tadpole-shaped 'monster'.

'A RIDDLE, WRAPPED IN A MYSTERY, INSIDE AN ENIGMA'

Is it a work of art? A gigantic graffiti? Or perhaps the world's most elaborate hoax?

All these possibilities, and others, have been suggested of the enormous desert carving of a hunter known as 'Marree Man' or sometimes 'Stuart's Giant'. The hunter wears a headdress, has initiation scars and a prominent penis.

First sighted by a helicopter pilot in 1998, the geoglyph, as such creations are known, appeared between 27 May and 12 June 1998 about 40 kilometres west of dry and dusty Marree, around 700 kilometres north of Adelaide. We can date the figure's origin so precisely from satellite images of the area taken before and after its appearance. Marree man is so big he can be seen from space. At over four kilometres long and covering an area of around 28 square kilometres, Marree Man is one of the largest pieces of earth art on the planet. It is also one of the biggest mysteries of modern times.

The Marree Man story embraces many themes, including First Nations culture and land rights, apparent links to

America, possibly including extreme religious views, mining, covert military operations, tourism and an apparently uncanny use of GPS long before such technology became widely available. It is 'a riddle, wrapped in a mystery, inside an enigma', as Winston Churchill said of Russia in the 1930s.

The fax messages began to arrive at the Marree Hotel just a few weeks after the figure was first spotted. The faxes were in the form of press releases and initially referred to the figure as 'Stuart's Giant', an allusion to the early explorer in the area. The first one suggested the figure had been created to promote tourism, including that related to local Arabana culture. The second message contained references to well-known large chalk figures in the landscape in England and a lesser-known Native American mound carving. It also mentioned the upcoming Sydney Olympics and gave directions for unearthing a 'dedicatory plaque' buried near the figure's head.

At one point, an American flag and a bottle containing a note on the religious sect known as the Branch Davidians were found. It seems that this message was never made public, possibly because of the violent clash between American authorities and a group of Davidians led by David Koresh at Waco, Texas, in 1993. More than 70 people died in the battle and subsequent conflagration.

Faxes then began to appear directing recipients to clues about the identity and purpose of the Marree Man creators. These clues were buried near the Cerne Abbas Giant and the Long Man of Wilmington in England. One note gave a clear explanation of the purpose of the mystery: 'As a permanent benefit to the state of South Australia through increased tourism, and also to honour the inherently athletic pursuits of the Indigenous people for the Sydney Olympiad', read one of the notes found buried in a glass jar.

And then the messages stopped as suddenly as they had begun. Media and popular speculation were running wild and theories came thick and fast.

The persistent American refences and some phrasing of the messages suggested some connection with the United States, though it was thought that this might have been a deliberately misleading ploy by the author or authors of the messages. Nevertheless, there were some joint Australian–American military operations at Woomera, a fact that provided some support for the USA connection.

Americans were also involved in mining-related works in the area. It was thought that the GPS technology necessary to survey and build such an enormous earthwork and the earth-moving equipment to do it could have been sourced from Western Mining, the company involved.

And then there was the faintly eccentric artist. Boasting the wonderful name of Bardius Goldberg, he was a well-known figure in Central Australia and had already carried out several similar, though much more modest, ground works. Goldberg did not deny his involvement and, after his death in 2002, some who knew him declared that he was the man responsible. But there is still no indication of how he managed to accurately draw the figure without GPS equipment or how he accessed the necessary earthmovers as well as the skills to drive them.

The local Arabana groups denied any knowledge of Marree Man, pointing out that he did not look like a man from their country but more like a Central Desert warrior. A long-running land rights claim effectively locked the Marrree Man site away from public access until 2012. At this point, the potential of the figure for attracting tourists came back into focus.

With this possibility in mind, the proprietors of the Marree Hotel restored the degrading image in 2016. But even with the advantage of much upgraded GPS technology they had great difficulty in completing the project. And then another message arrived. This one came by email and contained information about the coordinates of the image that could only have come from the original survey. Today, the hotel promotes a scenic flight over the Marree Man, which is now part of Arabana land.

Entrepreneur, adventurer and one-time hoaxer himself, Dick Smith spent a couple of years trying to track down the true story of Marree Man. When this was unsuccessful, a $5000 reward was offered for anyone who could come up with the truth.

What, if anything, does it all mean?

Maree is located at the junction of two important inland routes, the Oodnadatta Track and the Birdsville Track. It was also the focus of a contested Native Title claim in 1998 between two groups of traditional owners. It owes its existence to a strategic location near springs discovered by a member of explorer John McDouall Stuart's expedition in 1859. Pastoral development began in the 1860s, followed by the Overland Telegraph and the railway. Camels and, later, motor vehicles connected Marree with Alice Springs, Innamincka and most of Central Australia, as well as with Adelaide.

Taken together, all these realities and theories suggest that Marree Man might say something about the complex history of the place where it is inscribed. What that might be is anyone's guess. There were hints in the mysterious messages of an artistic intention behind Marree Man's creation. If one purpose of art is to draw our attention to the unnoticed or hidden and so raise previously unasked questions, Marree Man is an outstandingly successful example of installation art.

Or it might just be someone's idea of a gigantic prank.

TUNNEL TALES

It doesn't matter how often historians debunk the stories, people just love a good secret tunnel yarn.

Most Australian cities have networks of subterranean passageways. These often carry the pipes, wires and tubes needed to keep everything going. Others are for waste or stormwater or simply for getting from place to place in a hurry or when the weather is inclement. In Ballarat the drains have become an impromptu art gallery, even though they are closed to the public for good safety reasons. But more than a few tunnels have no obvious reason for being or their original purpose has long passed.

Darwin's group of tunnels is usually said to be associated with military activities during World War II. The fear that Japan intended to invade Australia was well advanced by the time Darwin was bombed in 1942, so the army had time to construct fortifications and defences that included surviving tunnels, some of which can be visited today. But others are not open to the public, leading to murmurings that ASIO is conducting some sort of covert operation in the damp and humid burrows.

Of course, Canberra is a prime suspect for subterranean spooks. There is said to be a tunnel running beneath Lake Burley Griffin from Old Parliament House to the Department of Defence. There is. But it is a service tunnel used for sending messages in metal cylinders whooshed through pipes by compressed air. These 'Lamson tubes' also connected to the General Post Office (GPO) and what was then the Government Printing Office in Kingston.

The Department of Defence does have a tunnel of its own, but it is simply for pedestrian access between buildings. A dead-end tunnel in University House was built during the early Cold War period and is thought to be nuclear bomb–proof. Fortunately, no one has needed to test this out.

Adelaide is riddled with tunnel tales. There is supposed to be an abandoned subway near North Terrace, passageways beneath the CBD connecting government buildings as well as an underground link from Old Parliament House to the Treasury. And, as usual, there are plenty of yarns about hidden bunkers and passageways from World War II. Historians and officials who work in these places are frequently asked about tunnels by seekers of mystery and intrigue. Alas, their responses are staid. Either the tunnels don't exist or, if they did, have long been filled in or blocked up. If they do exist, they are simply service conduits. Nothing to see here.

Outside Sydney, in the suburb of Newington, there are indeed wartime tunnels that were very secret when they were built. In this case, they were constructed before World War I and when New South Wales was still a colony and Australia had no national defence forces. Established in 1897, the Royal Australian Navy Armaments Depot (RANAD), as it came to be known when Australia did get a navy, was designed to store shells, bullets and torpedoes. When ships returned from active duty tours, their ammunition would be unshipped in Sydney Harbour then sent by barge up the Parramatta River to RANAD. Here, the weaponry was carefully unloaded and taken by a small railway network to wherever it was to be safely stored in the sprawling arsenal. The facility was used in both world wars by Australian forces and, in the 1940s, by American forces. It was active until 1999 when the expansion of Sydney made it unsafe to have an enormous bomb situated in the middle of a residential suburb.

The city of Sydney has its own tunnel network as well. Naturally there are unused and forgotten tunnels beneath the inner reaches of the harbour, dating from the 1890s. In addition, a large tunnel runs from Angel Arcade, under Martin Place and into the basement of what was the GPO. In the 1960s it was used for delivering packages and allowing employees to move between buildings.

St James railway station boasts not only tunnels, but a bomb shelter and even a lake. Hard to top that, though there are said to be many hidden tunnels beneath Central station. Some of these are used for baggage handling and worker access, though others are locked, even to those who work there. No one knows why the doors are locked or what might lie behind them.

But things get much spookier than that. In the 1970s, platforms 26 and 27 were built where the old Devonshire Street Cemetery once stood. The platforms are not used but workers inspecting the structure have reported hearing voices echoing through the concrete caverns and the distant sounds of children playing.

There are many more underground oddities around the country. In some ways, they are the urban equivalent of 'Alien Big Cat' stories (see The Cryptid Files) so often heard in rural areas. Citizens love to tell tales about the odd or unexplained aspects of their hometowns. Telling these yarns is a badge of belonging and identity. Nothing mysterious about that.

THE POINCIANA WOMAN

Was there ever a Poinciana Woman? Darwin folk have long speculated about the truth of this distinctive local mystery embodied in local tradition since at least the 1950s.

The story is known in many versions, but the most consistent telling is that the East Point Reserve is haunted by the ghost of a woman who was raped, became pregnant and hanged herself from a poinciana tree near the scene of her assault. Her ghost can be encountered there, or even summoned, and she appears in a long white gown to men unwise enough to be in the area at night. Beautiful and long haired, she transforms into a shrieking spectre, slicing open the entrails of her victims, which she eats while they are still warm and quivering.

The details of the legend vary. Sometimes the woman is said to be Asian or Aboriginal and her attackers are soldiers, often Japanese, or Asian fishermen. The Poinciana Woman, or Lady, is also connected with women who have died in giving birth.

Could this sad and grisly legend have some basis in fact? If so, who could the Poinciana Woman have been? Attempts to track down the truth of this unsettling tale have revealed a long and complicated backstory. It begins, not in Australia but in the monster traditions of south Asia and beyond.

In Malay belief, one of the many demons troubling humans is known as a *pontianak*, a spirit associated closely with childbirth. By a variant of this name or by others, a similar figure appears in many south Asian mythologies. She is described as originally being a very beautiful woman who died in childbirth and become a *pontianak*. In the version collected in the late nineteenth century, she is said to perch in a tree in a robe of green with long black hair and very long and sharp nails. She is also a vampire who sucks the blood of children through a hole in the back of her neck. There is more, but these are the essential characteristics that lie at the base of Darwin's Poinciana Woman.

Darwin has always been a culturally diverse city, with residents and visitors from south Asia, including Malays and those from the many other islands in and around what is now Indonesia. It also has a strong Filipino community with similar tales to tell.

By the time Darwin was bombed by the Japanese in World War II, the spooky ghost story added the element of soldiers as the rapists. Although the Japanese did not set foot in the Northern Territory, the fear that they would was a traumatic one for the Darwin community.

Towards the end of the twentieth century, the ethnic identity of the Poinciana Woman seems to have changed from the vague 'Asian' to Aboriginal. This depiction has continued in various ways and is an example of how legends pick up new elements as they grow and are seen to be meaningful to new groups of people. Yet another introduced element is what is known as 'legend tripping'. The story of the Poinciana Woman is so widely known in Darwin that night visits to the site are considered a form of initiation and it has become a custom among Darwin's youth to go there and attempt to summon the wraith by incantation and turning three times in a circle.

The supernatural theme of vengeful spirits returning from the grave is widespread in world folklore. There are also quite similar stories known in the Cocos (Keeling) Islands and Queensland and probably elsewhere in Australia. But with its multicultural layers of community and history, the Poinciana Woman could belong only to Darwin.

So, the mystery would appear to be solved. It's all just a hoary story derived from interacting traditions in a particular place over a long period of time. True. But why are versions of the same story told not only in Australia, south Asia and even some European traditions? That is the real mystery.

Juanita Nielsen, fashionable Sydney girl, heiress to the Mark Foy retail dynasty and crusading newspaper editor, disappeared on 4 July 1975. Through her determined campaigning for the 'green bans' that saved many of Sydney's heritage buildings, she put enormous pressure on local developers. Was that her undoing?

7

VANISHINGS

THE PHANTOM ISLAND

In January 1841, the Hobart *Courier* ran an article titled 'The Antarctic Continent'. It was a report of the progress of the United States exploring expedition, a fleet of four ships tasked with confirming the existence of the continent of Antarctica. The expedition had left Sydney the previous December and headed for Macquarie Island, approximately halfway between Tasmania and the frozen southern seas.

The expedition was the prequel to what would later become the great age of Antarctic discovery, producing such heroic characters as Ernest Shackleton, Douglas Mawson, Roald Amundsen and Robert Falcon Scott, together with those who went with them. One of the aims of the American expedition was to confirm the existence of a mysterious island said to be located near Macquarie Island.

A sealing ship out of London, the *Emerald*, first sighted the island in December 1821, when she landed 25 men on Macquarie Island to catch and kill seals. The men would not be collected until September the following year. The 'supercargo'— Christopher Nockells—noted that 'At 11 a.m. we saw the semblance of an island bearing east by north about 25 miles from our position. It appeared high with peaked mountains—about 30 miles long—the longer axis direct north-east and south west.'

Nockells was an experienced navigator and not likely to mistake an iceberg for an island. But when the later American expedition sailed to the coordinates given by the *Emerald*, the island was 'not found where laid down', as missing things were described in nautical language. Although they could not find the island, the Americans did confirm that 'there can scarcely be a doubt of the existence of the Antarctic continent extending the whole distance of seventy degrees from east to west' and that there were plenty of seals and whales to be found there, a situation that generations of sealers and whalers worked hard to reverse.

Phantom islands are not unknown in the history and lore of the sea. Their sightings are often put down to mirages in tropical climes or the cold climate equivalent known as a 'fata morgana'. Emerald Island was consigned to the lengthy list of mistaken observations.

But in 1890, it was reported that an unnamed sea captain had found an island at the original coordinates, describing it as 'a small, high, rocky island'. He sailed around it but found nowhere to land. The mystery had deepened.

Nearly twenty years later, another opportunity to solve it arose. In 1909 the polar explorer Ernest Shackleton sent the *Nimrod* to look for Emerald and other missing islands (Royal Company's Islands, Nimrod Islands, Dougherty Island). Chief Officer J.K. Davis found no Emerald Island nor any of the other islands he was seeking. When the ship passed over the charted position of the island, 'it was a fine, clear moonlight night—had any land been in the vicinity, it would have been sighted to a certainty. There was a high sea running, and sounding was impracticable', meaning that he was unable to search for a possible sunken island.

On balance, the score for Emerald Island was now two for and two against. This was a confusing state of affairs that resulted in mapmakers including the island on charts into the 1980s. Since then, though, the consensus is that the island does not exist. But how could the mistake have been made, and more than once?

The optical illusion explanation is feasible, but doubtful. The American expedition of 1841 noted the 'sluggishness' of their compass needles the closer they got to what they assumed at the time to be the South Pole. Could this be the explanation? A simple matter of incorrect coordinates due to the more primitive navigation equipment of the 1820s and the distorting effect of the magnetic pole. This might still have been a factor in the 1890 sighting.

A theory only, of course. But, if it were correct, that means Emerald Island really could exist. Somewhere south.

MYSTERY BAY

Why would London's Metropolitan Police advertise a £300 reward for information about a missing man in New South Wales? The answer to that question is fairly straightforward, but the fate of Lamont Young and four other men has remained a baffling mystery to this day.

On Saturday 9 October 1880 the 29-year-old geological surveyor with the colony's department of mines arrived on what were then known as the Montreal goldfields near Bermagui. Lamont Young was accompanied by an assistant named Max Schneider. After introducing themselves to the authorities in charge of the gold rush, the two men said they intended to look around the coast and a local island, and so would need a boat. Lamont Young went in search of one to hire for an outing the following day. Then 'he went to his tent, or camp, and after that he disappeared as thoroughly as if he had been a "materialised spirit"'.

The following Sunday afternoon, a farm worker riding near the beach noticed something 'shining' on the rocks. He went to investigate, finding an abandoned green fishing boat with disturbing signs of a disaster. He rode to a local dairy farm and returned with the owner.

Although the sails were lashed securely to the boat, rocks had been piled into the stern, along with bedding and clothing and some geology books. One of the books had the name 'Lamont Young' penned on the flyleaf. Next morning, the police and authorities arrived and conducted a search. They found another book signed by Young, food, a compass and a coat and pipe belonging to Schneider. The boat's planks were stoved out from the inside, suggesting a deliberate act rather than an accident, and the anchor and stern ropes were gone. Some tools were scattered in the sand. Someone had vomited in the stern of the boat, but no signs of blood or other violence were then found.

Oddly, the police constable conducting the search became ill with vomiting and a fever and needed to take sick leave. During his absence, a campfire and the remains of a meal were discovered near the boat, along with other evidence suggesting foul play, including several bullets. An extensive land and sea search failed to find anything relevant.

Some modest local rewards had already been offered by the time the Scotland Yard reward was posted, £200 of which was contributed by Lamont's father, a major general. It was thought by then that Young and Schneider were dead, murdered by all or some of the three men who were in possession of the only boat known to be in the vicinity. Their names were Tom Towers, William Lloyd and Daniel Casey, all from Batemans Bay. They had also disappeared.

Where were the bodies and where were the suspected murderers? What was the motive?

The official investigation was hamstrung by administrative problems caused by uncertain lines of authority in policing the Montreal gold strike. Even then, the police were strangely reticent to declare foul play, preferring, with little evidence or apparent motivation, a kidnapping scenario. The inspector-general reported:

Nothing has, I am satisfied, been left undone to clear up the mystery. I do not say that the circumstances were not suspicious, but I believe the party fell victims to some fatal mischance, and this is the opinion of nearly all the officials who have given thought to the case.

The press and public were mostly convinced that the three boatmen had murdered the geologist and his assistant. Investigations commissioned by the government also concluded that the men had been murdered: 'we are also of opinion . . . that the bodies have not been buried on land, but that they have been carefully rolled up in the sail . . . and dropped in the strongest current that runs off the coast'.

Other investigators provided similar opinions to the New South Wales Legislative Assembly inquiry into the case that reported in 1883. The police disagreed with the results of the other investigations, though they were thoroughly castigated by the press. Despite all the effort expended in solving the mystery, no sign of any of the missing men was ever found.

The discovery of human bones near Bermagui in 1887 sparked further interest in the case. Old theories were again canvassed, and new developments discussed. Rumour had it that a local selector had provided hospitality to two unknown men who called at his home. His dogs had later come out of the bush smelling of human flesh. This gory story was quickly refuted and put down to the man's depressed state of mind at failing to secure the reward. The bones were not connected with the disappearances but the story remained in popular circulation, not only locally but also in the colony and beyond.

All this hearsay, supposition and guesswork has continued to the present day. The failure to find an answer to the puzzle is acknowledged in the naming of the area where the boat was found 'Mystery Bay', gazetted in 1972. A memorial was built there in 1980 to inform tourists of the little that is known about the disappearance of the 'Bermagui Five'.

LEGENDS OF THE LAKE

In 1828, settlers around Lake George, New South Wales, reported an earthquake followed by a 'hurricane'. It was an early indication that the area might have some unusual characteristics. It may also have signalled the displeasure of Budjabulya, creation serpent of the Ngunawal people, at the invasion of his traditional home in Ngungara, the 'flat water'. Budjabulya made the lake as well as the land and the people, plants and animals within it, especially the rivers and other water bodies.

Europeans first found Lake George in 1820, or possibly earlier, and settlement around its vast waters began within a few years. By the 1830s, the lake began to exhibit the mysterious behaviour it is now known for—its waters are continually disappearing and, mostly, reappearing. In 1842, passers-by reported that the lake was 'now quite dry, not a drop of water in it! Which may perhaps astonish such of your readers as may have seen the lake in former times.' Yet, by the 1870s, the lake was so full and flourishing with fish that a commercial trawler worked the waters and regattas were being enjoyed.

And then the waters dried up again. This unpredictable sequence has been the usual course of events for the million-year-old lake ever since. Scientific explanations for the vanishing waters include aquifers connecting the lake to rivers; wind action moving the water from one end of the long, shallow basin to another; as well as the effects of evaporation. But while the liquid on the surface disappears, there is always water—saline water—hidden beneath the lake floor.

Folkloric explanations for these phenomena include the suggestion that the lake waters drain to such improbably distant places as Peru, or New Zealand or Siberia. There have also been a few accounts of a Loch Ness–type monster in the lake, possibly related to the Budjabulya tradition, or not. While durable, lake lore is as murky as the water itself.

Whatever the reasons, scientific or otherwise, the unusual behaviour of the lake has given it a mysterious image.

Several tragedies have also contributed to the area's disturbing atmosphere, as projected in stories about UFOs and alien abductions. The death of five Duntroon cadets in the 1950s led to a persistent but inaccurate belief that the bodies had never been recovered. A girl also drowned in the lake during the 1950s, probably giving rise to one of Lake George's most unsettling traditions.

In this legend, a young girl dressed all in white hitchhikes along the Federal Highway that passes the lake. A car stops to give the girl a lift and she asks to be driven to her grandmother's place, usually said to be in Queanbeyan. When they arrive at the address the girl has given, the driver gets out and knocks on the door. An elderly woman answers and he tells her that he has her granddaughter in the back of the car. Taken aback, the elderly woman gasps out the name of the girl, saying that she drowned in the lake 30 years ago. The astonished driver returns to the car only to discover that the little girl in white has disappeared.

The details of this widespread modern legend, often known as the 'Vanishing Hitchhiker', differ from telling to telling, but it can be heard frequently in Canberra and surrounding areas.

For a final bit of weirdness, there is another Lake George where strange things happen. This one is in New York. At the Lake George Village Visitors Centre, there is a blue map of the lake painted onto a circular platform. Various compass bearings are laid across the map in metal. They cross at a point in the middle of the map, and if visitors stand exactly on that 'X' spot and shout or sing they hear that sound echo back to them. But no one else can hear it. The echo is only audible at that precise point.

There are various scientific explanations for this effect, mostly involving the sound of the voice reflecting back from the curved stone wall that surrounds part of the site. There is also said to have been a Native American deity who once materialised at that spot, which echoed his wise words around the lake itself.

Maybe this is where our Lake George waters go when they disappear?

VANISHING STARS

Perhaps it was fate. There were a number of unusual messages and statements made by film star Brian Abbot (George Rikard Bell) and others associated with the movie he was making on Lord Howe Island in 1936. Along with nineteen other cast and crew, Abbot sailed from Sydney to Lord Howe Island to make a feature film. It was the first movie production of the Commonwealth Film Laboratories and told a tale of shipwreck and murder, with a romantic subplot. The location and facilities of Lord Howe, then in the early stages of its role as a tourist resort, were ideal for the script and the required authentic Pacific island setting.

To keep the fans back home informed of their progress, leading man Abbot wrote an article for the *Australian Women's Weekly*. He began with a series of questions to tantalise his readers: 'Why does a film company take away a staff of artists and technicians to an island in the South Pacific, and what takes place in such circumstances? How does the unit go about making the film? Do the artists work all day long? How are the leisure hours passed?'

Readers were thrilled to hear about a typical day on the island paradise, which usually began with a pre-breakfast 'plunge into the warm waters of the sparkling lagoon'. The film had a musical angle, so the actors had to practise the theme song. After breakfast it was all into a boat bound for a beach on the far side of the island for a day's shooting. Abbot wrote that they drank a lot of billy tea on location, returning to their accommodation with fishing lines cast, bagging a 20 pound (9 kilogram) kingfish.

After a dinner of fish, they rehearsed, then relaxed with some music on harmonica, concertina and ukulele: 'We sing, we have supper, we stroll or we yarn or we dance, and at length we sleep.' Sounds very pleasant, so no wonder Abbot wrote that 'this lovely isle has completely captivated its film-invaders'.

It wasn't all cups of tea and kingfish, though. Abbot mentions storms at sea and an overnight marooning of some of the group on an islet due to rough weather. Despite the subtropical surroundings and relaxed leisure time, they were working hard to make a sound film on location and not to 'stay at home and fake the whole thing'.

Around this time, Brian Abbot wrote a cryptic private letter to the *Women's Weekly*. He informed the editors that 'I shall be attempting a very adventurous voyage in October. However, there are strong personal reasons for no word of this trip of mine to be published until it has actually begun.' The editors of the magazine later said they had no idea what this might mean and neither did anyone else—then.

The film was completed, and arrangements were made to leave the island. Brian Abbot and fellow actor Desmond Hay (Leslie Hay-Simpson) decided that they would not return to Sydney with the rest of the cast and crew. Instead, they would take Abbot's small skiff, the *Mystery Star*, specially shipped to the island for this purpose, and voyage home independently. Seasoned sailors on Lord Howe pointed out that the almost 800 kilometre crossing to Sydney was notoriously dangerous and was best not attempted in a small 16 foot (4.9 metre) craft and with only a compass for navigation.

This trip was presumably what Abbot was referring to in his note to the magazine. Perhaps he was being intentionally mysterious to garner some potential publicity? He had always been an adventurer and attention seeker with a history of daring sea trips, two of which ended in near disaster.

Whatever their motivations, the pair ignored the advice and loaded up for what they anticipated would be just a six- to eight-day journey. With food, petrol, luggage and the two passengers, locals thought that the *Mystery Star* was riding very low in the water. Not long after the two stars departed, the weather turned rough. Ten days later, they had still not reached Sydney.

A massive air and sea search was mobilised, including a Royal Australian Navy destroyer and two Royal Australian Air Force amphibious aircraft, as well as a monoplane. After a few unsuccessful days of scanning the waves, the two men were declared lost and the search abandoned. Relatives pleaded for efforts to continue, favouring a possibility that the skiff had made it to the mainland coast and possibly wrecked. The men might be stranded on an island, desperate for help. It was suggested by those who knew the waters that, if their motor had run out of fuel or failed, they might have drifted southwards.

Sadly, the men were never found, nor any trace of their boat. The disappearance of the two stars has remained a mystery ever since. What was the meaning of the odd note Abbot wrote to the *Women's Weekly*? And why would you send such a note, requesting confidentiality, to a media organisation! Were there troubles between cast and crew, belying Abbot's sunny reports? Or were the two missing men simply the victims of foul weather and foolhardiness?

The movie in which Brian Abbot and Desmond Hay had both featured was released the following year as a support film for main features. Reviewers praised the scenery but panned the sound quality and the lack of suspense. The *Sydney Morning Herald* critic acknowledged that 'Brian Abbot, whose tragic disappearance followed so soon on the making of the film, is the hero'. Like the unfortunate stars, the movie vanished without trace. It was called *Mystery Island*.

THE LADY OF THE SWAMP

Margaret Clement's disappearance on 22 May 1952 was described by the Melbourne coroner as 'one of the great unsolved mysteries'. The coroner was speaking more than 40 years later, and the case remains as baffling as ever today.

Margaret was born into a wealthy family in 1881. The Clements were part of Melbourne society, travelling widely and enjoying a leisured lifestyle. With her sister, Jeanie (sometimes 'Jenny'), Margaret purchased Tullaree, a Gippsland property at Tarwin Lower, Victoria, in 1907. Their purchase of the troubled property was assisted by their brother, Peter. When he married and moved away in 1912, Margaret and Jeanie were left to run the station together.

It did not go well. Within ten years, the sisters found themselves in difficult financial circumstances. It seems that poor management, an inability to live within their depleted means and a series of expensive legal cases led to Tullaree being mortgaged and nearly lost to them altogether. The property was surrounded by what was then known as Tullaree Swamp, but 'drains silted, floodwaters backed up and spread over the pastures' and the area became 'nothing but a desolate swamp haven for wildfowl, deer—and the two recluse sisters, living on their own in a world of memories'.

The two women were supported by relations and, as they aged, became increasingly isolated and eccentric. Jeanie died in 1950. A neighbour had to wade through the swamp waters to collect her body and take it for burial in the family vault.

Margaret was left to carry on alone as best she could, but she put a brave face on her situation:

My sister and I were very happy; nobody bothered about us and we bothered nobody. Maybe the future will be lonely for me, but I have no regrets and no fears. After all a person has only one life to live and I'm enjoying mine in my own way ... I have my memories, my books (mostly thrillers), Dingo (a dog and her constant companion) ... I'm just going to carry on until my time comes.

When Margaret's time came, barely two years later, a massive search was carried out over several months. Several hundred police and civilians joined in 'on horseback and on foot, wading at times shoulder deep in the icy cold, muddy water, we searched every part of that swamp'. But there was no trace of the reclusive woman. Had she been abducted? Had she been murdered? Had she committed suicide? With no leads and no body, a frustrated police force began another search of the extensive Tullaree Swamp. Once again, no trace of the missing woman was found.

At this point, *Argus* journalist Barney Porter wrote about the case. He had covered the story of Jeanie's death, got to know Margaret Clement and became familiar with the area and its few residents. He began with a description of Tullaree's nearest neighbours, Stan Livingstone, 'former Port Melbourne and Footscray ruckman, farmer, and contractor', and his 'attractive wife Esme, ex-Alfred Hospital trainee'.

The Livingstones had come to the area some years before. Stan had work dredging Fish Creek to further the larger project of draining the swamp. He and Esme became close friends of Margaret. Eventually, they purchased Tullaree from her on the understanding that they would build her a suitable residence outside the boggy part of the property that 'guaranteed her a home, free from worry, for the rest of her life'. They reportedly paid as little as £16,000, a bargain even at that time. After paying off her debts, Margaret was left with only £3000.

According to the Livingstones, Margaret's friendship with them gave her a new interest in life: she 'went on trips with them to Leongatha, Wonthaggi, and Cowes'. On the weekend of her disappearance, Margaret was due to join Esme Livingstone for a shopping trip but did not turn up for the outing. When Stan Livingstone called at the home, he found it empty: 'Supplies left a few days previously had not been put away. Miss Clement's bed was made and had not been slept in. The stick she always took when she went wading through the swamp was in its customary place beside the door. And that is the last seen, heard, or known of Margaret Clement.'

It was Stan who informed the police of Margaret's disappearance. The police had a number of theories. A few years earlier,

Margaret had collapsed in the swamp and only survived with the help of a local boy who found her. Perhaps it had happened again and she had not been so lucky? Or someone with an interest in the property had stolen her away? Or, distraught over her troubles, she just wandered off and drowned somewhere in the swamp?

But the most favoured theory, both of the police and the public, was that the defenceless recluse had been murdered and her body dumped in a part of the swamp where it would have been washed down Fish Creek and then out to sea. Police found a note in a bag in Margaret's room reading: 'I will rise above my enemies and fools. They will not defeat me.' Some scriptural quotations and other notes were also found. The fact that the missing woman had left her faithful stick behind in the house could also suggest foul play. Or it could suggest suicide. The case was truly baffling.

As well as the main plot in this mystery, there were several subplots. One concerned a Gippsland yarn in which a trove of gold sovereigns stolen in 1877 had been cached at Tullaree as the thief sought to escape (see Gippsland Gold). A large part of the loot remained unrecovered and rumour had it that it was somewhere in, beneath or around Tullaree.

And then there were the relatives. Margaret's financial troubles and the unrealised value of her decaying property drew interest not only from the Livingstones, but members of the extended Clement family. A nephew claimed Margaret had promised in 1945 to leave the property to him at her death. But he was unable to make his case in court and the Livingstones were duly confirmed as the owners of the property. In 1956 they reportedly sold it for £67,500 and went overseas, though other accounts say they lived there until the 1960s and bought island property in Queensland with their profits.

While the mystery lingered, along with years of litigation over ownership of the property, the police persisted with their investigation. They favoured the theory that the Livingstones murdered Margaret Clement and, somehow, somewhere, disposed of her body. Esme Livingstone was interviewed several times. On the last occasion, after husband Stan had passed away, she told the police that although she would like to help, she was too frightened to do so. She allegedly told a friend that Stan extracted a signature from Margaret at gunpoint, transferring ownership of Tullaree to himself. Later he arranged for her murder by a couple of Melbourne hitmen. Esme died in 1993, along with whatever secrets she held.

Despite the passing of almost 70 years, we are none the wiser about what happened to the lady of the swamp. Whether she was murdered, fatefully lost or a suicide, where are her remains?

Since then, the swamp has been drained. Tullaree has had several new owners and been renovated into a stunning display home, sometimes open to the public for tours. No one seems to have found any gold sovereigns under the floorboards, but Margaret's ghost is still with us. The old woman is sometimes seen near Tullaree or carrying an old sugar bag as she trudges the scrub near Inverloch.

WHO KILLED HARRY?

'I picked it up and turned it around and I see two open eye sockets looking at me.'

Glenelg, New South Wales, farmer Ted Markham was holding a human skull. In 2004, he'd been spraying the grass-hoppers out of his paddocks when he noticed a 'white thing on the side of the road'. He backed the ute up, stepped out and bent down: 'I got a surprise when I picked it up and turned it around', he recalled in a masterpiece of understatement. Ted was looking at the mortal remains of William Henry Lavers. Flash flooding in the area had washed the skull down from a nearby cave where the rest of the skeleton was then found.

'Harry', as Lavers was known, ran the roadside store and petrol station at Glenelg, near Grenfell, New South Wales, and had last been seen on the morning of 5 September 1936.

At around 6 a.m. he told his wife, 'I better go feed the horses.' It was a couple of hours before his wife became concerned and went to look for him. She did not find him and nor could anyone else until 75 years later in 2004.

When Harry Lavers first disappeared, the police mounted a murder investigation. Human blood and hair were found on the handle of the petrol pump and 'a car was heard to race away from the place', according to the press. But the police failed to find either Harry's body or a murderer. Until ten years later.

In 1946, an itinerant shearer with a taste for the grog was named by police as the murderer. Fred McDermott confessed to a heated conversation with his girlfriend, Florrie Hampton, in which she had called him 'a damm murderer . . . you murdered Lavers . . . you cut him up'. McDermott replied: 'I didn't. It was we not I.' This was a reference to another man who had been accused of assisting him. During another quarrel, Florrie had said, 'You killed Lavers for seven gallons of petrol. And put his body in the car and drove out to the old Grenfell sheep-yards, cut it up with an axe and buried it.' McDermott replied: 'Yes of course I killed Lavers for seven gallons of petrol, put his body in the car and drove out to the old Grenfell sheepyards, cut it up with an axe and buried it.'

McDermott was also shakily identified from some question-able photographs by a travelling mind-reader, Essie May King, who, unknown to the jury, shared in the reward money. On this flimsy evidence, the Crown argued McDermott had killed Lavers and buried his body in a paddock—somewhere. He was found guilty and sentenced to death, later commuted to life in prison.

Without access to alcohol, Fred's faculties returned and he began agitating for release. He collected evidence to support his innocence and was also able to convince the Anglican chaplain of Long Bay Gaol, as well as his warders, that he did not kill Lavers. This resulted in several appeals and, in 1951–1952, a Royal Commission into the case. After years in prison,

Fred McDermott was released. But his conviction was never officially quashed and he lived the last 25 years of his life as an accused and convicted murderer.

Following Ted Markham's remarkable find, scientists used DNA and facial reconstruction techniques to confirm that the remains were indeed those of Harry Lavers. Together with strong representations from the legal fraternity, these facts led to a petition to the Court of Criminal Appeal. In 2012 the court ruled that a miscarriage of justice had occurred and quashed Fred McDermott's wrongful conviction. This was the first time an Australian had been posthumously acquitted of murder. Justice had, eventually, been served, to the relief and happiness of Fred McDermott's family, who had long campaigned for this result.

But what did happen to Harry Lavers in the two hours between telling his wife he was off to feed the horses and the discovery of his disappearance? Had one or more travellers stopped at the bowser on the isolated road and murdered the man serving them? To murder a man just to steal a tank of petrol seems extreme, as McDermott himself implied to Florrie Hampton in his mock confession. The bloody body, alive or dead, would then need to have been bundled into the car, driven to a difficult-to-access cave and concealed. This sequence of events seems to be very unlikely. On the other hand, one person, or more probably several persons, transported Harry Lavers from his shop to the cave. Who could they have been?

THE PRIME MINISTER VANISHES

People have always disappeared, of course, but in the modern era vanishings seem to have become much more frequent. This may simply be due to the ability of technology to keep track of us and to quickly raise an alarm when someone is not where they are supposed to be.

But on the other hand, the information technologies we now all rely on for almost everything have made it easier for people to assume, or steal, identities. Disappearing has become so popular in Japan that companies exist to help people drop from sight and start completely new lives.

Around 40,000 Australians go missing each year. Many turn up alive and well, some don't and quite a few remain disappeared, usually forever. On 17 December 1967, Australia's seventeenth prime minister vanished.

Harold Holt became prime minister in 1966 when Robert Menzies retired from the position. Holt was a lawyer who became a Member of the House of Representatives in 1935, at the age of 27. He rose through the ranks of the United Australia Party and its successor, the Liberal Party, serving as a minister and treasurer. A career politician, he was the unopposed choice of his party to succeed his predecessor.

Robert Menzies was always going to be a hard act to follow, though Holt did well at first. It was the era of the Vietnam War and his party supported Australia's alliance with America and consequent involvement in that conflict. But public opinion on Australia's role in Vietnam was turning away from Holt's enthusiastic endorsement of the USA and he came under increasing pressure from the Opposition and some of his own party when he mishandled several controversies, including the impartiality of the Australian Broadcasting Commission (now Corporation) as well as a second inquiry into the controversy over the sinking of the *Voyager*. Electoral setbacks in late 1967 further fuelled Liberal party concerns about Holt's leadership.

With these political troubles surrounding him, Holt, a keen ocean sportsman, went swimming with a friend at Cheviot Beach, Victoria. The water was rough, but Holt confidently swam far from the shore. An eyewitness saw him in a 'flat, swirling mess of water'. He seemed unworried and made no signs of distress, even though he had been in the water for some time. When he did begin to swim back to shore, 'the water seemed to boil into colossal waves where he was [and] he couldn't come back . . . and then there was nothing'.

A vast search failed to find any trace of the prime minister and no definitive answers to his fate could be offered by police. It was not until a coronial inquest in 2005 that Harold Holt was declared to have been accidentally drowned.

But, as with all unanswered questions, we have to have a narrative, no matter how reasonable, radical or simply ridiculous. In the years between Holt's fatal swim and a final official pronouncement on his fate, many guesses, rumours and conspiracies circulated among Australians. Even today, references to the story can crop up in everyday conversation.

Many believed the prime minister was taken by a shark, a reasonable assumption but one unsupported by any evidence. Some claimed he had been assassinated by the American Central Intelligence Agency (CIA). Given Holt's support for Australia's participation in the Vietnam War as an American ally, this seems very unlikely. A favoured explanation was that Holt had been taken away by a Chinese submarine because he wished to defect to that country. Why the prime minister of Australia would do such a thing is never explained.

Harold Holt was in politically difficult circumstances at the time of his disappearance. Perhaps he committed suicide? Those who knew him as an active and enthusiastic lover of life considered this to be highly unlikely. So maybe he managed to find a way to simply vanish and live out the rest of his life under a new identity?

Or maybe not. Whatever explanations or pseudo-explanations are offered, Harold Holt's body is still missing. Despite the existence of a spoof Facebook group named the 'Harold Holt Disappearance Re-enactment Society' dedicated to unravelling the puzzle, kind of, the whereabouts of Australia's only vanishing prime minister will probably remain a mystery forever.

FLIGHT OF THE MOTH

Why were His Royal Highness Prince Philip and Tasmanian Premier Eric Reece yelling at each other in 1972?

In the 1970s, the island state had serious problems of unemployment, undereducation and poverty. The government of the day, with the support of the Tasmanian Hydro-Electric Commission and many business interests, believed that the solution to these problems was to increase Tasmania's production of electricity to encourage the development of heavy industry. The best way to do that, they concluded, was to flood Lake Pedder, a startlingly beautiful body of water with a unique beach of pink quartz. This involved damming the Huon and Serpentine rivers.

Largely in response to this threat, the world's first Green political party was founded in Hobart in March 1972. A 'Save Lake Pedder' campaign was launched, and the party contested state elections. They were very effective, even attracting HRH Prince Philip to support the cause. In his role as president of the Australian Conservation Foundation, the prince met with Premier Reece over the issue. Loud, angry voices were heard in the corridors of Parliament House. Despite both royal and popular opposition, the Tasmanian government determined to proceed with the Lake Pedder scheme. The Greens needed to take their fight to the federal level.

Committed environmentalist and Hobart socialite Brenda Hean, 62, together with a barnstorming pilot, Max Price, decided to fly a rebuilt World War II Tiger Moth biplane to Canberra. There, they planned to skywrite 'Save Lake Pedder' above the capital to raise awareness of the campaign, hoping to have some influence on the 1972 federal election. Asked by a reporter when she would give up the cause, Brenda replied, 'Never. There's a lot of British spirit in us yet, you know?' Asked by the same reporter if he thought he might outlast his old aeroplane, Price replied, 'Oh! Ah, well, that's a toss up, really. Uh, I think the aeroplane will last a long time yet. I hope to. Whether me licence will last as long as the aeroplane, I don't know.'

The Tiger Moth took off later than scheduled, shortly after 10 a.m. Max radioed to say all was well and the plane flew up the east coast, bound for a scheduled refuel stop at Flinders Island. A family holidaying at the Eddystone Point Lighthouse saw the Tiger Moth heading out to sea around 1.30 p.m. There did not seem to be any trouble with the engine. The flyers should have made it to Flinders Island about 45 minutes later.

They never did. Ten days of searching found no wreckage or any other sign of the biplane. What happened?

Before the flight, Brenda Hean had received a threatening telephone call in which an unidentified man asked, 'Do you want to go for a swim?' The night before the flight, the Tiger Moth's hangar was broken into. It was later discovered that the plane's emergency signalling device had been removed and possibly hidden in the hangar.

Investigators theorised that the plane had caught fire, possibly caused by the extra fuel it was carrying for the flight. But they allowed there was also a possibility that the strong rumours of sabotage that circulated after the crash might be true. Sugar in the fuel tanks was, and for many still is, the most favoured explanation. The perceived lack of interest of the Tasmanian government in pursuing the tragedy raised suspicion, as did the absence of a coronial inquest, at this time not a requirement in Tasmania. Nor was there ever an official inquiry.

These suspicions and uncertainties have fuelled the mystery of Brenda Hean and Max Price's disappearance ever since. Articles, a book, a documentary film and an ABC investigation in 2004 have kept the case alive, as has environmentalist Bob Brown, who spoke about the mystery in federal parliament and believes the Tiger Moth was sabotaged.

These events took place ten years before the much better known Franklin River campaign of the 1980s. But Brenda Hean and Max Price did not die in vain. As the first environmental martyrs, their sacrifice convinced many to support the Green cause, leading to the formation of a new party to balance Australian politics.

BLACK MOUNTAIN MYTHS

The massive jumble of rocks south of Cooktown in Queensand looks unnatural. It has some unusual physical characteristics and some tricks of the light that give it an ominous, even menacing presence in the landscape. Wind blowing through the sacred stones between Mareeba and Cooktown is said to sound 'like howling souls trapped inside'. This brooding mass has been called a 'Bermuda Triangle', after the area of the Caribbean notorious for unexplained disappearances, but its disturbing history is much older.

Kalkajaka, meaning 'spear', is a place of conflict and violence in the stories of the traditional owners of Far North Queensland's Black Mountain. Several groups of Aboriginal people, known as the Kuku Yalanji, have custodianship of the mountain and its dark traditions. Giant spirits fought each other here, while many people died in wars between the totemic black and white cockatoos.

Today, as with Uluru, the custodians feel it is disrespectful and positively dangerous for people to walk on Kalkajaka. They tell of those who do transgress this sacred bora, or ceremonial site, suffering from illness and spiritual torments. One group of adventurers who did explore the mountain found it to be a forbidding and dangerous labyrinth of darkness, unsettling sounds and slippery stones. Once lost inside this maze, an unfortunate interloper would 'never again find his way to the light of day'.

In modern times, settlers, fugitives, policemen, prospectors and travellers have been going missing around Black Mountain since at least the 1870s, when Cooktown was established as a port for the gold rush along the Palmer River. At first, the inexplicable disappearances were often classed as suicides or misadventures. Although the records of the period are few and murky, it seems that the mountain became associated with unexplained events in the 1880s and 1890s. In the twentieth century, people were also said to have disappeared there in the 1920s and 1930s. Some were eventually found shot dead.

Black Mountain was by then firmly established as a place where strange things occurred. Highly embroidered versions of traditional stories were published in newspapers and magazines, fostering a growing fascination with the place. Popular newspapers still print articles about Black Mountain, all rehashing the same unsteady 'facts' and further contributing to the legend. There are few weird things that are not alleged to have happened on the mountain.

As well as the earlier disappearances, whole herds of livestock are said to have somehow melted into the rocks. The Queensland Tiger, an 'Alien Big Cat' (see The Cryptid Files), is said to stalk the area and it is also said that overflying aircraft experience strange interferences to their electronic equipment, as in the original 'Bermuda Triangle'. The unusual structure of the mountain has also inspired a belief that it is not natural at all but was somehow built by aliens. All these yarns can be found living a robust life on the World Wide Web.

Mountains do feature strongly in mysterious disappearances. The difficult to access Wonnangatta Valley in Victoria's high country has a reputation for unsolved murders, dating back to World War I. More recently, it has become a popular bush destination for more intrepid campers, hunters and walkers. Over 2019 to 2020 four of them disappeared without trace. Intensive searches and investigations have failed to find the missing people, leaving police baffled. Locals and regular visitors mutter about hidden marijuana crops and an odd character who wanders through the area. But, like Black Mountain, this rugged region has, so far, refused to reveal its secrets.

TIGER TALES

The puzzles surrounding the fate of the Tasmanian tiger, or thylacine, continue to perplex many people. Sent extinct by careless zookeeping in 1936, the 'Tassie tiger', as it is usually affectionately known, has an extraordinarily large following of admirers. And not just in Tasmania. Thylacine fanciers are found around the world, keeping up interest in the fate of the creature and its lengthy afterlife in blogs, books and articles.

Some are even trying to hunt a thylacine down in the wild, true believers in the continued existence of the animal somewhere in the Tasmanian wilderness or even on the mainland. A couple of recent discoveries have sparked a major rethink of the thylacine's physical characteristics and these should provide new insights for tiger hunters to pursue.

For decades, scientists have believed that the average weight of the thylacine was around 30 kilograms. But researchers have discovered that this is an overestimation. The average weight of the tigers was more than 10 kilograms lighter: 'Our calculations unanimously told a very different story from the 19th century periodicals, and from the commonly used estimate. The average thylacine weighed only about 16.7 kg—not 29.5 kg.'

So what? This discovery has major implications for the feeding patterns and habitat of the stripy beasts. It means that those attempting to locate and photograph, or even catch, tigers believed to be hiding in the wild are probably looking in the wrong places.

Shortly after this news broke, another discovery was made, this time in New Zealand. Back in 1923, a Kiwi natural history collector purchased a thylacine pelt. It was stored for decades in a drawer, followed by another 50 years or so on the wall of a canoe and taxidermy shop. A photo of the pelt was shared on Twitter, where Launceston conservator David Thurrowgood spotted it. Knowing its potential significance, David visited Whanganui and brought the pelt home.

What a surprise souvenir it turned out to be.

Most of the tiger skins in museums have been exposed to light and air for very long periods. They have gradually lost their natural colour and are also deteriorated in other ways, often due to tanning processes. Because the New Zealand pelt had been protected for so long and not tanned, it retained its full hues: 'rich chocolate browns on the stripes and honey colours, down to really beautiful greys on the underside of the animal', said David Thurrowgood.

As well as its beauty, the condition of the pelt enabled DNA confirmation of its authenticity, along with a rare examination of its hair. It seems that thylacines have eight different hair types arranged in layers. Some of these are hollow and helped keep the animals warm in the chilly Tasmanian winters.

And that was not the end of the thylacine surprises. In 2021 scientists discovered that Tassie tiger pups had skulls more akin to those of wolves than other marsupials. They posited that the wolves and tigers last shared a common ancestor some 160 million years ago.

So science and serendipity have now combined to throw a little more light on the thylacine. It's a shame that we could not have been more enlightened in the past. Blamed for attacking farm animals—some of which it could not possibly have challenged—the thylacine was hunted to extinction with the help of generous government bounties, ignorance and prejudice. In 1926, the London Zoological Society delivered itself of the learned opinion that thylacines were 'slinking and cowardly animals, but will defend themselves savagely. They seem to have a low intelligence. They were sometimes said to have tusks and to attack when cornered.' In fact, thylacines were timid, preferring flight to fight.

These projections of fear, and even hate, are perplexing to most people today. We lament the extinction of a unique native species, the world's largest marsupial predator, and have even tried to bring it back through DNA cloning. Perhaps that is why the thylacine continues to exert an enigmatic fascination over so many.

BENEATH THE THREE UGLY SISTERS?

This is a story with a distinctively Sydney plot and characters. The cast includes rabid developers, dodgy politicians, crooked cops and desperate chancers prepared to do anything if the price is right. The heroine of the tale is a crusading newspaper editor, Juanita Nielsen.

Heiress to the fortunes of the Mark Foy's retailing dynasty, Juanita Nielsen was born in 1937. She was expensively educated and worked at the family business as a glove model for some years before taking off on a travel adventure in 1959. While she was abroad Juanita married, though the union lasted only a few years. She returned to Australia and to her previous place of work, where she ran a boutique featuring the trendy new fashions of the 1960s.

At that time, Sydney was in the throes of an extensive redevelopment fervour. Old buildings were being knocked down to make way for much larger new ones, especially apartment blocks. There were demonstrations, forced evictions and intimidation as developers acquired rented properties by one means or another and there was an increasingly vociferous resistance to what many saw as the dismissal of property rights, the despoliation of heritage and environment and the corruption of officials and politicians. Eventually, the building trade unions became involved, leading to the imposition of 'green bans' by the New South Wales branch of the Builders Labourers Federation (BLF) in the 1970s. The bans blocked union and non-union labour from working on sensitive heritage sites slated for demolition by property developers. Pickets, protests, scuffles and arrests of prominent unionists and their supporters followed.

In the midst of this turmoil, Juanita Nielsen was running a local newspaper, purchased on her behalf by her father. Initially a hobby, NOW was located in the gentrifying eastern suburbs and quickly became a voice for urban conservation and against the redevelopment of areas such as Kings Cross and Potts Point. The stylishly dressed and coiffured Juanita campaigned ceaselessly against the developers and their cronies. As the green bans put in place by the BLF denied developers the trades and labour they needed to demolish and rebuild, some became worried. In particular, developer Frank Theeman was heavily in debt to underworld figures for the financing of his grandiose plans for a Kings Cross apartment complex.

To build this, the developer needed to evict many tenants from the nineteenth century terrace houses in Victoria Street, where Juanita Nielsen lived at number 202. With the support of the BLF, Nielsen and local tenants refused to leave their homes. Despite intimidation, legal threats and ongoing harassment by an ex-detective and others, the residents held out until the BLF changed leadership in 1974 and removed the green ban. Another union then took up the cause, and by 1975 the costs involved in the delayed clearance and building were mounting dramatically.

Juanita Nielsen had been documenting events in Victoria Avenue and effectively kept the issue in the news through her paper. She was becoming a serious problem to Theeman, to his backer, rumoured to be 'Mr Sin', Abe Saffron, and to others with a financial interest in the redevelopment. Nielsen became worried about her safety but, nevertheless, on 4 July 1975 she attended an appointment at the Carousel Club in Kings Cross (previously Les Girls) to discuss advertising in her newspaper. The club was owned by Saffron. What happened there is the subject of many stories, testimonies and statements. Whatever the truth, or not, of these, Juanita Nielsen was never seen again.

Popular belief in Sydney was, and is, that the fashionable journalist was murdered by those in the pay of the developer or 'Mr Sin', who then disposed of her body. Juanita Nielsen's whereabouts are variously said to be beneath the second runway at Mascot (Sydney) Airport, then under construction, or at the bottom of Sydney Harbour. The favoured theory, though, is that her body is in the foundations of the three-tower block that Theeman eventually built in lower Victoria Street, known locally as the 'three ugly sisters'.

Subsequent inquiries could only conclude that Juanita Nielsen was dead. Police corruption was noted but no one has ever been charged over her disappearance, although New South Wales police offered a one million dollar reward in 2021.

Such a sensational mystery has attracted the attention of writers, filmmakers and journalists for years, though as the characters in the story are now all dead it is unlikely we will ever know the truth about what happened to the brave Juanita Nielsen. Her memory lives on, not only in Sydney lore and legend but also in the house where she lived and published *NOW*. Number 202 Victoria Street survived the redevelopment and is now a heritage-listed building. There is a Juanita Nielsen Community Centre at Woolloomooloo run, somewhat ironically, by the Council of the City of Sydney.

It is said that the truth about Juanita Nielsen's disappearance is in the diaries of Abe Saffron. These were in the possession of his son, Alan, who died in 2020. His widow, Genevieve, has been quoted stating, '"I want redemption", to respect his wishes and for the facts to be revealed.' The diaries are now thought to be under lock and key with a Sydney publisher.

'GOOD NIGHT. MALAYSIAN THREE SEVEN ZERO'

The disappearance of Malaysian Airlines flight MH370 is considered the most puzzling aviation mystery of all time. It is also one of the worst aviation tragedies, with 239 passengers and crew believed dead. Almost half the passengers were Chinese, 38 were Malaysian and the remainder from twelve other countries, including six from Australia.

The bare facts of the MH370 mystery are few and simple. The Boeing 777 took off from Kuala Lumpur bound for Beijing on 8 March 2014 at 42 minutes past midnight. The last human communication with the plane was around 1.20 a.m. from Captain Zaharie responding to a call from Lumpur Radar, which he acknowledged with the signoff 'Good night. Malaysian three seven zero'. The last sound of MH370 was heard by satellite seven hours later. Apart from some wreckage later washed up on various Indian Ocean shores, everything else about the fate of the flight and those aboard is speculation.

We have sought to fill that void of unknowing with science, technology, logic, rumour and conspiracy theories of all kinds. As with all disappearances, the earliest red herrings are usually reported sightings. There were several of these, from the Maldives, from Indonesian fishermen, from oil rig workers and, later, a solo yachtswoman in the Indian Ocean who reportedly saw a burning aircraft. These sightings fitted with the early predictions about MH370 disappearing somewhere in South-East Asia.

Initial searching was carried out on this assumption until the middle of March, when a joint Malaysian and Chinese operation under Australian management began searching much further south in the Indian Ocean. Debris began to turn up and some items were assessed to be definitely from MH370, their location consistent with being carried by ocean currents from somewhere south of the Western Australian coast. These finds raised some hope that the plane might be located, but despite extensive and expensive operations this search was suspended in January 2017. A year later, a private American contractor undertook to locate MH370, but without success. Since June 2018, no further searches have so far been made. The fate of MH370 remains unknown within a mire of international recriminations, mourning and legal actions by relatives of the lost, as well as competing theories about what might have happened.

Were the people aboard MH370 the victims of terrorism, instigated by a crew member, a passenger or even one or more of the pilots? A bomb in the cargo? Was there an accident? Loss of power? An event that knocked out passengers and crew, leaving the plane to fly on until fuel ran out?

Beyond these rational possibilities, conspiracy theories proliferated. The plane did not crash but was hijacked and flown to a secret destination. Who might have done this, why and where are questions usually answered with the all-purpose explanation of 'terrorists'. A favoured destination is the British Indian Ocean Territory island of Diego Garcia, on which there is an American air base. The plane is usually said to have been dismantled and dumped in the sea. Another hypothesis has it that the flight was, accidentally or otherwise, shot down by some sort of joint Thailand and United States operation. Alien abduction and North Korean hijackers also feature in these fantastications. There are others, even more absurd. None are helpful.

Among all the methods suggested for locating MH370, the most intriguing is the use of 'prediction markets', or the wisdom of crowds. This involves sampling opinions of many people, expert and inexpert. These are then combined in sophisticated statistical analysis to come up with a likely answer. Sounds like another conspiracy theory, but it turns out that this is a respectable and reasonably reliable technique with a track record that includes the stock market reaction to the *Challenger* space shuttle disaster of 1986 and locating the lost United States submarine *Scorpion* in 1968.

At the time of writing, there seems to be no active search for MH370. The Malaysian government has said it will consider credible proposals and suggestions. There is considerable anger among relatives of those believed to be lost, and diplomatic tensions between the main countries involved. So far, the only positive things to come out of these sad events have been the discovery of two ships that went missing in the nineteenth century and a great deal of new information about the depths of the Southern Ocean that will assist scientific research.

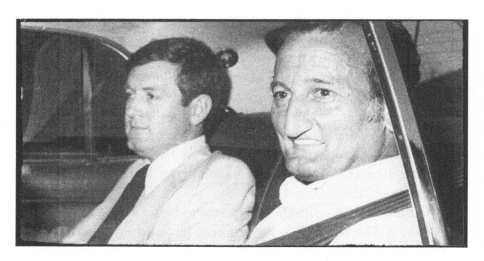

*In 1971, British national Peter Macari ('call me "Mr Brown"') held
Qantas to ransom for $500,000, claiming he had placed a bomb on
a plane. Qantas handed over the money, and the plane landed with
only sixteen minutes of fuel left. Is the unrecovered quarter of
a million still stashed somewhere in Sydney? Was Macari a
murderer as well as a modern-day highwayman?*

8

UNSOLVED

A QUEENSLAND RIPPER?

Three violent crimes committed in Queensland between 1898 and 1902 raise suspicions about a possible serial killer.

On 7 January 1899 a boy's badly decomposed body was found concealed beneath branches at Darra. He had been shot in the back of the head. His piebald pony also lay dead in a paddock a little way from him. Alfred Hill was only fifteen years old when he was murdered in December 1898. Edward Linton Cairns Wilson, a troubled one-time Ipswich school teacher, was tried for the murder. Evidence was conflicting and witnesses, including that of Wilson's crippled son, were contradictory. In the end, Wilson was acquitted. No one else has ever been charged with the seemingly pointless murder.

Early in 1902, Aboriginal tracker Sam Johnson led Constable George Doyle and station manager Albert Dahlke to the campsite of Patrick and James Kenniff at Lethbridge Pocket, Queensland. Doyle and Dahlke were pursuing the notorious bushrangers. Exactly what happened there remains unclear but Doyle and Dahlke were killed and only Sam Johnson escaped. The Kenniffs had disappeared. Police later located a quantity of charcoal mixed with human remains at the camp and a large manhunt began.

Arrested in June 1902, the brothers were charged with the murders and their attempt to conceal the crime by burning the bodies. After prolonged legal proceedings, including an appeal to the Privy Council in Britain and considerable community concern that the police had the wrong men, Patrick Kenniff was hanged in 1903. His brother's death sentence was commuted to life imprisonment.

The bodies of Michael Murphy and his younger sisters, Norah (Honora) and Ellen (Theresa), were found in a paddock 2 kilometres from Gatton, Queensland, on 27 December 1898. They had been savagely murdered and the girls raped. The bodies were posed along an east-west orientation and the horse that drew the sulky carrying them home from the cancelled Boxing Day evening dance they had travelled to attend also lay dead between the shafts of the sulky.

Each of these crimes has been surrounded in mystery and speculation since they were committed.

The man thought most likely to have murdered the Murphys was an itinerant worker known as Thomas Day (a.k.a. Theo Farmer) who lived near to the murder scene. He was interviewed by police but set free soon after. No one else was ever arrested for this especially horrific and baffling crime, usually known as the 'Gatton murders'.

Just as nature abhors a vacuum, so people hate unresolved mysteries. Rumour, speculation and, sometimes, complete fantasy flow in to fill any information voids. Who killed the Gatton victims and arranged their bodies in what has been called a 'ritualistic' pattern? Why?

Not many motives have been left unrehearsed. Almost as many suspects as those in the famous English 'Jack the Ripper' case have been named, as mostly amateur sleuths investigate the archives, newspaper reports and folklore surrounding these events. The Gatton case in particular has thrown up many names, from that of the shifty Day to members of the victims' extended family. Motives have included love trysts and disappointments, including incest, robbery, envy, maniacal rage and almost anything else.

One theory even has the famed Harry the 'Breaker' Morant in the frame. This is based on Morant's movements immediately before enlisting to fight in the Boer War, where he met his ignominious but fabled end. In this investigation, the horseman and poet is revealed as an alcoholic depressive with a very mean streak, feared and even reviled by some of those who knew him best. His later murder of unarmed enemy prisoners in South Africa, whatever the circumstances, is seen as a further indication of his dark side.

But the most intriguing possibility to be raised concerning these cases is the chilling suggestion that they—and possibly even more—were all the work of one killer. Several investigations of the cases and the records of their mostly inept treatment by the police of the time have resulted in books and television shows making the case for a previously unsuspected serial killer—a kind of 'Queensland Ripper'.

Supporting arguments are based generally on circumstantial evidence. These include real or alleged similarities in the methods of the murderer, the likelihood of suspects being in the right place at the right time and other tantalising possibilities and clues. As with the ever-expanding mythology of Jack the Ripper, other unsolved, apparently unrelated cases have also been connected to the Gatton murderer. There is even the possibility of conspiratorial official cover-ups to protect the Gatton and Oxley murderer, also a feature of the Jack the Ripper legend.

What can we conclude? Probably not much more than the police and other law officials at the time these crimes were committed. The most likely Gatton murderer was Day, though poor policing allowed him to escape. Alfred was probably murdered by the man tried for the crime and one or both of the Kenniffs killed and probably burned their pursuers; they were bushrangers, after all, and only a very few of these characters were 'gentlemen robbers'.

Yet, we cannot now ever be completely sure. The mystery continues to intrigue us and to compel us to find answers—any answers.

NED KELLY'S SKULL

The ongoing mystery of Ned Kelly's skull has more twists and turns than a bushranger's getaway track. Most of them are great stories in their own right, all going to prove that the facts and the fictions about the heroic villain continue to intrigue Australians.

The larger epic, of which the mystery is now an established element, begins in 1878 when Ned Kelly took to the bush with his younger brother Dan, Steve Wright and Joe Byrne. Whether in self-defence or not, Ned Kelly shot dead Sergeant Michael Kennedy, Constable Michael Scanlan and Constable Thomas Lonigan at Stringybark Creek, Victoria. 'The Kellys were out', as it was often said.

After a now mythic eighteen months or so of robbing banks and evading the considerable forces sent to hunt them down, the gang was finally cornered in their emblematic armour at Glenrowan. Three died a fiery death in and around the Glenrowan Hotel and their leader was badly wounded but captured alive. He was nursed back to health and tried for murder. No one was much surprised at the guilty verdict, and despite a strong public campaign for clemency Edward Kelly was hanged at Old Melbourne Gaol on 11 November 1880.

Then the mystery began.

In accordance with the practice of the time, the body was taken down and decapitated so the skull could be studied for what were then thought to be good scientific purposes of identifying criminal types by their physical features. As part of this procedure, a death mask was also cast for future reference. The skull and the rest of the body were buried outside the walls of the gaol along with other executed criminals.

Old Melbourne Gaol was redeveloped in the late 1920s and the remains of the executed criminals needed to be relocated.

When the graves were dug up, the skeletons were more or less intact. Souvenir hunters bagged many of the bones, but the contractor carrying out the excavation managed to save the skull. The remains were reburied, but without Ned Kelly's head.

The skull was kept, it seems, in official hands until 1931, when it was housed at the Australian Institute of Anatomy in Canberra, occasionally coming out for display to an eager public fascinated by the ever-growing mythology of the long-dead bushranger. Continued interest later saw the skull placed on permanent display, along with the death mask, at what was by then the Old Melbourne Gaol museum. In 1978 the skull disappeared, stolen—it has been said—by a Roman Catholic clergyman wishing to give the remains a decent burial.

Whatever the truth of this possibility, at some point after its disappearance a skull came into the possession of Kimberley farmer and Kelly enthusiast Tom Baxter. Tom kept the relic in a plastic box and spent many years talking about it around the country. Many were sceptical, but Tom insisted he had the real deal. I had several contacts and communications with Tom and it was clear that he genuinely believed he had the famous skull.

This went on until 2009, when archaeologists discovered a mass of skeletons at Pentridge Prison, the site of the 1929 reburial of the bones. Were Ned's bones in this lot? DNA testing might prove conclusive and, if so, Tom Baxter's skull could be examined to see if it matched. With much fanfare, Tom handed the skull to the scientists on 11 November 2009. After almost two years of testing, including the DNA of a Kelly family descendant, the scientists determined that Tom Baxter's artefact was not Ned Kelly's skull. But they were at least able to identify the rest of the bushranger's bones and to re-assemble them into a fairly complete skeleton.

But his skull is still missing. Where is it?

Various theories have emerged. Perhaps it was kept as a souvenir by one of the skull-seeking scientists? Or it may have been destroyed in the 1929 excavations. These are plausible explanations. Just as plausible is the possibility that it might be lying, long forgotten, in someone's garden shed. We may never know.

But there remains one small piece of evidence that could yet solve this mystery. The scientists reassembling the skeleton also found a small piece of skull bone that definitely is Ned Kelly's, probably removed as part of the original decapitation and examination process.

So if you're on the trail of Ned's skull, and some are, look for one with a hole in the head. If that one can be matched with the piece in the box of bones, the mystery will be solved. Though this final proof may entail yet another interference with the mortal remains as these were finally buried in the Kelly family's home ground at Greta in 2013.

The amount of expertise, time and presumably money that has been spent on trying to solve this mystery is perplexing to some. The scientific work involved the Commonwealth Scientific and Industrial Research Organisation (CSIRO), overseas DNA labs, excavations and DNA testing of Kelly descendants. We now know that the skull said to be Ned's was definitely not. We have his bones and a fragment of the true skull. We also have an enduring enigma that resonates with an almost religious fervour. Why? Because Ned Kelly, rightly or wrongly, has become a potent and enduring symbol of Australian identity, along with 'Waltzing Matilda' and the Anzacs.

Which is why Ned Kelly continues to generate intriguing stories, long after his life, death and skeletal resurrection.

THE DYING LIGHT

When young Albert Dann arrived in Lismore the local kids wanted him to take their initiation ritual. Newcomers would be given a penny if they had the gumption to read the name inscribed on a strangely glowing gravestone in the local cemetery. Years later Albert evocatively recalled his attempt to be accepted into the Lismore children's community:

I will never forget that bright moonlit night so long ago when with awful thoughts of ghosts and things unseen, I set out to earn my penny. I paused for a while at the little gate to what was then called the Pioneer Cemetery, and gazed fearfully at the grim lonely graves on the black slope. Forcing myself to move towards the main gate, suddenly, as I edged closer, a dazzling beam of white blinding light flashed from the centre of the cemetery and struck me fair in the eyes.

I was rooted to the spot with a horrible fear, still indescribable to this very day. Somehow or other, I remember forcing my unwilling body about and with every horrible ghost and devil after me, I sprinted back along the metalled road . . . to the comfort of a glowing gas lamp.

Albert had encountered William Steenson's glowing cross, a mystery that has spanned the decades and remains unexplained even today.

There was nothing unusual about William Steenson's death. A family man, keen Mason and member of the Casino–Lismore–Tweed Railway Employees Picnic committee, the 29-year-old Billy, as he was known, died in a shunting accident at Mullumbimby in 1907. The family buried him in Lismore cemetery beneath a cross of Balmoral red granite. An everyday tragedy.

But then something quite extraordinary happened. After a few years, locals noticed that Billy Steenson's memorial cross was glowing at night. The first public mention of this phenomenon was around the end of World War I in 1918. The cross above the grave reportedly glowed for several weeks. It has continued to shine at various times since.

In 1978, a visitor witnessed the cross glowing once again. The national press got hold of the story and there was a rush of sightseers to Lismore wanting to see the glow for themselves. Sure enough, the cross was glowing. Not quite as dramatically as Albert Dann remembered, but definitely giving off a strange luminescence.

The faithful hoped for a miracle or some kind of divine sign. The sceptics sought rational scientific explanations. Perhaps the cross was positioned to catch and reflect the moonlight? Perhaps it was some geological effect involving the quartz and feldspar content of Balmoral red granite? No reports of anything similar occurring with this popular monumental material were found, nor did the other gravestones made of the same material shine. Someone suggested prehistoric glow-worms fossilised in the ancient stone, but that was rejected by just about everyone.

Eventually, the luminescence faded, along with public interest, though the cross of light was well embedded in local folklore. In the 1980s, the stone was first vandalised and then stolen. There are rumours that it was destroyed or thrown in a river, but whatever the truth it is still missing. A replica was erected after an anonymous donation to pay the cost. People are still trying to locate the original cross, rightly considering it to be an important artefact of local history.

Can rocks glow? In particular, Balmoral red granite? Well, according to some research they can emit radon, a form of radioactivity, and Balmoral red does have a particularly high level of radon radiation. Whether that could illuminate the piece of it that formed Billy Steenson's cross remains an unanswered question.

THE CRYPTID FILES

Also known as a 'cryptoid' in popular culture, 'cryptid' is the scientific name for a creature thought to exist but of which there is no credible confirmation. Nevertheless, many people not only believe in abominable snowmen or yetis, but actively search for them. In Australia, we are not short of these cryptozoological mysteries, some of which began at the start of European settlement.

The bunyip is probably the most familiar of our cryptids. Variously said to be feathered, or not, often it is described as a hybrid of native animals. Sometimes it can even fly! One of the most consistent features of bunyip stories is that the creature is mostly water-dwelling. It originates in Aboriginal traditional stories but, over the years, has taken on one or two characteristics of British water-dwelling monsters, such as sharp teeth and claws.

A newspaper article of the 1840s sums up the various versions of the bunyip. Along the Murrumbidgee it was described as having 'a head and neck like an emu, with a long and flowing mane—feeding on crayfish (with which the river abounds)'. It was also said to devour the odd human.

At Paika Lake near the confluence of the Lachlan and Murrumbidgee rivers, the bunyip went under the local name of the oddly Irish-sounding 'kine pratie'. But whatever it was actually called by the Aboriginal people of the area, it lived in the lake and ate people. They were reluctant to go near its dwelling place.

The Burrawang bunyip is a good example of this type of yarn. Burrawang is in the Southern Highlands, south of Sydney in New South Wales, and boasts a large area of swampland in which the bunyip was said to live. People knew it lived there because it made a lot of roaring noises, often described as bull-like but a lot louder. The bunyip's roar was so intense that it could shake bottles off the shelf of the local pub. They say.

A section of the peat swamp was drained in the 1970s and the Burrawang bunyip has not been heard since. The reason for this is that there is now less of the peat, which is of a type that swells and shrinks as the temperature changes. It was the sucking and gurgling of the peat that produced the bull-roaring of the bunyip. Hmm.

Although bunyips have a pretty fearsome image, we are now so familiar with the creatures that they have become almost cuddly. In fact, there are bunyip soft toys, as well as children's books. Burrawang Public School even calls its newsletter the 'Burrawang Bunyip'. This cryptid has been thoroughly colonised.

A very different image is presented by the yowie. Also going by other names, such as Yahoo, Whowee and, in the Victorian High Country, the little-known Oona Poona, the yowie also has a fluid form. Sometimes it is a very tall, hairy creature that stands upright on two legs. Or it may be a much shorter creature, around a metre or so tall. In either case, it lives in the bush and is usually only seen when disturbed while hunting. Occasionally, a yowie turns up in someone's garage or backyard.

Yowies, or yowie-like creatures, have been spotted since pioneering days and also feature in First Nations stories. There is an extremely large and active community of dedicated yowie hunters around the country, all of whom feature on their websites' extensive lists of yowie sightings and encounters. Despite these efforts, nobody has yet produced any incontrovertible evidence of the yowie's existence.

Other well-known cryptids are sometimes known as 'phantom cats' or 'Alien Big Cats' (ABCs for short). The 'Alien' bit here refers to the fact that the animals are not native to Australia, not to any alleged interstellar origin—though it is just a matter of time before we hear about this angle.

ABCs are said to exist in many bushy parts of the country—which is most of it. People frequently report seeing very large cat-like creatures sloping around in search of food. They are often described as resembling exotic wild cats, such as pumas, tigers or leopards. Leaving aside the issue of how many average folk would know what any of these creatures looked like in the wild, the most likely resolution of the mystery is that most ABCs are large feral cats.

But, never wanting to let an opportunity for a good yarn pass by, there are plenty of explanations for the origins of ABCs. The favoured rationale is that they are escaped circus animals or escaped mascots of American soldiers stationed here during World War II. Some American units reportedly kept exotic animals as good luck charms. A recent embellishment is that the creatures, and their descendants, might have been left over from the gold rush era as Chinese diggers allegedly kept such troublesome creatures as pets.

As with other cryptids, ABCs have legions of fanciers and followers. There are regular sightings, often with supposedly incontrovertible photographic or other proof that they exist. These murky shots of vague shapes and indistinct plaster casts of paw prints are just as regularly dismissed by scientists. On the other hand, there are also some unexplained aspects of DNA and other physical indications that suggest overgrown feral cats are not the only predators out there.

THE PYJAMA GIRL

She lay for years in a zinc-lined tub full of formalin. Before a brutal end took her body to such a forensic resting place, she was Linda Agostini (née Platt). Or perhaps she wasn't. The intriguing arabesques of the Pyjama Girl case continue to mystify and trouble us, almost as much as they did when it began in 1934.

A local farmer found the burned remnants of a young woman wrapped in a towel and sack stuffed into a culvert on the Howlong Road about 8 kilometres west of Albury, New South Wales. The woman had been wearing silk pyjamas. These details were just about the only verifiable facts the police had from 1 September, when the remains were first found, until a decade later. In the meantime, the 'Pyjama Girl', as the media dubbed the body, waited in her formalin bath for an investigative breakthrough. The public became as intensely fascinated about the Pyjama Girl as they would be about the Azaria Chamberlain debacle many decades later.

A coroner's inquest in 1938 was unable to establish an identity for the corpse and it was not until 1944 that she was identified by dental evidence as the wife of Antonio Agostini, an Italian migrant who worked as a waiter and sometimes as a journalist. Linda had migrated from England via New Zealand and worked as a cinema usherette, though there were suggestions that she might have been a prostitute. When the couple married in Sydney in 1930, Tony was 27 and Linda was 25. Their marriage was stormy. Linda drank too much and too often, making Tony feel shamed among the Italian migrant community. The couple moved to Melbourne in 1933, where Linda found work as a hairdresser and Tony, a committed fascist, worked for an Italian-language newspaper.

During the decade between the discovery of the Pyjama Girl and an arrest for her murder, Tony Agostini had moved around the country and been interned as an enemy alien until 1944. He was not long free and back at work in Sydney when New South Wales police commissioner 'Big Bill' MacKay interviewed him.

William John MacKay was a tough Scot who had worked his way through the ranks to the top job by diligence, efficiency and a certain amount of guile. Coincidentally, he had known Agostini when the Italian worked at a restaurant MacKay frequented in the 1930s. Using this personal connection and his well-developed interrogatory skills, MacKay convinced Agostini to sign a shaky confession.

Agostini said that he and Linda had argued in bed, she had a pistol and it accidentally went off as they struggled. In panic, he wrapped her body up and drove from Melbourne to Albury, where he deposited the bundle in the culvert and set it alight. He was tried for murder but convicted only of manslaughter with a sentence of six years hard labour. In 1948 he was released under a 'Peace Remission' amnesty and deported. He died in Sardinia in 1969.

Agostini's conviction and sentence seemed to be the end of the Pyjama Girl mystery, all loose ends neatly tied up and justice done. But as the years wore on some began to have doubts, particularly about Big Bill MacKay's role in the case. Never popular with his own police force, the overbearing MacKay was a fierce scourge of political extremism, both of the left and the right. He was particularly concerned about women with British nationality marrying aliens who then became naturalised Australians and so, he believed, potential threats to national security. His interest and track record in these matters led to his appointment as the head of the Commonwealth Security Service in 1942, the organisation that preceded today's Australian Security Intelligence Organisation (ASIO). He did not last long in that position, but in taking the appointment he revealed his deep interest in national security matters. Did Tony Agostini's support for fascism cause MacKay to frame him?

Eventually, historian Richard Evans brought these and other doubts and inconsistencies together in a book about the case. Evans went back over the records, old and new, and checked newspaper reports to seriously undermine the case against Agostini. He unravelled an unsettling tale of lies, half-truths, hidden agendas, coronial mismanagement, police ineptitude and probably perjury, forensic incompetence and myth making.

In a chilling prefiguration of the Azaria Chamberlain case, Evans highlighted the inability of the media and police to accurately establish and communicate even the most basic facts. Essential details of eye colour, hair and clothing were frequently misreported by journalists, police and even the supposed forensic experts.

Together with the extensive national and international hunt for the killer, the convolutions of the Pyjama Girl mystery generated massive media interest in the 1930s and 1940s, including a 1939 documentary and several others since. And as with the Chamberlain case, there were jokes and popular parodies including, to the tune of 'Funiculì Funiculà':

My name is Antonio Agostini
And I'm in strife,
I killa my wife.
It was down in sunny Melbourne
I do her in,
I shoot poor Lyn . . .
My head is losing every curl,
Just because I killed the Pyjama Girl!

Despite that long-ago ditty, the mystery of the Pyjama Girl remains. We cannot be sure that the woman in the chemical coffin was killed by Antonio Agostini or by someone else. Nor do we know if Big Bill MacKay deliberately miscarried justice. We probably never will.

THE UNKNOWN MAN

He is known by various names, none of which belonged to him. A couple of jockeys exercising their mounts found his body crumpled against the sea wall on Somerton Park beach, near Adelaide, South Australia, so he was given the name 'Somerton Man'. Later discoveries led to him becoming known as 'Taman Shud'. And he is often simply called the 'Unknown Man', as inscribed on his gravestone. More than 70 years later, we know little more about this man than we did in 1948. Was he a criminal? A fugitive Nazi? A spy? He might even have been an American ballet dancer.

Like most mysteries based on very few verifiable facts, this one has grown to enormous proportions. It has been called Australia's most baffling unsolved crime and one of the world's most perplexing cold cases and has developed more twists and turns than a fictional thriller plot.

When police began to investigate the case, they were quickly confronted with a puzzling array of peculiar events. The man had arrived in Adelaide by train on the morning of 30 November 1948 and purchased a ticket to Henley Beach. He did not catch that train but walked to the City Baths, where he showered and shaved, then returned to the station, depositing his brown leather suitcase in the cloakroom. He bought a bus ticket on a service that had already departed, though he may well have walked to a further stop and boarded the bus there. However he arrived, he was in Glenelg later that morning, not too far from the home of a woman who would feature prominently in subsequent events (see The Secret Watchers). He remained in the area for the rest of the day.

At some point, he ate a pastie. Then he turned up dead the following morning.

The coroner suspected poisoning but no traces could be found, suggesting something very rare and restricted, the most likely substances being digitalis and strophanthin. The body had dental and other irregularities, including unusually well-developed calf muscles suggesting the man was an acrobat or even a ballet dancer. Most of the labels in his good-quality clothing had been removed and there were no identification documents of any kind upon him.

In January 1949, a leather suitcase the man had left at Adelaide's main station cloakroom was discovered. It contained some curious tools related to merchant shipping tasks, and some orange thread that had been used to repair the dead man's trousers. A tailor identified stitching in the coat as American in style. All potentially useful identifying labels had been carefully removed from the case and its contents.

This discovery stimulated further investigations of the dead man's clothing that revealed a fragment of paper rolled into a concealed pocket in the waistband of his trousers. On the paper were the words 'Tamám Shud' printed in an exotic font. The phrase is from the usual ending of the *Rubaiyat of Omar Khayyam*, a book of Persian poetry very popular in English translations. The phrase means 'It is ended' or 'Everything is finished'. ('Tamám Shud' was misprinted as 'Taman Shud' in some newspapers, a mistake that has persisted in the name that was given to the dead man.)

Unable to take the investigation much further at that point but hoping that more details might emerge, the police had the decomposing body embalmed and made a death mask of the face. They were lucky. Eight months after the discovery of the body, a man handed in a copy of the *Rubaiyat* found in the back seat of his car the previous December. A section of the last page containing the words 'Tamám Shud' was missing. Closer scrutiny of the book revealed an unlisted telephone number that turned out to belong to a young nurse living near

Somerton beach whom the police codenamed 'Jestyn'. On being interviewed, she told detectives that she had once given a copy of the *Rubaiyat* to a man in New South Wales. Expecting a breakthrough, police were disappointed to find the man alive and well and still with his intact copy of the book. Somerton Man was someone else.

When Jestyn's telephone number was discovered in the dead man's *Rubaiyat*, police also discovered the faint impressions of what looked like an alphabetic code. But no one, not even the skilled decryptionists at Naval Intelligence, was able to decipher the code and neither has anyone since.

The book itself is also the source of further questions in this ever-unfolding mystery. It turned out that the particular edition found in the car and thought to belong to Somerton Man never existed. Even more perplexingly, Professor Derek Abbott later discovered that the death of another man involved a copy of the *Rubaiyat*. The edition in this other man's possession also appears never to have been published.

With a range of puzzles and riddles that would delight Agatha Christie, it is no surprise that this case has continued to draw the attention of investigators, particularly retired policemen Gerry Feltus and Derek Abbott. They have, together and separately, followed up overlooked details and faint clues.

For whatever reasons, the original police investigation declined to publicly name 'Jestyn'. She was obviously a person of considerable interest whose shocked reaction on being shown the death mask of Somerton Man raised suspicions about what she knew and what she was not revealing. But she was apparently never seriously interrogated and never charged. Gerry Feltus tracked down her identity and Derek Abbott later located a photograph that enabled her to be identified as Jo Thomson. But it was too late; she had died two years earlier.

However, she had given birth to a son, Robin. Derek Abbott discovered he had been a ballet dancer, but he was dead by the time he was identified through photographic and physical evidence showing similarities between him and Somerton Man. Abbott then discovered that Robin had a daughter, Rachel Egan. Hoping to find a DNA connection with Somerton Man, he met with Rachel, Jo Thomson's granddaughter. In a romantic twist to the tale, they married shortly after.

Through Rachel's DNA, a connection with America has been established. In 2020 a virtual reality specialist in America created a facial reconstruction of Somerton Man and a forensic genealogist has also taken up the case. The body was exhumed in 2021 and is undergoing scientific examination.

Despite the efforts of Gerry Feltus and Derek Abbott, there is considerable controversy about their conclusions, between each other, among experts, as well as from online opinioneers. It is not impossible that Somerton Man committed suicide, even though the use of the suspected drugs would be a painful way to die. And where would he have obtained them? If he was murdered, why—and who did it? Who was he and why did he take so much care to confuse his movements? That city's proximity to the top-secret experiments then proceeding at Woomera and elsewhere suggests he might have been a spy of some sort, presumably for Soviet Russia, active in Cold War espionage in Australia. Or something completely different.

Without answers to these and many other questions, the body on Somerton beach will remain the Unknown Man.

THE WEEPING WOMAN

The typed ransom letter was addressed to the then Victorian Minister for the Arts and began:

We have stolen the Picasso from the National Gallery as a protest against the niggardly funding of the fine arts in this hick State and against the clumsy, unimaginative stupidity of the administration and distribution of that funding.

The loss of the painting was discovered early in August 1986. It had not long been purchased for the eye-watering sum of $1.6 million, the highest price an Australian gallery had ever paid for a work up to that time, and was the pride and joy of the National Gallery of Victoria (NGV) collection. Then gallery director, the flamboyant Patrick McCaughey had only launched the wonderful new acquisition eight months earlier, declaring that the beautiful rendition of Picasso's mistress, Dora Maar, 'would haunt Melbourne for the next hundred years'. He was probably right about that, though not in the way he meant.

The note announcing the unauthorised removal of the masterpiece went on to make two demands that needed to be met for the painting to be returned. The artnappers wanted arts funding increased by ten per cent, with an independent committee to oversee distribution, and they wanted a new annual prize for painting by five artists under 30, each to be worth $5000. Cheekily, the prize was to be called the 'Picasso Ransom'.

These conditions were to be met within seven days—or else. A used safety match was included with the note. Clearly, the hijackers of the work had issues.

Pandemonium followed. McCaughey made a desperate search, hoping it was just a prank and that the painting had simply been hidden in the building. The police turned the gallery and grounds upside down and turned over artists' studios. There was consternation in artistic and government circles and when the theft was reported—three days after the event—outcry and angst among the public. Worse, the painting was not insured as the premiums for such a tempting item were too high for the government to contemplate paying.

Then a second note arrived, dated a week after the theft. It called the minister a 'pompous fathead' and stated that 'if our demands are not met, you will begin the long process of carrying about you the smell of kerosene and burning canvas'. Two days later the minister's office received a third letter, including another burned match and notification that 'Phase two begins shortly'.

The original seven-day deadline was now long past and it was not until almost three weeks after the heist that an anonymous phone caller told the press and police to go to locker 227 at Spencer Street (now Southern Cross) railway station.

And there it was.

A brown paper package measuring the same as the missing picture. The package was taken directly to the police forensic laboratory, carefully unwrapped and, to the relief of all, the artwork was found to be unharmed. Another note was with it, stating that the perpetrators had not expected their demands to be met but that their aim had been to call attention to the plight of artists.

The *Weeping Woman* soon returned to her former splendour on a prominent wall of the NGV. But the mystery was not resolved. Who were the thieves?

In place of the missing painting, they left a registration card stating that it had been taken 'to the A.C.T'. This turned out not to be the Australian Capital Territory but the 'Australian Cultural Terrorists', a previously unknown group. Fifty thousand dollars were offered as a reward for information leading to their unmasking and conviction, but there were no takers.

The police suspected it was all a front for a criminal operation, though insiders considered that the thieves were knowledgeable about painting and likely to have been artists themselves, or persons closely involved in the art industry. It was speculated that the theft was a form of homage saluting the notorious theft of the *Mona Lisa* from the Louvre in 1911. Picasso himself was once suspected, incorrectly, of being involved in this caper.

Director McCaughey believed that the theft of the *Weeping Woman* was, to some extent at least, an inside job. Evidence to support these suspicions includes the fact that the masonite board backing the painting, to which notes on its provenance were attached, was not recovered and remain missing. And, in removing the painting from its frame, the thieves needed to use a specialised screwdriver.

Today, the identity of the Australian Cultural Terrorists is still unknown. There are rumours and suspicions, but none have yet come forward or been unmasked as the culprits. Perhaps they never will.

DOING A LORD LUCAN

In November 1974, Sandra Rivett was bludgeoned to death with an unknown weapon in the basement of the Lucan family home in London's swanky Belgravia. Sandra was the 'nanny', or child carer, for the three children of Veronica and Richard John Bingham, the Seventh Earl of Lucan. The no longer happy couple were separated and there had been a custody battle for the children, which Lucan lost. He became increasingly obsessed and began what would today be called 'stalking' his lost family.

On the fatal night, Lucan broke into the family home, murdered Sandra Rivett and attempted to murder Veronica. She managed to escape and he fled to rural Sussex, where he was last seen. At least, that was the last confirmed sighting of the lord.

This very English murder mystery has intrigued the press and public for nearly 50 years. And while the missing Lord Lucan has since been supposedly spotted in many parts of the world, there is a persistent Australian connection with the story. Part of the appeal of the sorry affair revolves around Lucan himself. A classic English aristocrat with the looks, bearing and education to match, he was once said to have been considered for the role of James Bond in one of the early films in the series. Photographs of Lucan show a tall, impeccably groomed and debonair gent. The reality was different.

Despite his breeding, Lucan was not especially wealthy. He was also a gambler, a drinker and, according to Veronica, a wife beater. The expensive trappings of a high lifestyle, including an Aston Martin, international travel and frequenting luxurious clubs, were mostly supported by debt and loans from long-suffering friends. As his custody case went from bad to worse, he became further addicted to gambling and drink and increasingly indebted. Friends became concerned about his mental state.

After the killing of Sandra Rivett and the attempt on his wife's life, Lucan drove around, contacted friends and wrote some letters reflecting his addled state, though denying his guilt and blaming a violent intruder. Bloodstained pipes were later found in his abandoned car, along with other incriminating evidence. His wallet, passport and other items were also found in the car. At the inquest, Lucan was declared the murderer of Sandra Rivett and subsequent legal proceedings dragged on for years. Lord Lucan himself was not officially declared dead until the issue of a certificate in 2016.

But was he? Many suspected suicide. The items left in the bloody car certainly pointed to that conclusion, but others were not so sure. These uncertainties provided unending fodder for media speculation and there are few places in the world where the disappearing aristocrat has not been 'seen', including several reports in Australia during the 1970s and some more recently.

In 2003, news broke that a former Scotland Yard detective had tracked Lucan down in Perth. He was said to be a folk musician playing with a popular local bush band. The incongruity between the image of the sophisticated lord and a scruffy fiddler was startling. The musicians in the band were uproariously amused and few others found the claim to be credible. They were right. It was a case of very mistaken identity. The fiddling 'Lord Lucan' had by then left the bush band and the country. When finally located in South Africa, he was exactly who he claimed to be.

Sightings of the fugitive lord have continued ever since. The latest was in early 2020, once again with an Australian connection. Media outlets reported that an Englishman named

Neil Berriman had discovered that he was the son of the murdered Sandra Rivett. He took it upon himself to investigate the Lucan case and to hunt down the man who had killed his mother. According to Berriman, Lucan, now an old and ailing man, was living in a suburban Perth share house as a bewhiskered Buddhist. This information has been passed to Scotland Yard though, at the time of writing, police have made no comment beyond stating that the case is still open.

The eventual issuing of the death certificate allowed Lord Lucan's son, George, to inherit his father's title and to sit in the House of Lords. Lady Lucan suicided in the family's Belgravia home in 2017, apparently wrongly believing that she was suffering from Parkinson's disease. When her will was read, it was found that she had disinherited all three of her children and left the estate to a charity for the homeless.

MR BROWN

Was it a hoax, or the real thing?

'Just call me Mr Brown', said the man who telephoned Qantas House in Sydney on 26 May 1971. He said that there was a bomb aboard Flight 755 from Sydney to Hong Kong. If he was not given half a million dollars it would explode as the plane and its nearly 130 passengers and crew landed. The caller had left a duplicate bomb in a locker at Mascot (Sydney) Airport as proof that he was serious.

He was. When police opened locker 84, they found a gelignite bomb connected to an altimeter and several notes, one saying that the plane would explode if it flew below 20,000 feet (6000 meters). The bomb in the locker was disarmed. The gelignite was replaced with a light bulb and the disarmed device rushed to another plane to confirm the exact altitude at which it would detonate. It turned out to be 5000 feet.

Aboard Flight 755, Captain William Selwyn, then over Dalby in Queensland, was told to keep his plane at 20,000 feet and divert to Brisbane. Crew began searching the aircraft, telling the passengers only that there was a technical problem. Brisbane airport refused to take the Boeing so Selwyn was directed back to Sydney, flying as slowly as possible while authorities on the ground negotiated with Mr Brown. Circling over the sea, Selwyn radioed that he would need to land no later than 7 p.m.

It was not until 5.45 p.m. that Captain R.J. Ritchie of Qantas emerged from Qantas House carrying two large suitcases. He went towards a yellow Kombi van waiting outside the building in Chifley Square and pushed the suitcases into the vehicle, as directed. Police were watching but, for some reason, were unable to follow the van and Mr Brown got clean away with half a million dollars.

But Captain Selwyn, with his planeload of people, was still circling Mascot, increasingly anxious about his fuel level. In the air and on the ground, everyone waited. Television news had picked up the story, and as the minutes ticked by the nation was transfixed. At last, Mr Brown called to say, 'There is no bomb aboard the plane. You can land her safely.' Selwyn had sixteen minutes of flying time left when he finally brought Flight 755 to a safe landing.

Attention now turned to tracking the mysterious Mr Brown. Police forces at home and abroad swung into action. A $50,000 reward was offered and an identikit face was created. Police even came up with a plastic replica of a bespectacled and moustachioed man looking disturbingly like the doll Barbie's male friend Ken. It was not until some months later that Mr Brown's accomplice, Raymond Poynting, began driving around in newly acquired luxury cars that the hunt ended. Suspicions were raised and reported. The police followed up with some surveillance and arrested Poynting, who quickly confessed.

But where was Mr Brown and who was he? Following Poynting's information, it wasn't long before police tracked down the elusive extortionist. He turned out to be a British migrant named Peter Macari. Charged together with Poynting, Macari claimed that there was a mysterious mastermind behind the crime and that he was only a dupe. He had given over $200,000 of the ransom to this man he called 'Ken'. Nobody believed him, including the judge, who gave him fifteen years and Poynting seven years.

Police had by then recovered just over half of the booty, secreted in various suburban locations around inner Sydney. But the rest is still missing. Local lore has it that the money is lying in a couple of metal containers or safes somewhere off Bondi Beach.

Macari was released from prison after serving eight years and deported, aboard a Qantas flight, to his homeland, the United Kingdom. He and his audacious crime were the subject of a 1985 movie and a folk parody that plays the hoax for laughs.

But the Qantas extortion was not the only Mr Brown mystery. Macari was using the alias William Day while enjoying the high living his loot allowed. William, or 'Billy', Day vanished in Queensland in 1970 while visiting that state together with Macari. Almost a quarter of a century after Day's disappearance New South Wales police interviewed Peter Macari, then running a fish and chip shop in Brighton, England. He claimed to know nothing about Billy Day, saying he had simply plucked the name out of the air. But there were several witnesses who remembered the two men living together in Australia. The police formed a view that Macari probably murdered Day and stole his identity.

It seems that there was not enough evidence to take the case any further. But there was still one more twist in this extraordinary tale.

Macari may also have murdered his own brother. George Macari went missing in England in 1962, before Peter migrated to Australia. It was five years before they found the body, but the case remained open. British police reviewed this murder in 2017 and nominated Peter Macari as the most likely killer. But by then Peter Macari, alias Mr Brown, alias William Day, had been dead for four years, taking his secrets with him to the grave.

LUNA PARK GHOSTS

The ghost train was one of the most popular attractions at Sydney's Luna Park. Around 10.15 on the night of 9 June 1979, a fire started inside the ride. Efforts to extinguish the blaze were futile and the entire structure was destroyed. When investigators were able to approach the site, they found the bodies of one man and six children.

Established in 1935, Luna Park quickly became an iconic attraction on the northern side of Sydney Harbour. Generations of Sydneysiders and visitors thrilled to the flashing lights, grinding music, whirling dodgems and laughing clowns. The striking entry to the fun was through the mouth of a giant face, thought to have been originally modelled on an early twentieth century nightclub in Paris called 'Hell'. Ownership of the park changed hands many times and the piece of harbourside real estate on which it stood became increasingly valuable and sought after by various interests.

One of these was Sydney 'identity' Abe Saffron, rumoured to have been the 'Mr Big' and also 'Mr Sin' of organised crime in the city (see Beneath the Three Ugly Sisters?). Saffron was known to use arson in pursuit of his business interests, though he denied involvement in the ghost train fire. After the tragedy, Luna Park was closed. Most of it was demolished but not all, and a new one constructed. The state government sold the site to a consortium that included Saffron's nephew, as well as others with links to Mr Big.

The police investigation into the fire had been perfunctory and the coronial inquiry little better. Electrical and other equipment faults were ruled out and there was no evidence of a carelessly extinguished cigarette. The inquiry arrived at the astounding conclusion that, while the owners had failed in their duty of care, there was not a sufficiently 'high degree of negligence necessary to support a charge of criminal negligence'. A National Crime Authority (NCA) corruption investigation reopened the case in the 1980s. The police investigation and the coronial inquiry were both criticised, but the NCA was unable to establish what, or who, had caused the fire. According to a statement made in 2007 by a niece of Abe Saffron, later retracted, Saffron was responsible for the fire, though the deaths were unintended.

This being a Sydney mystery, crime, corruption and suspicion are to be expected. In the case of the ghost train tragedy, these elements were fused with a slightly satanic aura. One of the dead children had been pictured in a newspaper with a man wearing a devil costume. In some quarters, this was linked to the ghostly and occult imagery and atmosphere of Luna Park and the ghost train itself.

Luna Park was reopened in the 1980s, closed again and, amid great public controversy and advocacy, eventually given legal protection by the state government. Subsequent owners developed and redeveloped the site, often in conflict with local residents taking legal action over noise and disruption to their amenity. Today, Luna Park remains a cherished part of Sydney lore and community heritage.

Memorials to those who died in the fire have been erected at various times and at various locations around the park. One by artist and Luna Park aficionado Martin Sharp is said to have disappeared during a refurbishment and at least one other has come and gone. There is a commemorative plaque naming the victims of the fire and a memorial in Art Barton Park at Milsons Point. It is a beautifully whimsical sculpture by famed cartoonist Michael Leunig atop a stone block. The inscription is simply the names of those who died in the ghost train fire:

John Godson
Damien Godson
Craig Godson
Richard Carroll
Jonathan Billings
Seamus Rahilly
Michael Johnson.

In 2021, a survivor of the fire, Jason Holman, broke decades of silence to speak about the trauma of the event and his later relationship with Martin Sharp. It seems that Sharp had collected a vast archive of relevant documents about the tragedy prior to his death in 2013. He did not believe the fire was accidental, nor do Jason Holman or Jenny Godson, the only survivor of her family. The two have carried on Sharp's work and made his evidence available to the ABC, which aired 'Exposed: The Ghost Train Fire' in March 2021. Once again, Mr Sin was named as a prime suspect. This led to a new investigation by the New South Wales police, the results of which will hopefully settle the matter and bring some consolation to the families of the victims. In July 2021, the New South Wales government offered a reward of one million dollars for further significant information about the incident.

WHERE'S PADDY?

In an isolated township of eleven people, one man goes missing. And then there were ten. Did he have an accident in the endless emptiness? Or was it a more sinister occurrence? Not too many suspects for police to interview. Should be an open and shut case.

As every Arthur Conan Doyle reader knows, the suave criminal mastermind Professor Moriarty was Sherlock Holmes's arch enemy. Paddy Moriarty, by contrast, was a knockabout bush character who disappeared from the Northern Territory hamlet of Larrimah without trace or reason. The vanishing of 70-year-old Paddy Moriarty and his kelpie, Kellie, is a case so puzzling that even the great fictional detective would be hard pressed to solve it.

On 16 December 2017, Moriarty and Kellie finished up their regular afternoon session at the Pink Panther Hotel and headed home to Paddy's place on his quad bike. They never came back. Next day, Barry Sharpe, the publican and Paddy's mate, went to find out what had happened. Paddy's reading glasses and hats were all in his home, together with the remains of some chicken given to him by a passing tourist. Everything was perfectly normal. But Paddy and Kellie were not there.

Paddy had still not turned up the next day, and on the nineteenth Barry reported the disappearance. Larrimah is on the Stuart Highway, more than 400 kilometres south-east of Darwin and several hours from the nearest police station. When police arrived, the locals were already out searching the scrub. The search was expanded with police and emergency services personnel and air support. They looked in searing heat until sunset on 23 December. Nothing. It was looking as if the 'Highway of Death', notorious for unexplained disappearances, had claimed another victim (see Highways of Death).

Paddy was known to be under treatment for a heart condition and it was feared he might have had an accident and, without his medication, perished. But what about Kellie? And why would he leave his hat at home if he went for a walk in the December heat? Checks on Paddy's bank showed he had not accessed his account since his disappearance. It didn't add up.

By the time detectives came onto the case Paddy had been missing for days, further complicating an already perplexing situation. But the police were sure of one thing: Paddy had not met with an accident. Nor had he been consumed by the crocodile known as 'Sneaky Sam', an attraction in the wildlife menagerie kept behind the Pink Panther for the amusement of tourists. The police checked. Someone, or someones, had murdered Paddy Moriarty.

A second, more focused search after Christmas failed to find anything relevant in the local tip, in dams, in any sinkholes or among the ruins of the World War II army staging camp nearby. Suspicion fell upon the remaining residents of Larrimah.

The tiny community rubbed along most of the time, it seems, but there were tensions. The otherwise jovial Paddy had an intense dislike of Fran Hodgetts who owned the Devonshire Tea House opposite his home. Her pies were famous, but Paddy was vociferous in expressing his dislike of them. Barry's pub also began to sell pies, which Paddy promoted with a provocative sign directing customers away from the Tea House and towards the Pink Panther, where he worked as well as drank. The feud intensified. At various times, dead 'roos had appeared beneath Fran's bedroom window and there was no love lost between the two.

While admitting that her relationship with Paddy was toxic, Fran denied any wrongdoing. Paddy could be argumentative, and she was not his only enemy in the settlement. But police investigated all the possible angles and have found no evidence against her. Or against anyone else.

Since Paddy's vanishing, Larrimah has begun to change. Some have left. Barry Sharpe died in 2019. The local Wubalawun people have won their native title claim, including a one square kilometre section of the township where Paddy's house is situated. They intend to build homes for their people with a view to the future running of Larrimah.

The quirky character of this mystery has attracted worldwide attention. It has been the subject of articles and documentaries and also featured in books of unsolved crimes. An award-winning podcast and a tenacious detective who has vowed never to give up on the case have also helped to keep the story in the public eye. It is very likely to remain there. In early 2021 the Northern Territory Police offered a $250,000 reward that may yet lead to Paddy Moriarty being found.

THE PORTUGUESE PLATYPUS AND THE SICILIAN COCKATOO

One of the many myths of *terra australis incognita*—the unknown south land—is that the Portuguese navigators made it that far south. There are wrecks and artefact finds that are claimed, by some, to be Portuguese and so to prove those adventurous mariners were present early along Australian coasts, as were the English and Dutch.

The navigational skills of Portuguese explorers were certainly extraordinary and provided the basis for what became a global empire, so it is certainly conceivable that they did visit Australia. The Spanish were also famed navigators and empire builders. Unfortunately, no one has yet found any incontrovertible evidence that either the Portuguese or the Spanish did reach Australia, despite some impressive manipulation and interpretations of old maps and charts.

Robert Bremner, himself a historian, lived for many years in Portugal and some years in Mozambique. He was once told by a long-time English resident of Lisbon that the sixteenth century choir stalls of Viseu Cathedral bore an extraordinary wooden carving. It was described by some as a 'duck-billed rat' and Robert was intrigued. He took the time to visit Viseu and found the choir stall, now apparently upstairs in the museum, and snapped a photograph or two. The carving certainly looks like a platypus, the odd creature unique to Australia. If it were, it would certainly strengthen the case for an early Portuguese encounter with the great south land.

And perhaps of even more unknown encounters with the native animals of the unknown south land.

Back in the thirteenth century, the Holy Roman Emperor was King Frederick II of Sicily. Like other rich and powerful monarchs of the time, he was a keen falconer and commissioned the writing of a book titled, in English, *The Art of Hunting with Birds*. Thought to have been put together in the 1240s, this book is now among the many riches held by the Vatican Library in Rome. Finnish scholars working on this manuscript in 2015 were intrigued to find four drawings of what could only be a cockatoo. These were 250 years older than what was then thought to be the earliest European representation of a cockatoo, which itself dated from centuries before the earliest known European contact with the continent we now know as Australia.

The bird in the book had been given to Frederick by another potentate, described as the 'Sultan of Babylon', actually the fourth Ayyubid Sultan of Egypt (al-Kamil), as part of the diplomatic backscratching that went on then, as it does today. So it seemed that the cocky had somehow got to Egypt first and then been transported north to the Mediterranean island of Sicily.

The bird could not have flown there, so how could this be?

Expert examination of the images suggested that the cocky was likely to have been a species from northern Australia, New Guinea or Indonesia, as we now know these islands. In recent years, evidence of extensive thirteenth century trade exchanges between China, India and the islands of south Asia has come to light as researchers gain access to previously unavailable historical sources. These distant places were connected to Europe through a network of routes often known as the 'Silk Road', passing through the Middle East. This was a relatively secure and efficient trade route, though it often took many years for goods to pass backwards and forwards along it.

Cockatoos, of course, are famously long-lived. It is surmised that this one was captured in its native habitat, possibly the northern tip of Australia, and carried carefully along the trade routes to Egypt. From there, she (probably) became an impressively exotic gift from one ruler to another, simultaneously signalling the wealth and prestige of the Sultan of Babylon and flattering Frederick II. It seems to have worked. There are four high-quality drawings of the cocky in Frederick's book of birds, suggesting that he thought a good deal of his present.

What happened to the cockatoo? We don't know. Frederick II died just a few years after his bird book was compiled. Most likely the cockatoo lived a long, if lonely, life only to be forgotten until researchers began to unlock another of the many mysteries of Australia, past and present.

ACKNOWLEDGEMENTS

For all kinds of help in the making of this book, my thanks to Maureen Seal, Kylie Seal-Pollard, Rob Willis, Robert Bremner and Warren Fahey, and to Elizabeth Weiss and staff at Allen & Unwin.

IMAGE CREDITS

CHAPTER 1

Portrait of Amata traditional owner Stanley Douglas at Cave Hill, Amata; 5 August 2017, photo by Wolter Peeters, Fairfax Media, IMAGE ID FXB321316.

CHAPTER 2

Brandard, Edward Paxman & Booth, Edwin Carton & Prout, John Skinner, 1874, *Old Whaling Station* [picture]/S. Prout; E. Brandard, National Library of Australia, nla.obj-138427282.

CHAPTER 3

Yankee Ned and his grandchildren, Torres Strait Island Region, 20 July 1911, Queensland State Archives, IMAGE ID ITM1443437.

CHAPTER 4

Three Austrian girls with a cart waiting for their ration allowance at the German Molonglo Internment Camp, Canberra, Australian Capital Territory, c. 1918 Australian War Memorial, IMAGE ID H17417.

CHAPTER 5

[Untitled studio portrait of an explorer ?], attributed to the Sydney photographer William Hetzer, c. 1870–81, Mitchell Library, State Library of New South Wales, IMAGE ID 889891.

CHAPTER 6

Inside the head keeper's quarters, the window facing south towards the lighthouse on South Solitary Island, Deb Masters/ Jo Young, 6 August 2019.

CHAPTER 7

Juanita Nielsen, 11 March 1968, photo by Richard John Pinfold, Fairfax Media, IMAGE ID FXB385923.

CHAPTER 8

Qantas bomb hoaxer Peter Macari (aka 'Mr Brown') is deported from Sydney, New South Wales, 12 November 1980, photo by News Ltd, Newspix, IMAGE ID NP1186031.

FRONT COVER

Campfire yarns, near Hay, New South Wales, 1954, taken by Jeff Carter, National Library of Australia, nla.obj-254407943.

NOTES

In order of reference within each tale

CHAPTER 1 MYSTERIES OF A NEW LAND

LOST AND FOUND CONTINENTS

Umberto Eco, *The Book of Legendary Lands* (trans. Alastair McEwen), MacLehose Press: London, 2013, pp. 182ff.

Patrick D. Nunn, *Vanished Islands and Hidden Continents of the Pacific*, University of Hawai'i Press: Honolulu, 2009.

Patrick D. Nunn and Nicholas J. Reid, 'Aboriginal Memories of Inundation of the Australian Coast Dating from More than 7000 Years Ago', *Australian Geographer*, 2015, Vol. 47, No. 1.

Zaria Gorvett, 'The Missing Continent it Took 375 Years to Find', *BBC Future*, 8 February 2021, bbc.com/future/article/20210205-the-last-secrets-of-the-worlds-lost-continent, accessed May 2021.

AN UNKNOWN SOUTH LAND

Mike Dash, 'Dreamtime Voyagers: Aboriginal Australians in Early Modern Makassar', *A Blast from the Past*, 31 October 2016, mikedashhistory.com/2016/10/31/dreamtime-voyagers-australian-aborigines-in-early-modern-makassar/, accessed August 2020.

John Perkins, 'The Indian Ocean and Swahili Coast Coins, International Networks and Local Developments', *Afriques*, June 2015, journals.openedition.org/afriques/1769; DOI: doi.org/10.4000/afriques.1769, accessed August 2020.

THE SEVENTH SISTER?

Efrosyni Boutsikas, Stephen C. McCluskey and John Steele (eds), *Advancing Cultural Astronomy: Studies in Honour of Clive Ruggles*, Springer International Publishing: Springer-Verlag GmbH, Heidelberg, 2021.

The National Museum of Australia has an online audiovisual presentation of the Aboriginal-led exhibition *Songlines: Tracking the Seven Sisters* available at nma.gov.au/exhibitions/songlines, accessed February 2021.

SACRED STONES

Badimia Land Aboriginal Corporation, badimia.org.au/badimia-heritage-surveys/, accessed May 2021.

Chee Chee Leung, 'Rocky Ways to Secrets of Skies', *The Age*, 2 August 2008, theage.com.au/national/rocky-ways-to-secrets-of-skies-20080801-3omb.html, accessed February 2020.

Ray P. Norris, Cilla Norris, Duane W. Hamacher and Reg Abrahams, 'Wurdi Youang: An Australian Aboriginal stone arrangement with possible solar indications', *Rock Art Research*, October 2013, Vol. 30, No. 1, pp. 55–65, aboriginalastronomy.com.au/wp-content/uploads/2020/02/Hamacher-2012-Wurdi-Youang.pdf, accessed February 2020.

Peter Randolph, 'Some Indigenous Stone Arrangements in the South of Western Australia', *Records of the Western Australian Museum*, 2011, Supplement 79, p. 56, museum.wa.gov.au/sites/default/files/5. Randolph.pdf, accessed February 2020.

Heather Threadgold and David Jones, 'What the Stones Tell Us? Aboriginal Stone Sites, Indigenous Landscapes and *Country's* in the Face of Urban Sprawl', UHPH 2018: *Remaking Cities: Proceedings of the 14th Australasian Urban History Planning History Conference*, apo.org.au/sites/default/files/resource-files/2018-06/apo-nid212851.pdf, accessed May 2021.

GONNEVILLE'S LAND

Margaret Sankey, 'The French and *Terra Australis*', 2003 Sonia Marks Lecture, University of Sydney, 15 April 2003, *Sydney Open Journals Online*, openjournals.library.sydney.edu.au/index.php/ART/article/viewFile/5628/6319, accessed October 2020.

THE *FLOWER OF THE SEA*

Mohd. Sherman bin Sauffi, 'Flor De La Mar: An Early Epilogue of the Lost Ship 1511', *Wrecksite*, 1 January 2009, wrecksite.eu/docBrowser.aspx?353?1?1, accessed February 2021.

Pascal Kainic, 'The Elusive Wreck of the Portuguese Carrack Flor do [sic] Mar', 2013 at *The Scuba News,* thescubanews.com/2013/09/30/the-elusive-wreck-of-the-portuguese-carrack-flor-do-mar/, accessed June 2017.

THE PHANTOM ROCKS

All Brookes's quotations from original correspondence in Jeremy Green, *Australia's Oldest Wreck: The Loss of the Trial, 1622*, British Archaeological Reports, Supplementary Series 27, 1977.

'A NEW RACE OF BEINGS'

Anonymous, 'Discovery of a White Colony on the Northern Shore of New Holland', *The Leeds Mercury*, 25 January 1834. The article also appeared in Australian newspapers, including *The Hobart Town Courier*, 25 July 1834, p. 4.

Thomas J. Maslen, *The Friend of Australia*, Smith, Elder & Co, Cornhill: London, 1830.

SPAIN SETTLES AUSTRALIA

Alison Bevege, 'How shipwreck hunter's search for a sunken galleon and lost engraved stone could rewrite Australian history by proving the Spanish landed more than a CENTURY before Captain Cook', *Daily Mail* (Australia), 13 April 2020, dailymail. co.uk/news/article-8199885/Man-hunts-lost-Spanish-galleon-engraved-stones-prove-Australia-settled-Spain.html, accessed February 2021.

Matt Neal, 'Mahogany Ship legend promised to rewrite Australian history, but is it just 19th-century fake news?', *ABC*, South West Victoria, 11 January 2020, abc.net.au/news/2020-01-11/mahogany-ship-legend-promised-to-rewrite-australian-history/11721884, accessed May 2021.

Hotli Simanjuntak, 'Resident finds gold coins dating back to ancient Aceh', *The Jakarta Post*, 13 November 2013, thejakartapost.com/news/2013/11/13/resident-finds-gold-coins-dating-back-ancient-aceh.html, accessed September 2016.

Kylie Stevenson, '"It Could Change Everything": Coin Found off Northern Australia May be From Pre-1400 Africa', *The Guardian*, 12 May 2019, theguardian.com/australia-news/2019/may/12/it-could-change-everything-coin-found-off-northern-australia-may-be-from-pre-1400-africa, accessed May 2021.

James H. Watson, 'The Spaniards at Port Curtis', *The Sydney Morning Herald*, 29 February 1912, p. 12.

THE HAIRY FOLK

Ernest Favenc, 'A Haunt of the Jinkarras. A Story of Central Australia' in *Tales of the Austral Tropics*, Osgood, McIlvaine & Co: London, 1894, pp. 39–55.

Tony Healey and Paul Cropper, 'Close Encounters With "Littlefoot", *Nexus*, April–May 2007, Vol. 14, No. 3, pp. 57ff.

Tony Healey and Paul Cropper, 'Pygmy elder faces eviction', *The Courier Mail*, 25 August 2007, https://www.couriermail.com.au/news/queensland/pygmy-elder-faces-eviction/news-story/7556feda80338ffcedda2c5ff9a1d351?sv=92d6483855d8b16adfe1b26eb0eacae8, accessed December 2020.

Austin Whittall, 'Australian Pygmies, fact and fiction', *Patagonian Monsters*, 13 October 2019, patagoniamonsters.blogspot. com/2019/10/australian-pygmies-fact-and-fiction.html, accessed February 2020.

MARK OF THE WITCH

William Allison's almanac and notebook, Tasmanian Archives, TAHO NS261/1/1.
Ian J. Evans, 'Defence Against the Devil: Apotropaic Marks in Australia', *Academia*, academia.edu/4148179/Defence_Against_ the_Devil_Apotropaic_Marks_in_Australia, accessed August 2020.
Meg Mundell, 'Spirit Levels: The Hidden Realm of Spatial Magic', *Meanjin,* Winter 2013, Vol. 72, No. 2, pp. 38–46.

CHAPTER 2 STRANGE SEAS

THE *FLYING DUTCHMAN* DOWN UNDER

George Barrington, *A Voyage to Botany Bay, with a description of the country, manners, customs, religion, &c. of the natives*, sold by H.D. Symonds: London, 1795.
Prince Albert Victor and Prince George of Wales, *The Cruise of Her Majesty's Ship 'Bacchante' 1879–1882. Compiled from the private journals, letters, and note-books of Prince Albert Victor and Prince George of Wales, with additions by J. D. Dalton*, Vol. 1, Macmillan and Company: London, 1886, p. 551.

THE DEADWATER WRECK

Joseph Catanzaro, 'Shipwreck hunter close to lost treasure', *The West Australian*, 8 September 2012, thewest.com.au/news/wa/shipwreck-hunter-close-to-lost-treasure-ng-ya-298181, accessed February 2021.
Rupert Gerritsen, 'An Historical Analysis of wrecks in the vicinity of the Deadwater, Wonnerup, Western Australia', Department of Maritime Archaeology report, Western Australian Museum, No. 97, 1995.
Helen McCall, 'Examination and evaluation of evidence relating to the Deadwater Wreck and other hidden wrecks in the Vasse–Wonnerup region', Maritime Archaeological Association of Western Australia Inc., static1.squarespace.com/static/56d7e469b6aa604e5de26ebf/ t/577ddde2d482e949405a75e8/1467866655256/ Deadwater+Wreck++Helen+McCall.pdf, accessed February 2021.
Adam Poulsen, 'Hunting for wrecks and bones: islands reveal their secrets', *Midwest Times*, 25 July 2019, midwesttimes.com.au/news/ midwest-times/hunting-for-wrecks-and-bones-islands-reveal-their-secrets-ng-b881265204z, accessed February 2021.

E.L. Grant Wilson, *Journey Under the Southern Stars*, Ablard–
Schuman Ltd: London, 1968, p. 75.

THE LOST WHALEMEN
'Miscellaneous Shipping', *The Hobart Town Daily Mercury*,
28 November 1859, p. 2.
S. Chamberlain, 'The Hobart Whaling Industry', PhD thesis, La Trobe
University, 1988.
C.H. Ringrose, 'Whaling Days', *The Age*, 21 September 1935, p. 6.
L.L. Robson, 'Tasmanian Songs', *Australian Tradition,* July 1965,
pp. 3–4; quoted in Mark Gregory, *Australian Folksongs,*
folkstream.com/reviews/robson.html, accessed May 2021. For
a recording and some details of the original interview see also
*J.H. Davies interviewed by Lloyd Robson in the Norm O'Connor
folklore collection*, sound recording, 1960, trove.nla.gov.au/
work/17761788?selectedversion=NBD6942460, accessed February
2021.
M. Nash, *The Bay Whalers: Tasmania's shore-based whaling industry,*
Navarine Publishing: Canberra, 2003.

THE SPECTRE OF ARMIT ISLAND
'The Phantom Sailor', *Bowen Independent*, 11 April 1941, p. 4.

THE HEADLESS ANGEL
'Collision with an Iceberg', *South Australian Register*, 6 February
1899, p. 6.
The Conradian: The journal of the Joseph Conrad Society (UK),
2007, Vols 32–33, The Society, p. 134.
A. Morgan, *The Shipwreck Watch: A Journal of Macquarie Island
Shipwreck Stories*, 1973–2000, Vol. 13, parks.tas.gov.au/fahan_
mi_shipwrecks/journals/Shipwrecks/swangel14.pdf, accessed
June 2018.

THE MYSTERY OF THE *MADAGASCAR*
'Shipping Intelligence', *The Argus,* 4 May 1854, p. 4.
Evening News (Sydney), 21 December 1872, p. 3.
John Earnshaw, 'Hayes, William Henry (Bully) (1829–1877)',
Australian Dictionary of Biography, National Centre of Biography,
Australian National University, adb.anu.edu.au/biography/hayes-
william-henry-bully-3737/text5879, published first in hardcopy
1972, accessed online 7 August 2020.
Ben Langford, 'In search of the Madagascar frigate's treasure',
Illawarra Mercury, 9 May 2014, illawarramercury.com.au/
story/2271487/in-search-of-the-madagascar-frigates-treasure/,
accessed February 2021.

Lurline Stuart, 'The Lost Gold Ship', *La Trobe Journal*, No. 67, Autumn 2001, www3.slv.vic.gov.au/latrobejournal/issue/latrobe-67/t1-g-t2.html, accessed August 2020.

AUSTRALIA'S *TITANIC*

Mike Dash, 'Waratah: a fresh look at the legend of the bloody swordsman', *A Fortean in the Archives*, 8 July 2009, aforteantin thearchives.wordpress.com/2009/07/08/waratah-a-fresh-look-at-the-legend-of-the-bloody-swordsman/, accessed February 2021.

Wikipedia contributors, 'SS Waratah', *Wikipedia, The Free Encyclopedia*, 12 May 2021, en.wikipedia.org/w/index.php?title=SS_Waratah&oldid=1022804311, accessed May 2021.

WRAITH OF THE *KØBENHAVN*

'SV København (+1928)' Wrecksite, wrecksite.eu/wreck.aspx?58328, accessed May 2021.

'Ocean Mystery Deepens', *Daily Standard*, Brisbane, 19 July 1929, p. 6. This report was later contradicted in *The Telegraph*, Brisbane, 6 September 1929.

'The København', Port Germein History, portgermeinhistory.com/KobenhavnDiaries.html, accessed May 2021 .

'Kobenhaven Theory Doubted', *Newcastle Morning Herald and Miner's Advocate*, 27 September 1935, p. 10.

Hamish A.C. Ross, 'The Key to the København Mystery', *Seabreezes*, 21 May 2013.

THE FATE OF *PATANELA*

Janice Jarrett, 'Operation Lilac: The Mystery of the *Patanela*', *Platypus News*, 36, July 1992, p. 14.

Paul Whittaker and Robert Reid, *Patanela is Missing: Australia's greatest sea mystery*, Bantam: Sydney, 1993.

FINDING *ENDEAVOUR*

Kristin Romey, 'No, Captain Cook's Ship Hasn't Been Found Yet', *National Geographic*, 19 September 2018, nationalgeographic.com/news/2016/04/20160504-Cook-Endeavour-shipwreck-discovery-Newport-underwater-archaeology/, accessed February 2021.

THE VANISHING WRECKS OF WAR

Kathryn Miles, 'The Thieves Who Steal Sunken Warships, Right Down to the Bolts', *Outside*, 2 May 2017, outsideonline.com/2168646/how-does-entire-shipwreck-disappear-bolts-and-all, accessed February 2021.

Tom Metcalfe, 'WWII Shipwrecks "Vanish" After Plundering by Illegal Scavengers', *LiveScience*, 22 November 2016, livescience.com/56965-wwii-shipwrecks-vanish-after-illegal-plundering.html, accessed February 2021.

CHAPTER 3 LOST TREASURES

YAMADA NAGAMASA'S HOARD

C.B. Christesen, *Queensland Journey*, Official Guide, Queensland
Government Tourist Bureau, P.A. Meehan Publicity Service, 1937,
p. 383.

TREASURE OF THE *GILT DRAGON*

Gilt Dragon Research Group, on Facebook, facebook.com/giltdragon.
com.au/photos/a.698138343629042.1073741854.125823890860
493/698138360295707/?type=1&theater, accessed October 2016.
At the time of writing no further word on the authenticity of the
documents had appeared.

THAT CURSED SHORE

'The Boyd incident', nzhistory.govt.nz/culture/maori-european-contact-
before-1840/the-boyd-incident (Ministry for Culture and Heritage),
updated 11 March 2014, accessed May 2021.

'The King of the Cannibal Islands' broadsheet, 18 September
1858, held in National Library of Scotland, deriv.nls.uk/
dcn3/7441/74414520.3.jpg, accessed November 2016.

Alexander Berry, *The Edinburgh Magazine and Literary Miscellany*,
1819, Vol. 83, p. 313.

Augustus Earle, *A Narrative of Nine Months' Residence in New
Zealand in 1827*, Whitcombe & Tombs Limited: London, 1909,
Chapter 11.

Eric Ramsden, 'The Massacre of the Boyd', *The World's News,*
29 April 1939, p. 6.

Ewan Stephenson, 'Boyd', *Archaehistoria,* archaehistoria.org/
new-zealand-sites/4-boyd, accessed November 2016.

THE *HOPE* TREASURE

'Loss of the Hope', *Colonial Times and Tasmanian Advertiser*, 4 May
1827, p. 2.

Captain Harry O'May, *Wrecks in Tasmanian Waters, 1797–1950*,
Tasmanian Government Printer: Hobart, 1956.

FATAL MYSTERIES OF THE *GENERAL GRANT*

William Sanguily narrative, http://www.wreckofthegeneralgrant.com/
page15.htm, accessed November 2016. Sanguily's full family name
was Sanguily Garrite.

Joseph Jewell to his father, Captain John Jewell, Clovelly, Devon,
16 July 1868, http://www.wreckofthegeneralgrant.com/page14.htm,
accessed November 2016.

James Teer, 'Narrative of a Passenger', *Otago Daily Times*, 4 February
1868, Issue 1902, p. 9 (Supplement), paperspast.natlib.govt.nz/
newspapers/ODT18680204.2.24.3, accessed November 2016.

'The Wreck of the *General Grant*', Maritime Archaeological Association of New Zealand, maanz.org.nz/projects/gengrant.html, accessed November 2016.

LOST AND FOUND IN THE TORRES STRAIT

'Sunken Treasure in Torres Straits', *The Brisbane Courier*, 7 April 1897, p. 6.

P. Gesner and G. Hitchcock, 'Two nineteenth century copper ingots from waters off Mabuyag, Torres Strait', in Ian J. McNiven and Garrick Hitchcock (eds), *Goemulgaw Lagal: Cultural and Natural Histories of the Island of Mabuyag, Torres Strait*, Memoirs of the Queensland Museum, June 2015, Vol. 8, Pt. 2, pp. 531–569.

BUSHRANGING BOOTY

'The Gold Escort Robbery', *Empire*, 24 June 1862, p. 8.

'Eugowra Gold Escort Robbery', *The Grenfell Record and Lachlan District Advertiser*, 11 June 1942, p. 1.

YANKEE NED'S PEARLS

'Torres Straits and Thursday Island Notes', *The Northern Miner*, 27 December 1912, p. 3.

'Yankee Ned—An Island Legend', *Stories from the Archives,* Queensland State Archives, 21 July 2016, blogs.archives.qld.gov.au/2016/07/21/yankee-ned-an-island-legend/, accessed February 2021.

C. Coral, 'Romance of a Yankee Sailor: An Episode of Torres Strait', *The Argus*, 11 March 1933, p. 6.

GIPPSLAND GOLD

Sarah Maunder and Rachael Lucas, 'Are Martin Weiberg's stolen gold sovereigns buried somewhere in Gippsland?', *ABC News*, 29 October 2019, abc.net.au/news/2019-09-19/what-happened-to-martin-weibergs-missing-treasure/11485278, accessed February 2021.

Annie O'Reilly, 'Buried Treasures', *Odd Australian History*, 6 September 2013, oddhistory.com.au/gippsland/buried-treasures/, accessed February 2021. This article also tracks down the history of Weiberg's family after his disappearance.

THE MOTHER SHIPTON NUGGET

'Mining Memoranda', *The Temora Star*, 17 September 1881, p. 3.

'Mother Shipton's Prophecy', handwritten document, National Museum of Australia, collectionsearch.nma.gov.au/ce/mother%20shipton%20prophecies?object=123740, accessed May 2021.

'News of the Day', *The Sydney Morning Herald*, 26 November 1885, p. 9.

'Notes from London', *The Kalgoorlie Western Argus*, 9 October 1906, p. 24.

NO TRACE OF THE MACE

'The Victorian Mace Stolen', *The Maitland Mercury and Hunter River General Advertiser*, 13 October 1891, p. 8.

Raymond Wright, *Who Stole the Mace?*, Victorian Parliamentary Library: Melbourne, 1991.

CHAPTER 4 RIDDLES OF WAR

LOST IN CELTIC WOOD

'On this day . . . 9 October', Australian Defence Department, webarchive.nla.gov.au/awa/20050801054049/http://pandora.nla.gov.au/pan/51715/20050801-0000/www.defence.gov.au/army/ahu/On_This_Day/October/9_October.htm, accessed February 2021.

Robert Kearney, *Raid on Celtic Wood: What Really Happened to Australia's 'Lost Company' in 1917?*, Digital Print Australia, 2017.

THE YOUNGEST ANZAC

'Our Youngest Soldier', *The Mirror* (Sydney), 20 December 1918, p. 6.

'Stowaway Boy Soldier', *Bendigo Advertiser*, 8 April 1916, p. 11.

'Adventurous Boy', *Leader* (Orange), 29 September 1916, p. 2.

Annie O'Reilly, 'The Youngest Anzac', *Odd Australian History*, 23 April 2015, oddhistory.com.au/other-areas-including-melbourne-the-western-district-and-overseas/the-youngest-anzac/, accessed May 2021.

THE SECRET WATCHERS

'Well-known Pearler', *The Brisbane Courier*, 24 June 1932, p. 13.

Norman S. Pixley, 'Presidential address: Pearlers of North Australia: The Romantic Story of the Diving Fleets', *Journal of the Royal Historical Society of Queensland*, 23 September 1971, Vol. 9, Issue 3, pp. 9–29.

Joey Watson and Ian Coombe, 'The secret missions of Australia's early spies', *ABC Radio National Late Night Live*, 14 February 2019, abc.net.au/news/2019-02-14/secret-missions-of-australias-early-spies/10785560, accessed May 2021.

FINDING THE LOST SUBMARINE

Henry Kinder, *Diary*, transcribed by Peter Ryan in 2011 based on materials supplied by the Kinder family. Kinder wrote his diary in later life.

John Foster, *AE1: Entombed but Not Forgotten*, Australian Military History Publications: Loftus, 2006.

James Hunter, 'Solving Australia's most enduring naval mystery', Australian National Maritime Museum, 18 September 2018, sea.museum/2018/09/18/ae1-found, accessed May 2021.

THE MOLONGLO MYSTERY

'Molonglo Internment Camp = A Notable Wartime Achievement', unsigned typescript [Mr Duncan], ArchivesACT, archives.act.gov. au/__data/assets/pdf_file/0011/706628/Daley-1940.pdf, accessed February 2021.

Frank Cotton, 'The Molonglo Mystery', *Labor News* (Sydney), 11 January 1919, p. 4.

Peter Monteith, *Captured Lives: Australia's Wartime Internment Camps,* National Library of Australia: Canberra, 2018.

Steven Trask, 'Conditions inside Canberra's Molonglo war camp revealed in century-old letters', *The Canberra Times*, 26 January 2018, canberratimes.com.au/story/6024093/conditions-inside-canberras-molonglo-war-camp-revealed-in-century-old-letters/, accessed February 2021.

WHY CAMP X?

'M Special Unit: Allied Intelligence Bureau', *Australia @ War*, ozatwar. com/sigint/mspecialunit.htm, accessed February 2021.

'Camp Tabragalba', Queensland WWII Historic Places, ww2places.qld. gov.au/place?id=1465, accessed May 2021.

DIAMOND JACK

'Valuable Matchbox', *The Kalgoorlie Miner*, 7 January 1943, p. 2.

'Diamonds Case', *The West Australian*, 30 April 1943, p. 4.

Emma Verheijke (ed), *Broome 3 March 1942–3 March 2012*, Embassy of the Kingdom of the Netherlands/Western Australian Museum, Canberra, 2012.

Tony Barrass, 'Broome's war heroics', *The Australian*, 2 and 3 March 2012.

THE BROOK ISLANDS EXPERIMENTS

Peter Dunn, 'Artillery Practice and Chemical Warfare Trails at Mission Beach', *Australia @ War,* ozatwar.com/chemicalwarfare/missionbeachcw.htm, accessed May 2021.

Peter Dunn, 'Australian Chemical Warfare Research and Experimental Section', *Australia @ War*, ozatwar.com/ausarmy/acwraes.htm, accessed May 2021.

Peter Michael, 'Defence investigating claims up to 50 US prisoners died in underground bunkers on atoll on Great Barrier Reef', *The Sunday Mail*, 10 February 2013, couriermail. com.au/news/queensland/us-prisoners-poisoned/news-story/f0b5d8db989157daa6c5ce1f77dba22c, accessed May 2021.

Emma Siossian, 'Rock engraving throws spotlight on Australia's top-secret World War II mustard gas program', *ABC News*, 10 January 2021, abc.net.au/news/2021-01-10/australia-world-war-two-secret-mustard-gas-chemical-program/13034000, accessed May 2021.

Sylvia Stolz, 'The Brook Island Trials During WW2', *Australia @ War*, ozatwar.com/brook island trial.htm, accessed May 2021.

'THERE'LL ALWAY BE A *SYDNEY*

War Cabinet Notebooks, meeting of 1 December 1941, notes by Shedden, quoted in Robert Summerell, *The Sinking of HMAS Sydney: A Guide to Commonwealth Government Records*, National Archives of Australia, revised edition 2010, NAA: A5954, 731/1.

James Eagles, 'HMAS Sydney and Intelligence Services in Australia WW2', SUBM.002.0156_R, to HMAS Sydney II Commission of Inquiry, 2007.

Glenys McDonald, *Seeking the Sydney: A Quest for Truth*, University of Western Australia Press: Crawley, 2005.

THE HANGED MAN

Peter Butt, *Final Rendezvous*, Blackwattle Films, screened August 2020.

Joey Watson, *The History Listen*, ABC Radio National, 12 August 2020.

Migrant Selection Documents for Displaced Persons who travelled to Australia per Fairsea departing Bremerhaven 6 October 1950, NAA: A12040, 203.

Philip Dorling, 'A Spy Like Horrie', *The Sydney Morning Herald*, 14 October 2013, smh.com.au/national/a-spy-like-horrie-20131013-2vgbd.html, accessed February 2021.

THE MISSING NUCLEAR FILES

NDA Archive Nucleus website, gov.uk/government/case-studies/nda-archive, accessed September 2020.

James Griffiths, 'Review or "cover up"? Mystery as Australia nuclear weapons tests files withdrawn', *CNN*, 11 January 2019, edition. cnn.com/2019/01/11/australia/uk-australia-nuclear-archives-intl/index.html, accessed September 2020.

Gillian Areia and Evelyn Leckie, 'Fallout from nuclear tests at Maralinga worse than previously thought', *ABC News*, 22 May 2021, https://www.abc.net.au/news/2021-05-22/maralinga-nuclear-particles-more-reactive/100157478, accessed May 2021.

Jon Agar, https://twitter.com/jon_agar/status/1082722513984151552, 9 January 2019, accessed May 2021.

CHAPTER 5 OUTBACK PUZZLES

THE LOST WELLS OF THE SIMPSON DESERT

Luise Hercus, 'Leaving the Simpson Desert', *Aboriginal History*, 1985, Vol. 9, pp. 22–43.

Amanda, 'Simpson Desert Aboriginal Culture', *Travel Outback Australia*, traveloutbackaustralia.com/simpson-desert-aboriginal-culture.html/, accessed May 2021.

Mark Shephard, *The Simpson Desert: natural history and human endeavour*, Royal Geographical Society of Australasia (South Australian Branch) and Giles Publications: Adelaide, 1992.

THE STONE FACE

Mike Dash, *Batavia's Graveyard: The True Story of the Mad Heretic Who Led History's Bloodiest Mutiny*, Crown Publishers: New York, 2002.

Ursula Frederick and Sue O'Connor, 'Wandjina, graffiti and heritage: The power and politics of enduring imagery', *Humanities Research*, 2009, Vol. XV, No. 2.

George Grey, *Journals of two expeditions of discovery in North-West and Western Australia during the years 1837, 38 and 39*, Vol. 1, T and W Boone: London, 1841, entries for 26 March 1838 and figure 16.

LEICHHARDT'S LAST QUEST

Darrell Lewis, *Where is Dr Leichhardt? The Greatest Mystery in Australian History*, Monash University Publishing: Clayton, 2013.

Henry Kendall, *Songs from the Mountains*, William Maddock: Sydney and London, 1880.

THE WAILING WATERHOLE

Bill Beatty, 'Wailing at the Wilga Waterhole', *The Sydney Morning Herald*, 4 January 1947, p. 10.

Philip Shields, 'In Search of the Wilga Ghost', 19 August 2017, ontologysite.wordpress.com/2017/08/19/in-search-of-the-wilga-ghost/, accessed February 2021.

LASSETER'S BONES

R. Ross, 'False Teeth', *Lasseteria*, lasseteria.com/HOME.htm, accessed May 2021, quoting Billy Marshall-Stoneking, *Lasseter, In Quest of Gold*, Hodder & Stoughton: Sydney, 1989.

R. Ross, 'Seventy Eight Days', *Lasseteria*, lasseteria.com/HOME.htm, accessed February 2021.

'Lassiter's [sic] body believed found in native grave', *Canberra Times*, 21 December 1957, p. 1.

Paul Wise, 'Historical Locations connected with Lasseter's Grave, Petermann Ranges, Central Australia', xnatmap.org/adnm/docs/1genmap/LASSETER/LHLasseter.htm, accessed February 2021.

'Harold Lasseter', Monument Australia, monumentaustralia.org.au/themes/people/exploration/display/93050-harold-lasseter, accessed May 2021.

IT'S RAINING FISH!

'Can it rain frogs, fish, and other objects?', *Everyday Mysteries*, Library of Congress, loc.gov/everyday-mysteries/item/can-it-rain-frogs-fish-and-other-objects/, accessed August 2020.

'Country News', *The Argus*, 12 September 1873, p. 7.

Ash Moore, 'Winton's mysterious fishy tale amid Queensland drought', *ABC Western Queensland*, 11 March 2016, abc.net.au/news/2016-03-11/wintons-mysterious-fishy-tale-amidst-soaking-rain-in-queensland/7239714, accessed February 2021.

Richard Shears, 'Residents stunned as hundreds of fish fall out of the sky over remote Australian desert town', *Daily Mail Australia*, 2 March 2010, dailymail.co.uk/news/article-1254812/Hundreds-fish-fall-sky-remote-Australian-town-Lajamanu.html, accessed February 2021.

SEEING THE LIGHTS

'UQ scientist unlocks secret of Min Min lights', *UQ News*, University of Queensland, 27 March 2003, uq.edu.au/news/article/2003/03/uq-scientist-unlocks-secret-of-min-min-lights, accessed May 2021.

Bill Bowyang, 'On the Track', *The Northern Miner*, 26 December 1928, p. 7

Karl Kruszelnicki, 'The Min Min Mystery', *Australian Geographic*, 9 August 2018, australiangeographic.com.au/blogs/dr-karl-need-to-know/2018/08/the-min-min-mystery/, accessed May 2021.

H.J.L. 'Strange Lights', *Saturday Journal* (Adelaide), 20 March 1926, p. 13.

D.B. O'Connor, 'The Light o' Min Min', *Townsville Daily Bulletin*, 20 December 1934, p. 4.

John D. Pettigrew, 'The Min Min Light and the Fata Morgana: An Optical Account of a Mysterious Australian Phenomenon', *Clinical and Experimental Optometry*, 2003, Vol. 86, No. 2, pp. 109–120.

A DESERT MIRACLE

Ben Martin, 'Great Survival Stories: Robert Bogucki', *The West Australian*, 13 October 2015 (first published in 2009), thewest.com.au/news/wa/great-survival-stories-robert-bogucki-ng-ya-130515, accessed May 2021.

Stephen Orr, *The Fierce Country: True Stories from Australia's Unsettled Heart, 1830 to Today*, Wakefield Press: Adelaide, 2018.

THE HAUNTED HOUSE AT HUMPTY DOO

'Australia Priest Says Strange Things Happening at Humpty Doo', *Catholic World News*, 2 April 1998.

Cropster, 'Tony & Paul Meet the Humpty Doo Poltergeist', *The Fortean*, 12 April 2020, thefortean.com/2020/04/12/tony-paul-meet-the-humpty-doo-poltergeist/, accessed January 2021.

Tony Healy and Paul Cropper, *Australian Poltergeist: The Stone-throwing Spook of Humpty Doo and Many Other Cases,* Paul Cropper, 2014.

HIGHWAYS OF DEATH

Rick Hind, 'Stuart Highway stretch among most dangerous', *ABC News*, 20 January 2012, abc.net.au/news/2012-01-20/20120120-stuart-highway-danger-stretch/3784778, accessed May 2021.

Ross Gibson, *Seven Versions of an Australian Badland*, University of Queensland Press: St Lucia, 2002.

THE HOLE FROM SPACE

Jemima Burt, 'Four-billion-year-old Wolfe Creek meteorite stolen from Queensland museum recovered', *ABC News*, 9 November 2020, abc.net.au/news/2020-11-09/stolen-wolfe-creek-meteorite-returned-to-atherton-museum/12864532, accessed February 2021.

Ben Lewis, 'Wolfe Creek Crater is way younger than we thought', *Australia's Science Channel*, 16 January 2020, australiascience.tv/wolfe-creek-crater-is-way-younger-than-we-thought/, accessed May 2021.

Kenneth McNamara, 'Unknown wonders: Wolfe Creek Crater', *The Conversation*, 16 May 2013, theconversation.com/unknown-wonders-wolfe-creek-crater-13709, accessed February 2021.

WHERE'S THE WATER?

Michael Slezak et al., 'The Mystery of the Murray–Darling's Vanishing Flows', *ABC News*, 3 September 2020. The study on which this article is based is Wentworth Group of Concerned Scientists, *Assessment of river flows in the Murray-Darling Basin: Observed versus expected flows under the Basin Plan 2012-2019*, 2020, wentworthgroup.org/2020/09/mdb-flows-2020/2020/, accessed February 2021.

CHAPTER 6 MYSTERIOUS PLACES

THE HAUNTED HAWKESBURY

'Haunted Hawkesbury', *Windsor and Richmond Gazette*, 27 January 1928, p. 11.

Richard Davis, *The Ghost Guide to Australia*, Bantam Books: Sydney, 1998, pp. 46–49.

Keith Whitfield, 'The Ghost of Greenman's Inn', *Peninsula Community Access News*, Issue 61, 25 February 2003.

THE VICAR'S TALE

'St Matthew's Anglican Church, Rectory, Stables & Cemetery', *New South Wales State Heritage Register*, NSW Office of Environment and Heritage, apps.environment.nsw.gov.au/dpcheritageapp/ViewHeritageItemDetails.aspx?ID=5045677, accessed May 2021.

Reverend Norman Jenkin, 'A Haunted Rectory', *Windsor and Richmond Gazette*, 3 March 1939, p. 3.

Jas. Steele, 'Chapter VII: The Church of England', *Early Days of Windsor N S Wales*, Tyrrell's Ltd: Sydney, 1916.

A CURIOUS CASTLE

'Ghosts of Early Adelaide', *The Advertiser* (Adelaide), 17 October 1929, p. 19.

Irene Altmann, 'Haunted By Children and Snakes', *The Advertiser* (Adelaide), 11 July 1947, p. 4.

'Lavender and Lace', 'More About the Ghost of Graham's Castle', *Chronicle* (Adelaide), 6 October 1938, p. 60.

W.G. Kendell, 'Graham's Castle', *The Register* (Adelaide), 28 March 1922, p. 9.

SATAN ON DEAD ISLAND

'Death of Mark Jeffrey', *Launceston Examiner*, 19 July 1894, p. 6.

Richard Davis, *The Ghost Guide to Australia*, Bantam Books: Sydney, 1998.

Mark Jeffrey, *Tales of the Early Days. A Burglar's Life or the Stirring Adventures of the Great English Burglar Mark Jeffrey*, Alexander McCubbin: Melbourne, 1900. Jeffrey's ghostwritten memoir was first published in Hobart in 1893.

Will Mooney, 'Ghost Stories', *The Companion to Tasmanian History*, utas.edu.au/library/companion_to_tasmanian_history/G/Ghost stories.htm, accessed May 2021.

THE CONCRETE CASKET

'The Late Miss Lydia Gow', *Newcastle Morning Herald and Miner's Advocate*, 26 November 1912, p. 6.

Helen Hemmons, 'The Keepers: David Robert Gow', South Solitary Island blog, southsolitaryisland.com.au/the-keepers#b6282e4c-1bd9-45e5-b446-dedcc490e555, accessed August 2020.

Melissa Martin, 'South Solitary Island Lighthouse haunted by ghost of girl buried in bathtub, former residents say', *ABC News,* 10 August 2019, abc.net.au/news/2019-08-10/lydia-gow-buried-in-a-bathtub-and-covered-with-concrete/11395174, accessed August 2020.

HERMITS OF THE REEF

'A Modern Crusoe', *Burra Record*, 9 January 1935, p. 1.

Frank Reid, 'Hermits of the Barrier Reef', *Kalgoorlie Miner*, 27 February 1932, p. 7. Reid also wrote about this story in his book *The Romance of the Great Barrier Reef*, Angus & Robertson: Sydney, 1954.

Mary T. Williams, *The Knob: A History of Yorkey's Knob*, M. Williams: Queensland, 1988.

THE GUYRA STONETHROWER

'A Staff Correspondent Recalls the Unsolved Riddle of Guyra's Ghost', *The Sydney Morning Herald* Magazine Section, 9 March 1954, p. 10.

'Guyra "Ghost" Mystery Solved', *The Register* (Adelaide), 27 April 1921, p. 9.

'Guyra Stone Thrower', *The Sydney Morning Herald,* 11 May 1921, p. 11.

THE HOOK ISLAND MONSTER

B. Heuvelmans, *In the Wake of the Sea-Serpents*, Hill and Wang: New York, p. 534.

Robert Le Serrec, *Autour du monde, 5 ans à la voile en thonier*, Arthaud: Paris, 1967.

Derrick Stone, *Walks, Tracks and Trails of Queensland's Tropics*, CSIRO Publishing: Canberra, 2016.

Darren Naish, 'The Amazing Hook Island Sea Monster Photos, Revisited', *Tetrapod Zoology*, 23 November 2013, blogs. scientificamerican.com/tetrapod-zoology/the-amazing-hook-island-sea-monster-photos-revisited/, accessed February 2021.

'A RIDDLE, WRAPPED IN A MYSTERY, INSIDE AN ENIGMA'

Hannah James, 'The Mystery of the Marree Man', *Australian Geographic*, 4 October 2018, australiangeographic.com.au/topics/ science-environment/2018/10/the-mystery-of-the-marree-man/, accessed February 2021.

James Vyver, 'An Outback Enigma', ABC Radio National *Earshot*, 24 August 2019, abc.net.au/news/2019-08-24/mystery-of-the-marree-man-in-australian-outback/11310330?nw=0, accessed February 2021.

TUNNEL TALES

Sonya Gee, 'Curious Canberra: Are there secret tunnels in Canberra?', *ABC News*, 28 April 2016, abc.net.au/news/specials/ curious-canberra/2016-01-31/abc-explores-secret-tunnels-under-canberra/7098382, accessed February 2021.

Malcolm Sutton, 'Curious Adelaide: Uncovering the truth about Adelaide's "secret" tunnel network (Part One)', *ABC News,* 2 February 2018, abc.net.au/news/2018-02-02/digging-up-the-truth-of-adelaides-tunnels/9232072, accessed February 2021.

Benedict Brook, 'Newington Armory, the suburban navy base that was vital to Australia's defence', news.com.au, 25 October 2019, news.com.au/technology/innovation/military/newington-armory-the-suburban-navy-base-that-was-vital-to-australiasdefence/ newsstory/4f0c6f866e47bf1773bda52e90a48e29, accessed February 2021.

THE POINCIANA WOMAN

Roland Dyrting, 'The Poinciana Woman of East Point: The truth behind Darwin's most popular urban myth', Crikey.com, 22 December 2017, blogs.crikey.com.au/northern/2017/12/22/poinciana-woman-darwins-east-point-roland-dyrting/, accessed May 2021. This account won the Charles Darwin University Essay Award in the Northern Territory Literary Awards, 2009.

Walter William Skeat, *Malay Magic: An Introduction to the Folklore and Popular Religion of the Malay Peninsula*, Macmillan & Co: New York, 1900.

CHAPTER 7 VANISHINGS

THE PHANTOM ISLAND

The Courier (Hobart), 12 January 1841, p. 3.

F.R. Chapman, 'The Outlying Islands South of New Zealand', read before the Otago Institute, 13 May 1890, *Transactions and Proceedings of the Royal Society of New Zealand*, 1890, Vol. 23, p. 520. Some sources give Charles Nockells.

J.T.K. Davis, 'Voyage of the S.Y. Nimrod: Sydney to Monte Video Via Macquarie Island, May 8–July 7, 1909', *The Geographical Journal*, December 1910, Vol. 36, No. 6, p. 701.

R.K. Headland, *Chronological List of Antarctic Expeditions and Related Historical Events*, Cambridge University Press: Cambridge, p. 123.

MYSTERY BAY

'More about the Bermagui Mystery', *The Brisbane Courier*, 5 July 1887, p. 7. There are some discrepancies with the dating of the disappearance, but 10 October is the date most frequently given.

'The Bermagui Mystery', *Illustrated Sydney News and New South Wales Agriculturist and Grazier*, 20 November 1880, p. 3.

'The Bermagui Mystery', *Queanbeyan Age*, 8 May 1883, p. 2.

LEGENDS OF THE LAKE

'Domestic Intelligence', *The Sydney Monitor*, 1 November 1828, p. 5.

Wally Bell, 'Today's Ngunawal culture and country: Archaeology from an Aboriginal perspective', *National Museum of Australia*, talk at National Museum of Australia, 19 April 2017, published 1 January 2018, nma.gov.au/audio/canberra-archaeological-society/transcripts/today-s-ngunawal-culture, accessed February 2021.

'Lake George', *Sydney Free Press*, 22 January 1842, p. 3.

'bhrbagenski', 'Lake George Mystery Spot', *Atlas Obscura*, nd, atlasobscura.com/places/lake-george-mystery-spot, accessed May 2021.

VANISHING STARS

'Brian Abbot's Mystery Plans', *Australian Women's Weekly*, 24 October 1936, p. 2.

'Sydney Men Missing', *The Sydney Morning Herald*, 17 October 1936, p. 17.

George Malcolm, *Mystery Island, Commonwealth Film Laboratories, 1937,* ozmovies.com.au/movie/mystery-island, accessed May 2021.

Nicole Cama, 'The Three Mysteries: A Film, a Voyage, a Disappearance', *Signals*, Australian National Maritime Museum, Sep–Nov 2013, Issue 104, pp. 30–37.

THE LADY OF THE SWAMP

'Swamp Lady's land sold for £67,500', *The Argus*, 26 October 1956, p. 3.

John Lack, 'Clement, Margaret (1881–1952)', *Australian Dictionary of Biography*, National Centre of Biography, Australian National University, adb.anu.edu.au/biography/clement-margaret-12845/text23189, published first in hardcopy 2005, accessed online 8 August 2020.

Barney Porter, 'Swamp Hopes Fade', *The Argus*, 29 May 1952, p. 1.

Barney Porter, 'Swamp Lady Hunt is on Again', *The Argus*, 30 January 1953, p. 2.

Jacob A. Stam, 'Swamp: The Muddied Waters of a Mystery Wrapped in a Riddle Inside an Enigma', *Applied Hermeneutics*, appliedhermeneutics.blogspot.com/2013/11/swamp-muddied-waters-of-mystery-wrapped.html, accessed February 2021.

Annie O'Riley, 'The Peculiar World of Margaret Clement', *Odd Australian History*, 28 April 2014, oddhistory.com.au/gippsland/the-peculiar-world-of-margaret-clement/, accessed February 2021.

'Wife Takes Swamp Lady Secret to Grave', *The Sunday Age*, 10 October 1993, p. 9.

'Bones May Be Lady of Swamp', *The Age*, 9 November 1978, p. 1.

Drew Sinton, 'Australian Gothic #121', Haunted Bookshop Facebook page, 21 May 2013, facebook.com/Haunted.Bookshop/posts/on-this-day-in-1952-the-ghostly-legend-of-australias-loneliest-woman-/519776914749046/, accessed May 2021.

WHO KILLED HARRY?

'Unsolved Crime List Grows', *Truth* (Sydney), 27 September 1936, p. 21.

Caroline Dobraszczyk, 'The Conviction of Frederick Lincoln McDermott', *Bar News*, Winter 2013, p. 66.

Chester Porter Q.C., 'The Conviction of Frederick Lincoln McDermott', *Bar News*, Summer 2013–14, pp. 74–75.

Tom Molomby, *The Shearer's Tale: A Story of Murder and Injustice in 1940s Australia*, ABC Books: Sydney, 2004.

THE PRIME MINISTER VANISHES

Samantha Bricknell, *Missing Persons: Who is at Risk?*, Australian Federal Police Research Report 08, Australian Institute of Criminology, 2017.

Andreas Hartmann, 'The companies that help people vanish', *BBC Worklife*, bbc.com/worklife/article/20200903-the-companies-that-help-people-vanish, accessed September 2020.

Bridget Judd, 'Inside the disappearance of Harold Holt—one of the largest search operations in Australian history', *ABC News*, 1 November 2020, abc.net.au/news/2020-11-01/disappearance-harold-holt-inside-search-operation-australia/12817236, accessed May 2021.

FLIGHT OF THE MOTH

Rachel Edwards, 'Lake Pedder protesters Brenda Hean, Max Price left Hobart in a Tiger Moth biplane bound for Canberra. They were never seen again', *ABC News*, 18 October 2020, abc.net.au/news/2020-10-18/lake-pedder-protesters-brenda-hean-max-price-disappearance/12660976, accessed February 2021.

Peter George and Lesley Holden, 'Lake Pedder: Missing in Action', *Rewind*, ABCTV, 15 August 2004, web.archive.org/web/20041125161856/http://www.abc.net.au/tv/rewind/txt/s1173814.htm, accessed May 2021.

BLACK MOUNTAIN MYTHS

Royce Christyn, 'Australia's Mysterious "Black Mountain": Evil Myths, Aliens and Fear', *News Punch*, 15 April 2015, newspunch.com/australias-mysterious-black-mountain-evil-myths-aliens-and-fear/, accessed May 2021.

Ivan Mackerle, 'Mountain of the Death', 1 August 2009, en.mackerle.cz/news/about-expedition1/, accessed February 2021.

Brendan Mounter and Adam Stephen, '"It'll haunt you forever": Traditional owners warn climbers of perils entering FNQ's "Bermuda Triangle"', *ABC News*, 21 October 2018, abc.net.au/news/2018-10-21/mysterious-black-mountain/10067072, accessed May 2021.

E. Grant Swan, 'Black Mountain: Cooktown Aboriginal Legend', *The Queenslander*, 16 October 1926, p. 11.

Elise Kinsella, 'Without A Trace', *ABC News*, 19 July 2020, abc.net.au/news/2020-07-19/how-four-people-disappeared-without-trace-in-victorian-mountains/12455124, accessed February 2021.

TIGER TALES

Kate Ainsworth and Laura Bevis, 'Baby Tasmanian Tiger Skulls More Similar to Wolf Pups Than to Other Australian marsupials', *ABC News*, 11 January 2021, abc.net.au/news/2021-01-11/tasmanian-tiger-pup-skulls-similar-to-wolves/13046480, accessed May 2021.

Pauline Conolly, 'The Tassie Tiger of Penguin', 27 March 2017, paulineconolly.com/2017/tiger-of-the-tasmanian-kind/, accessed February 2021.

Belinda King, 'Tasmanian tiger pelt found in New Zealand reveals rich colours of the extinct thylacine', *ABC Northern Tasmania*, 29 August 2020, abc.net.au/news/2020-08-29/tasmanian-tiger-thylacine-colourful-pelt-from-nz-reveals/12597682, accessed February 2021.

Douglas Rovinsky, Alastair Evans and Justin Adams, 'The Tasmanian tiger was hunted to extinction as a "large predator"—but it was only half as heavy as we thought', *Lens*, Monash University, 20 August 2020, lens.monash.edu/@science/2020/08/20/1381106/the-tasmanian-tiger-was-hunted-to-extinction-as-a-large-predator-but-it-was-only-half-as-heavy-as-we-thought, accessed February 2021.

BENEATH THE THREE UGLY SISTERS?

Andrew Woodhouse, 'Murder mystery may soon be solved', *City Hub*, 29 April 2020, cityhubsydney.com.au/?s=murder+mystery+may+soon+be+solved, accessed August 2020.

Warren Fahey, folklorist, private correspondence, 31 July 2021.

Richard Morris, 'Nielsen, Juanita Joan (1937–1975)', *Australian Dictionary of Biography,* Australian National University, adb.anu.edu.au/biography/nielsen-juanita-joan-11241/text20047, published first in hardcopy 2000, accessed August 2020.

'GOOD NIGHT. MALAYSIAN THREE SEVEN ZERO'

Graham Kendall, 'How to Unleash the Wisdom of Crowds', *The Conversation*, 10 February 2016, theconversation.com/how-to-unleash-the-wisdom-of-crowds-52774, accessed February 2021.

Leighton Vaughan Williams, 'What Happened to MH370? Prediction Markets Might Give Us the Answer', *The Conversation*, 4 August 2015, theconversation.com/what-happened-to-mh370-prediction-markets-might-give-us-the-answer-45528, accessed February 2021.

Wikipedia contributors, 'Malaysia Airlines Flight 370', *Wikipedia, The Free Encyclopedia*, 29 May 2021, en.wikipedia.org/w/index.php?title=Malaysia_Airlines_Flight_370&oldid=1025749802, accessed May 2021.

CHAPTER 8 UNSOLVED

A QUEENSLAND RIPPER?

Stephanie Bennet, *The Gatton Murders: A True Story of Lust, Vengeance and Vile Retribution*, Pan Macmillan: Sydney, 2004.

Neil Raymond Bradford, *Oxley–Gatton Murders: Exposing the Conspiracy*, BookPal: 2015.

Cheryl Fagan, *Murder & Misconduct*, InHouse Publishing: Queensland, 2016.

John Meredith, *Breaker's Mate: Will Ogilvie in Australia*, Kangaroo Press: Kenthurst, 1996.

Queensland Police Service, 'From the Vault—Police Trackers', mypolice.qld.gov.au/museum/2014/07/08/vault-police-trackers/, accessed May 2021.

NED KELLY'S SKULL

Craig Cormick (ed), *Ned Kelly Under the Microscope*, CSIRO Publishing: Canberra, 2014.

Graham Seal, *Tell 'em I Died Game*, Hyland House: Melbourne, 1980.

THE DYING LIGHT

The Lismore Chronicle, 1 October 1907, p. 2.

The Northern Star (Lismore), 17 February 1978, p. 3.

The Sydney Morning Herald, 21 February 1978, p. 3.

Nash Soonawala, 'Which Types of Granite Emit the Most Radon?', *Sciencing*, 25 October 2017, sciencing.com/which-types-of-granite-emit-the-most-radon-12304959.html, accessed August 2020.

Joseph Trainor, *UFO Roundup*, 26 February, 2003, Vol. 8, No. 9, http://www.ufoinfo.com/roundup/v08/rnd0809.html, accessed January 2020.

THE CRYPTID FILES

'The Bunyip, or Kine Pratie', *Sydney Chronicle* (from the *Port Phillip Patriot*), 23 January 1847, p. 2.

Jewel Topsfield, 'The hunt for big cats in Australia', *The Sydney Morning Herald*, 5 July 2020, smh.com.au/national/the-hunt-for-big-cats-in-australia-20200703-p558qg.html, accessed February 2021.

D. Waldron and S. Townsend, *Snarls from the Tea-Tree: A History of Victoria's Big Cat Folklore*, Australian Scholarly Publishing: Melbourne, 2012.

THE PYJAMA GIRL

Antonio Agostini, prison record, prov.vic.gov.au/sites/default/files/files/media/vprs_515_p0_central_register_male_prisoners_unit_97_agostini_page_307_1.jpg, accessed May 2021.

Richard Evans, *The Pyjama Girl Mystery*, Scribe: Melbourne, 2004.

Mark Finnane, 'Controlling the "alien" in mid-twentieth century Australia: the origins and fate of a policing role', *Policing and Society*, 2009, Vol. 19, Issue 4, pp. 442–67.

THE UNKNOWN MAN

Ben Cheshire, 'Dancing With the Dead', *Australian Story*, ABC TV, 14 October 2019.

Mike Dash, 'Tamám Shud', *A Blast from the Past*, 12 August 2011, mikedashhistory.com/2011/08/12/tamam-shud/#more-956, accessed February 2021.

G.M. (Gerry) Feltus, *The Unknown Man: A Suspicious Death at Somerton Beach*, Greenacres: South Australia, 2010.

THE WEEPING WOMAN

Bridget Judd, 'A Picasso painting was stolen from a Melbourne gallery—and we still don't know who did it', *ABC Retrofocus*, 20 September 2019, abc.net.au/news/2019-09-14/retrofocus-picasso-weeping-woman-famous-unsolved-art-heist/11498936, accessed August 2020.

Patrick McCaughey, *The Bright Shapes and the True Names: A Memoir*, Text Publishing: Melbourne, 2003.

DOING A LORD LUCAN

Duncan McNab, 'Lord Lucan mystery: Is the alleged nanny killer hiding out in Australia?', *7News*, 4 February 2020, 7news.com. au/original-fyi/crime-story-investigator/lord-lucan-mystery-is-the-alleged-nanny-killer-hiding-out-in-australia-c-674211, accessed February 2021.

Wikipedia contributors, 'John Bingham, 7th Earl of Lucan', *Wikipedia, The Free Encyclopedia*, 28 May 2021, en.wikipedia. org/w/index.php?title=John_Bingham,_7th_Earl_of_ Lucan&oldid=1025662685, accessed May 2021.

MR BROWN

Malcolm Brown, 'Selwyn, William (1922–2010)', *Obituaries Australia*, National Centre of Biography, Australian National University, oa.anu.edu.au/obituary/selwyn-william-16909/text28797, accessed May 2021.

Bridget Judd, 'The true story of the 1971 Qantas bomb hoax—one of Australia's most audacious heists', *ABC Retrofocus*, 23 February 2019, abc.net.au/news/2019-02-23/qantas-bomb-hoax-1971-the-great-plane-robbery-australia/10807510, accessed February 2021.

Duncan McNab, 'Planes, bombs and murder: The curious case of the Peter Macari Qantas hoax', *7News*, 27 August 2019, 7news.com. au/original-fyi/crime-story-investigator/planes-bombs-and-murder-the-curious-case-of-the-peter-macari-qantas-hoax-c-365924, accessed February 2021.

LUNA PARK GHOSTS

'Ghost Train (Luna Park Sydney)', enacademic.com, https://enacademic. com/dic.nsf/enwiki/7044215, accessed December 2020.

Richard Cooke, 'Hellfire', *Sydney Review of Books*, 8 December 2017, sydneyreviewofbooks.com/essay/hellfire-richard-cooke/, accessed May 2021.

Caro Meldrum-Hanna et al., '"Luckiest boy alive": Luna Park Ghost Train fire survivor breaks his silence', *ABC News*, 10 March 2021, abc.net.au/news/2021-03-10/luna-park-ghost-train-fire-survivor-breaks-silence/12224530, accessed May 2021.

WHERE'S PADDY?

Justine Ford, 'An Outback Whodunnit: The Baffling Disappearance of Paddy Moriarty', *Unsolved Australia: Lost Boys, Gone Girls*, Pan Macmillan: Sydney, 2019.

Anna Henderson and Neda Vanovac, 'Could the disappearance of Paddy Moriarty end up unravelling an entire town?', *ABC News*, 3 December 2018, abc.net.au/news/2018-12-03/a-dog-act-homicide-on-the-highway/10575078, accessed February 2021.

THE PORTUGUESE PLATYPUS AND THE SICILIAN COCKATOO

Robert Bremner, private communication to author, September 2019.

Heather Dalton, 'How did a cockatoo reach 13th century Sicily?', *Pursuit*, University of Melbourne, pursuit.unimelb.edu.au/articles/how-did-a-cockatoo-reach-13th-century-sicily, accessed September 2020.